# The Secretary's Deskbook of Practical Business Math

Earl B. Hitchcock

*A James Peter Book*
*James Peter Associates, Inc.*

Prentice-Hall, Inc.
Englewood Cliffs, NJ

Prentice-Hall International, Inc., *London*
Prentice-Hall of Australia, Pty. Ltd., *Sydney*
Prentice-Hall Canada, Inc., *Toronto*
Prentice-Hall of India Private Ltd., *New Delhi*
Prentice-Hall of Japan, Inc., *Tokyo*
Prentice-Hall of Southeast Asia Pte. Ltd., *Singapore*
Whitehall Books, Ltd., *Wellington, New Zealand*
Editora Prentice-Hall do Brasil Ltda., *Rio de Janeiro*
Prentice-Hall Hispanoamericana, S.A., *Mexico*

© 1986 *by*
Prentice-Hall, Inc.
Englewood Cliffs, N.J.

**Library of Congress Cataloging-in-Publication Data**

Hitchcock, Earl B.
  The secretary's deskbook of practical business math.

  "A James Peter book."
  Includes index.
  1. Business mathematics.   I. Title.
HF5691.H57  1986     513'.93'024651     86-8159

ISBN 0-13-797523-6

Printed in the United States of America

# How This Book Will Help You Solve Everyday Math Problems

Business math is applied math. It's nothing more than using the skills you already have to solve business problems. However, business math problems are seldom stated in operational terms, such as multiply this number by that number and then subtract it from another. If they were, life would be quite easy, indeed.

The goal of this book is to make the math portion of your secretarial life easy to handle. To do this, I have taken virtually all the business math problems you could possibly face and have presented them in easy-to-follow, step-by-step formats. You will see exactly what is required, and what has been done every step of the way. And to make your mathematical life even easier, I have included worked-out and illustrated examples with every mathematical operation. There is no need to master any complicated formulas; you don't even have to learn the language of math. This is a practical book—a book that you will use wherever and whenever the need arises.

### Find Your Answers Instantly

To find the help you need quickly, I have created a multilevel index—a fast guide to math problems as well as to solutions. I call it the Math-O-Matic Guide. (See page 235.) If you already know what kind of help you need, just turn to the appropriate heading in the Guide. For example, if you want to discover how to compute compound interest, just look under the word *interest*. If, however, you don't understand the term, but know that interest is a percent of another figure, the word *percent* will locate the help you need. You will also find help under the word *finance,* and other terms as well.

In short, you can find the help you need regardless of your knowledge of mathematics.

## For Secretaries Only

This is the only book devoted entirely to math for secretaries. There are other business math books available, but none of them approaches the subject entirely from the secretary's point of view. This book is your own personal guide to business math. With it you will be able to...

- Solve problems you could not solve before
- Solve problems faster than ever before
- Check the accuracy of your answers instantly
- Understand the procedures and handle the calculations for virtually every business math problem
- Find the help you need quickly with the multi-level Math-O-Matic Guide
- Solve your own math problems just by substituting your numbers for those in the examples, and doing basic arithmetic.
- Do much more than the basics with a calculator
- Solve problems with and without a calculator using many of the unique shortcuts that are carefully explained
- Face every business math problem with confidence

## A Ready Reference Whenever You Need It

This is a desk book, a complete reference you turn to whenever you need help with a mathematical problem. One chapter doesn't build on another; you don't have to read the book from cover to cover. Each section is written so that you can relate your own problems to the instructions, and then to the solved problems and examples instantly. Then, it's just a matter of doing the arithmetic. And because the problems are developed step by step, you can check your answers by reviewing each individual step. There's no need to do the problem over completely to check your answers.

## Brush Up on Your Skills Quickly and Easily

The only section of the book you should read thoroughly is Chapter 1, which reviews basic arithmetic. Read it for two reasons: First, you can use the material and the exercises to sharpen your skills. Second, this is the section in which I have included the time-saving shortcuts. For example, I have described a simple technique on page 6 that allows you to add a column of complex numbers using a much easier method than the one which is taught in most schools. In addition, it allows you to test the accuracy of your answer much more easily than by re-adding, which is the only way to handle the chore when you add numbers the conventional way.

## HOW TO USE THIS BOOK

This book is organized functionally. It's designed to help you find the solution you need with the Math-O-Matic Guide, and then to take you through the math quickly and easily.

Each chapter is organized this way:

*Topic introduction*—In the beginning of every chapter, I have included a general introduction to the topic. This will put your problem and the material that follows into perspective. If you already understand the topic, simply skip the introduction and turn directly to the specific information you need.

*How to do it*—This is the core of each section. Real-world business problems are created, and you are shown how to solve them. The solutions are developed step by step, and you are given all the help you need to solve similar problems on your own.

Unlike other math books that present procedures in an uninteresting recipe format, the information is given in a case history style—a method that is used by major universities when they train top executives. Not only does this method make it easier to learn, but it makes the entire process a lot more interesting.

*Solved problems and examples*—The material that follows each how-to-do-it section identifies typical business problems, sets up practical situations, and allows you to practice the skills you have learned by actually solving the problems. The answers are given for each problem.

The best way to learn is to learn by doing. There is no better way to master business math, or any other subject for that matter, than by actually working through typical problems. Even if you have no intention of becoming a mathematician, you can at least assure yourself that you can solve your day-to-day problems by working out the examples that have been included. They are real-world business problems, and you work them through as though you were facing them on the job—not in an abstract situation, such as a classroom.

In short, this book will make you a mathematical whiz without the need for tedious study and without having to memorize anything. Considering the complexities of the business world today, this is a critical skill. And all you have to do to be skillful is to turn to the Math-O-Matic index and locate the instructions and the solved problems. It's as simple as 2 + 2.

# Table of Contents

# CHAPTER 1

# How to Master All the Math You Will Ever Need to Know

You are probably already very familiar with most of the basic arithmetic operations that will be covered in this first chapter. So we'll just review them quickly to refresh your memory and sharpen your present skills. First, you'll see how to do them with paper and pencil. Then we will show you shortcuts that you can use to save time, such as estimating tricks that allow you to figure answers in your head. In Chapter 2, you'll learn how to use a calculator to speed and simplify arithmetic operations.

After reading these two chapters, you will have the confidence and ability to solve all your business and personal arithmetic problems quickly and accurately. Best of all, you can use this information as a reference that you can come back to whenever you need a refresher.

We'll start by looking at the decimal numbering system, which is a pretty handy and ingenious way to count and record numbers up to quantities too big to grasp.

## HOW THE DECIMAL SYSTEM MAKES OFFICE MATH EASY

Before we look at the basic arithmetic functions, it will be helpful to recall a few facts about our numbering system. It is composed of 10 symbols (including zero), yet it can easily express numbers in the billions and trillions.

This capability is due to the principle of position or place value. For example, the figure six by itself represents the fingers on one hand plus one. But the figure 60 is ten times greater, and the figure 600 one hundred times greater. Thus, all numbers can be written with the use of ten digits.

Here is a number which shows how our numbering system accommodates numbers into the trillions:

$$5\ 6,\ 7\ 8\ 5,\ 0\ 4\ 2,\ 6\ 0\ 0,\ 9\ 3\ 7$$

Now let's start by talking about the four basic operations in arithmetic.

## HOW TO ADD NUMBERS QUICKLY AND ACCURATELY

This is the most basic operation of all. In fact, the other three operations are variations of addition, as we shall see later.

People could count before they knew how to use arithmetic. They discovered that by counting the fingers on each hand, they had ten. After they learned how to add, they found a shortcut. Observing that they had five fingers on each hand, they added

$$\begin{array}{r} 5 \\ +5 \\ \hline 10 \end{array}$$

and of course got the same result.

The electronic calculator, which makes arithmetic so easy, performs addition by counting at an extremely rapid rate. The abacus, used by Orientals as a rapid calculator, works in the same way.

Since we can't count that fast, we do addition by memorizing combinations of the numbers from 0 to 10, like these:

$$
\begin{array}{cccccc}
2 & 3 & 2 & 6 & 7 & \\
\underline{+2} & \underline{+4} & \underline{+1} & \underline{+2} & \underline{+0} & \text{etc.} \\
4 & 7 & 3 & 8 & 7 &
\end{array}
$$

Although there are 100 such combinations, memorizing is made easier if you realize that 45 of them represent the reverse of one another:

$$
\begin{array}{ccc}
2 & 6 & \\
\underline{+6} & \underline{+2} & \text{etc.} \\
8 & 8 &
\end{array}
$$

and 20 of them call for adding 1 or 0:

$$
\begin{array}{ccc}
3 & 2 & \\
\underline{+1} & \underline{+0} & \text{etc.} \\
4 & 2 &
\end{array}
$$

For your convenience in reviewing combinations, a table is included on page 5. Adding long columns of numbers can be tedious if you don't have these combinations at your fingertips.

Test your memory of combinations by adding these columns. If you have to hesitate as you add, you may want to review some of the more difficult combinations $(9+6, 8+7, 8+9, \text{etc.})$

$$
\begin{array}{cccc}
3 & 1 & 4 & 8 \\
4 & 6 & 5 & 9 \\
7 & 9 & 8 & 6 \\
2 & 8 & 2 & 1 \\
9 & 2 & 3 & 7 \\
\underline{6} & \underline{3} & \underline{6} & \underline{5} \\
31 & 29 & 28 & 36
\end{array}
$$

In adding these columns, try to say the sum of the numbers to yourself as you go through the column. Column 1 for instance should be added: **7, 14, 16, 25, 31.**

**Carrying:** In adding columns of figures, it is necessary to carry a figure from one column to the next whenever the sum of the column exceeds 10.

*EXAMPLES:*

| Carry figure –> 1 | 1 | 11 | 2 |
|---|---|---|---|
| 36 | 75 | 589 | 89 |
| 45 | 68 | 753 | 77 |
| 81 | 143 | 1342 | 66 |
| | | | 232 |

Here are several examples of practical business situations requiring the addition of large columns of numbers.

(1) The Wilson Sales Company has five salesmen. Their reported sales for the month of June were as follows:

| Ed Wilson | $ 7,854 |
|---|---|
| Roy Edwards | 8,250 |
| Walt Averill | 11,672 |
| Tony Aorilla | 9,046 |
| Ray McGee | 4,228 |

What were total sales for June?                    (*Answer:* $41,050)

(2) Bill Terhune turned in the following expense account for May:

| Airline tickets | $225.50 |
|---|---|
| Mileage allowance | 87.70 |
| Hotel bills | 378.56 |
| Phone calls | 67.27 |
| Entertainment | 112.15 |
| Parking & tolls | 23.30 |

What were his expenses for May?                    (*Answer:* $894.48)

## ADDITION COMBINATIONS

| 0 | 1 | 2 | 3 | 4 | 5 | 6 | 7 | 8 | 9 |
|---|---|---|---|---|---|---|---|---|---|
| +0 | +0 | +0 | +0 | +0 | +0 | +0 | +0 | +0 | +0 |
|  | 1 | 2 | 3 | 4 | 5 | 6 | 7 | 8 | 9 |

| 0 | 1 | 2 | 3 | 4 | 5 | 6 | 7 | 8 | 9 |
|---|---|---|---|---|---|---|---|---|---|
| +1 | +1 | +1 | +1 | +1 | +1 | +1 | +1 | +1 | +1 |
| 1 | 2 | 3 | 4 | 5 | 6 | 7 | 8 | 9 | 10 |

| 2 | 8 | 6 | 1 | 5 | 3 | 7 | 0 | 3 | 9 |
|---|---|---|---|---|---|---|---|---|---|
| +2 | +2 | +2 | +2 | +2 | +2 | +2 | +2 | +2 | +2 |
| 4 | 10 | 8 | 3 | 7 | 5 | 9 | 2 | 5 | 11 |

| 1 | 4 | 0 | 7 | 3 | 5 | 9 | 6 | 8 | 2 |
|---|---|---|---|---|---|---|---|---|---|
| +3 | +3 | +3 | +3 | +3 | +3 | +3 | +3 | +3 | +3 |
| 4 | 7 | 3 | 10 | 6 | 8 | 12 | 9 | 11 | 5 |

| 4 | 7 | 3 | 9 | 5 | 1 | 2 | 6 | 8 | 0 |
|---|---|---|---|---|---|---|---|---|---|
| +4 | +4 | +4 | +4 | +4 | +4 | +4 | +4 | +4 | +4 |
| 8 | 11 | 7 | 13 | 9 | 5 | 6 | 10 | 12 | 4 |

| 0 | 2 | 8 | 1 | 6 | 3 | 9 | 5 | 7 | 4 |
|---|---|---|---|---|---|---|---|---|---|
| +5 | +5 | +5 | +5 | +5 | +5 | +5 | +5 | +5 | +5 |
| 5 | 7 | 13 | 6 | 11 | 8 | 14 | 10 | 12 | 9 |

| 2 | 8 | 6 | 1 | 5 | 3 | 7 | 0 | 4 | 9 |
|---|---|---|---|---|---|---|---|---|---|
| +6 | +6 | +6 | +6 | +6 | +6 | +6 | +6 | +6 | +6 |
| 8 | 14 | 12 | 7 | 11 | 9 | 13 | 6 | 10 | 15 |

| 1 | 4 | 0 | 3 | 5 | 9 | 7 | 2 | 8 | 6 |
|---|---|---|---|---|---|---|---|---|---|
| +7 | +7 | +7 | +7 | +7 | +7 | +7 | +7 | +7 | +7 |
| 8 | 11 | 7 | 10 | 12 | 16 | 14 | 9 | 15 | 13 |

| 4 | 7 | 5 | 9 | 3 | 6 | 1 | 8 | 0 | 2 |
|---|---|---|---|---|---|---|---|---|---|
| +8 | +8 | +8 | +8 | +8 | +8 | +8 | +8 | +8 | +8 |
| 12 | 15 | 13 | 17 | 11 | 14 | 9 | 16 | 8 | 10 |

| 2 | 9 | 3 | 7 | 1 | 6 | 0 | 5 | 4 | 8 |
|---|---|---|---|---|---|---|---|---|---|
| +9 | +9 | +9 | +9 | +9 | +9 | +9 | +9 | +9 | +9 |
| 11 | 18 | 12 | 16 | 10 | 15 | 9 | 14 | 13 | 17 |

(3) The Reynolds Valve & Fitting Company reported the following amounts of excess inventory at year end:

| | |
|---|---:|
| Brass water valves | $7,650 |
| Drain cocks | 4,021 |
| 1" metal hose | 3,960 |
| Miscellaneous steel pipe fittings | 720 |
| Pipe hangers | 852 |

What is the value of the excess inventory?            (*Answer:* $17,203)

## How to Check Your Addition Instantly

The accepted way to check the accuracy of your addition, particularly in long columns, is to add the columns in reverse. Since many people have trouble keeping their place in adding such columns, there are several ways to make the task easier.

One way is to divide the column into a number of subtotals, then adding the subtotals, to reach the grand total. This method avoids the problem of adding long columns in your head. For example:

| | |
|---|---|
| 352 | |
| 419 | |
| 721 | |
| 202 | 1492 subtotal |
| 521 | |
| 610 | |
| 825 | 1333 subtotal |
| 170 | |
| 241 | |
| | 1236 subtotal |
| 4061 | grand total |

## Addition Shortcut

Another way to make this addition problem easier is to use angular addition. Instead of adding each column and carrying to the next, separate the problem into three individual columns and add them:

then use angular
addition to get the total

| 3 | 5 | 2 | 352 |
|---|---|---|-----|
| 4 | 1 | 9 | 419 |
| 7 | 2 | 1 | 721 |
| 2 | 0 | 2 | 202 |
| 5 | 2 | 1 | 521 |
| 6 | 1 | 0 | 610 |
| 8 | 2 | 5 | 825 |
| 1 | 7 | 0 | 170 |
| 2 | 4 | 1 | 241 |
| 38 | 24 | 21 | 21 |
| | | | 24 |
| | | | 38 |
| | | | 4061 |

## How to Estimate the Sum When You're in a Hurry

Often it is unnecessary to obtain the exact answer in addition. If you're adding mileages on a map or estimating expenses for a budget, you can save time by rounding off each number in the column. For example:

(Estimate by rounding off each number
to the nearest 10)

| 22 | becomes | 20 |
|----|---------|----|
| 33 | becomes | 30 |
| 45 | becomes | 50 |
| 58 | becomes | 60 |
| 158 | | 160 |

Note that the estimated answer is reasonably close to the exact answer.

Obviously if you are dealing with numbers in the 100s, you would round off to the nearest 100:

| 121 | becomes | 100 |
|-----|---------|-----|
| 576 | becomes | 600 |
| 832 | becomes | 800 |
| 375 | becomes | 400 |
| 1904 | | 1900 |

Estimating is also a quick way to check the approximate accuracy of your work in adding a column of figures.

## HOW TO SUBTRACT NUMBERS QUICKLY AND ACCURATELY

Subtraction is the reverse of addition. In adding, you increase one number by combining it with a second. In subtracting, you take away the smaller number from the larger.

For example, if you leave the house with $5 in the morning and your friend Lois repays the $10 she owes you, you now have $15. If you buy lunch for $5, you subtract it from the $15 and you have $10 left.

Since the electronic calculator performs all operations by adding, it subtracts by adding two numbers, one of which has a negative sign. This is how it works:

In subtracting 5 from 15, the calculator first counts to 15 in one direction, then reverses itself and counts to 5 in the opposite direction.

$$\longrightarrow$$

$$1 \quad 2 \quad 3 \quad 4 \quad 5 \quad 6 \quad 7 \quad 8 \quad 9 \quad 10 \quad 11 \quad 12 \quad 13 \quad 14 \quad 15$$

$$5 \quad 4 \quad 3 \quad 2 \quad 1$$

$$\longleftarrow$$

Answer (10)

In subtraction, you have to memorize the same 100 combinations used in addition but in reverse.

$$
\begin{array}{cc}
3 & 6 \\
-1 & -4 \\
\hline
2 & 2 \\
\end{array}
\qquad \text{etc.}
$$

Again, the task is made easier by the combinations involving 1 or 0. See how well you remember the combinations by performing these subtraction examples:

$$
\begin{array}{ccccccc}
5 & 8 & 9 & 11 & 14 & 15 & 17 \\
-1 & -3 & -5 & -2 & -7 & -6 & -9 \\
\end{array}
$$

If you want to review them, a table of subtraction combinations is on page 10. This list includes only those combinations which may give you difficulty.

Subtraction operations can be quickly checked for accuracy. Simply add the lower figure back to the number being subtracted to get the top number. For example:

$$\begin{array}{r} 521 \\ -310 \\ \hline 211 \end{array} \qquad \begin{array}{r} 310 \\ +211 \\ \hline 521 \end{array}$$

**Borrowing:** Some subtraction problems are not as easy as the one above. Look at the example below. Although 2 can be subtracted from 4, 8 cannot be subtracted directly from 6. We can, however, borrow from the 5 in the left column:

$$\begin{array}{r} 564 \\ -282 \\ \hline 2 \end{array} \quad \text{then} \quad \begin{array}{r} \text{Borrow 1 from 5} \\ \text{\& add 10 to 6} \\ 4^{1}64 \\ -282 \\ \hline 282 \end{array}$$

In effect, we have increased the 6 to 16, permitting us to subtract 8 from 16. This process can be continued if necessary:

$$\begin{array}{r} 235\overset{1}{6} \\ -1767 \\ \hline \end{array} \longleftarrow \text{First, } \textit{borrow } \text{1 from 5}$$

$$\begin{array}{r} 234\overset{1}{6} \\ -1767 \\ \hline 9 \end{array} \text{ then } \textit{borrow } \text{1 from 3}$$

$$\begin{array}{r} 2\overset{1}{2}46 \\ -1767 \\ \hline 89 \end{array} \text{ then } \textit{borrow } \text{1 from 2}$$

$$\begin{array}{r} 1246 \\ -1767 \\ \hline 589 \end{array}$$

Prove your answer by adding:
$$\begin{array}{r} 589 \\ +1767 \\ \hline 2356 \end{array}$$

## SUBTRACTION COMBINATIONS

| 11 | 11 | 11 | 12 | 11 | 12 | 11 |
|----|----|----|----|----|----|----|
| 2  | 9  | 8  | 9  | 3  | 3  | 7  |
| 9  | 2  | 3  | 3  | 8  | 9  | 4  |

| 12 | 13 | 11 | 12 | 13 | 11 | 12 |
|----|----|----|----|----|----|----|
| 8  | 9  | 4  | 4  | 4  | 6  | 7  |
| 4  | 4  | 7  | 8  | 9  | 5  | 5  |

| 13 | 14 | 11 | 12 | 13 | 14 | 13 |
|----|----|----|----|----|----|----|
| 8  | 9  | 5  | 5  | 5  | 5  | 7  |
| 5  | 5  | 6  | 7  | 8  | 9  | 6  |

| 14 | 15 | 13 | 14 | 15 | 15 | 16 |
|----|----|----|----|----|----|----|
| 8  | 9  | 6  | 6  | 6  | 8  | 9  |
| 6  | 6  | 7  | 8  | 9  | 7  | 7  |

| 14 | 15 | 16 | 16 | 17 | 16 | 18 |
|----|----|----|----|----|----|----|
| 7  | 7  | 7  | 8  | 9  | 9  | 9  |
| 7  | 8  | 9  | 8  | 8  | 7  | 9  |

Here are a series of subtraction problems involving borrowing. Try to solve them. See if you understand the process thoroughly and how the answers were obtained:

|   340.57 |   423.13 |   553.75 |
|---------:|---------:|---------:|
| − 120.98 | − 276.34 | − 141.87 |
|   219.59 |   146.79 |   411.88 |

Now prove the answers are correct by adding the result to the lower number. Note that the same estimating process used in addition can be applied to subtraction problems.

For example, when you return from your vacation you have $167 left. If you took $780 on the trip, you can estimate your expenses by subtracting $200 from $800 leaving $600 as your estimate. The exact expenditure was $613, very close to your estimate.

## HOW TO MULTIPLY NUMBERS QUICKLY AND ACCURATELY

This operation is really a short form of addition. Think again about the electronic calculator which only knows how to add. If you present the calculator the problem of multiplying 5 × 6, it will simply add $6+6+6+6+6=30$. The calculator works so fast it can handle such problems as $65 \times 37$ this way, but we will use a different method.

To perform multiplication problems easily, it is essential to remember your grammar school multiplication tables:

$$5 \times 3 = 15, \quad 6 \times 7 = 42, \quad 9 \times 8 = 72, \text{ etc.}$$

See how well you remember them by answering these samples:

$$6 \times 8 = ? \quad 7 \times 8 = ? \quad 7 \times 7 = ?$$
$$5 \times 9 = ? \quad 9 \times 9 = ? \quad 9 \times 6 = ?$$

A set of multiplication tables is on page 13 if you need a review. If you're rusty you'll need to brush up on multiplication, particularly the 7s, 8s, and 9s, the hardest ones to remember.

Fortunately, some numbers are very easy. To multiply by 10, for instance, simply add a zero to the number:

$$72 \times 10 = 720$$

To multiply by 100, add 2 zeros; by 1000, 3 zeros, and so on.

When multiplying by 5, remember that your answer will end in zero if the number is even and in 5 if it's odd:

$$12 \times 5 = 60 \qquad 15 \times 5 = 75$$

And, if you multiply by 0 you'll always get 0 for an answer.

To multiply numbers with two, three or more digits, make use of the fact that any large number can be broken down. Thus:

$$23 \text{ is the same as } 20 + 3$$
$$128 \text{ is } 100 + 20 + 8$$

To multiply 122 by 23, for example, we proceed as follows. First, multiply 122 by 3, then by 20 and add up the results:

$$
\begin{array}{r}
122 \\
\times 3 \\
\hline
366
\end{array}
\qquad
\begin{array}{r}
122 \\
\times 20 \\
\hline
2440
\end{array}
$$

(since 20 is 2 × 10, we can multiply 122 by 2 and add a zero)

$$
\begin{array}{r}
366 \\
+2440 \\
\hline
2806
\end{array}
$$

**An Easy Way to Understand Carrying in Multiplication**

When we multiply larger numbers, the process is slightly more complicated. If the result of an individual multiplication is a product (answer) greater than 9 (in other words has two digits), the left-hand digit must be carried to the next place (the result of the next multiplication) and added to the product of that place. To see how it works, let's multiply 137 by 4:

$$
\begin{array}{r}
137 \\
\times 4 \\
\hline
28 \\
12 \\
4 \\
\hline
548
\end{array}
$$

[Note: Each of these products is moved one place to the left to account for the fact that we are first multiplying units (4 × 7 = 28), then tens (4 × 3 = 12), then hundreds (4 × 1 = 4)]

We can shorten this process by carrying

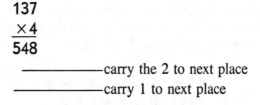

$$
\begin{array}{r}
137 \\
\times 4 \\
\hline
548
\end{array}
$$

————————carry the 2 to next place

————————carry 1 to next place

## MULTIPLICATION TABLES

| | | | |
|---|---|---|---|
| $2 \times 1 = 2$ | $3 \times 1 = 3$ | $4 \times 1 = 4$ | $5 \times 1 = 5$ |
| $2 \times 2 = 4$ | $3 \times 2 = 6$ | $4 \times 2 = 8$ | $5 \times 2 = 10$ |
| $2 \times 3 = 6$ | $3 \times 3 = 9$ | $4 \times 3 = 12$ | $5 \times 3 = 15$ |
| $2 \times 4 = 8$ | $3 \times 4 = 12$ | $4 \times 4 = 16$ | $5 \times 4 = 20$ |
| $2 \times 5 = 10$ | $3 \times 5 = 15$ | $4 \times 5 = 20$ | $5 \times 5 = 25$ |
| $2 \times 6 = 12$ | $3 \times 6 = 18$ | $4 \times 6 = 24$ | $5 \times 6 = 30$ |
| $2 \times 7 = 14$ | $3 \times 7 = 21$ | $4 \times 7 = 28$ | $5 \times 7 = 35$ |
| $2 \times 8 = 16$ | $3 \times 8 = 24$ | $4 \times 8 = 32$ | $5 \times 8 = 40$ |
| $2 \times 9 = 18$ | $3 \times 9 = 27$ | $4 \times 9 = 36$ | $5 \times 9 = 45$ |
| | | | |
| $6 \times 1 = 6$ | $7 \times 1 = 7$ | $8 \times 1 = 8$ | $9 \times 1 = 9$ |
| $6 \times 2 = 12$ | $7 \times 2 = 14$ | $8 \times 2 = 16$ | $9 \times 2 = 18$ |
| $6 \times 3 = 18$ | $7 \times 3 = 21$ | $8 \times 3 = 24$ | $9 \times 3 = 27$ |
| $6 \times 4 = 24$ | $7 \times 4 = 28$ | $8 \times 4 = 32$ | $9 \times 4 = 36$ |
| $6 \times 5 = 30$ | $7 \times 5 = 35$ | $8 \times 5 = 40$ | $9 \times 5 = 45$ |
| $6 \times 6 = 36$ | $7 \times 6 = 42$ | $8 \times 6 = 48$ | $9 \times 6 = 54$ |
| $6 \times 7 = 42$ | $7 \times 7 = 49$ | $8 \times 7 = 56$ | $9 \times 7 = 63$ |
| $6 \times 8 = 48$ | $7 \times 8 = 56$ | $8 \times 8 = 64$ | $9 \times 8 = 72$ |
| $6 \times 9 = 54$ | $7 \times 9 = 63$ | $8 \times 9 = 72$ | $9 \times 9 = 81$ |

Here are two problems worked out. See if you can arrive at the same answers.

```
     312
    ×64
    1248      (multiply 312 × 4)
    1872      (multiply 312 × 6 and move answer one place to the left)
  19,968
```

This is a slightly more complicated problem. Try to follow it completely.

756

×87
-----
5292          (multiply 7 × 756)
  34
6048          (multiply 8 × 756 and go left one place)
  44
-----
65,772

The small figures are the numbers carried to the next place to the left.

### How to Check the Accuracy of Your Multiplication

Checking multiplication is usually done by reversing the numbers being multiplied and repeating the process (756 × 87, then 87 × 756).

### Four Multiplication Shortcuts

There are few shortcuts in multiplication, but these suggestions may be helpful:

1. To multiply by 99, use 100 instead and subtract the number.
2. To multiply by 101, use 100 and add the number.
3. To multiply by 25, use 100 and divide by 4.
4. To multiply by 50, use 100 and divide by 2.

## HOW TO DIVIDE NUMBERS QUICKLY AND ACCURATELY

A division is the inverse operation of multiplication. A calculator performs division by subtraction. For example, to arrive at $48 \div 12 = 4$, the calculator would subtract 12 from 48 four times. However, there is a shorter way. First, you'll need to remember your division combinations:

$$8 \div 4 = 2$$
$$10 \div 5 = 2, \text{ or}$$
$$10 \div 2 = 5, \text{ etc.}$$

As you review these combinations, remember that you can't divide by zero, so you'll have fewer to remember. (Refer to page 17 for division tables.)

The simplest division problems involve single numbers:

$$
\begin{array}{r} 123 \\ 3\overline{)369} \end{array}
\qquad \text{or} \qquad
\begin{array}{r} 36 \\ 4\overline{)144} \end{array}
$$

The second problem requires that you carry a remainder. Since 4 goes into 14 three times with a remainder of two, that number is added to the next place making it 24 (the two is 10 times greater than the number to its right).

Here is another problem using remainders. Follow the solution to see that you understand the method.

$$
\begin{array}{r} 2618 \\ 3\overline{)7854} \end{array}
$$

## How and When to Use Long Division

When dividing by numbers with two or more digits, the process is slightly different. Follow the example below:

$$
\begin{array}{r}
23 \\
71\overline{)1674} \\
\underline{142}\phantom{00} \\
254\phantom{0} \\
\underline{213}\phantom{0} \\
41\phantom{0}
\end{array}
$$

We start by estimating how many times the first digit of the divisor (71) goes into 16. The answer is 2, and that number is written on the top line. It is the first digit of the answer.

Next, multiply the whole divisor (71) by 2 (the figure above the line). Write the answer 142 under 167. Subtract 142 from 167 and get 25.

Bring 4 down from 1674 and write it alongside 25.

Now estimate how many 7s there are in 25. Write the answer, 3, alongside the 2 on the top line.

Multiply 71 by 3 and write 213 under 254. When you subtract, the answer is 41, the remainder (since 71 is larger than 41).

The solution to the problem is written 23 remainder 41, or 23 41/71.

To check your work, multiply the answer by the divisor. Add the remainder to 1633:

$$
\begin{array}{rr}
23 & 1633 \\
\times 71 & +41 \\
\hline
23 & 1674 \\
161 & \\
\hline
1633 &
\end{array}
$$

If you find that you estimated too high a number for the answer, you'll need to reduce your estimate and try again:

$$
\begin{array}{r}
3 \\
65 \overline{)1821} \\
195 \\
\hline
\end{array}
$$

Here we estimated 3 since 6 goes into 18   3 times. However, 195 is greater than 182, so our answer is wrong. Erase 195 and 3.

$$
\begin{array}{r}
28 \\
65 \overline{)1821} \\
130 \\
\hline
521 \\
520 \\
\hline
1
\end{array}
$$

Using 2 as the estimate, we multiply 65 × 2 = 130. Bring down 1 and estimate 8 as the next digit in the answer.

The answer is 28, remainder 1, or 28 1/65.

Sometimes we estimate the answer too low as in this example:

$$
\begin{array}{r}
3 \\
37 \overline{)1590} \\
111 \\
\hline
48
\end{array}
$$

Since 48 is larger than 37, we realize that we should increase 3 to 4. Erase, 3, 111 and 48.

$$
\begin{array}{r}
42 \\
37 \overline{)1590} \\
148 \\
\hline
110 \\
74 \\
\hline
36 \text{ remainder}
\end{array}
$$

Multiply 4 × 37, subtract 148 from 159 and bring down 0 to add to 11.

## DIVISION TABLES

| | | | |
|---|---|---|---|
| 2 ÷ 2 = 1 | 3 ÷ 3 = 1 | 4 ÷ 4 = 1 | 5 ÷ 5 = 1 |
| 4 ÷ 2 = 2 | 6 ÷ 3 = 2 | 8 ÷ 4 = 2 | 10 ÷ 5 = 2 |
| 6 ÷ 2 = 3 | 9 ÷ 3 = 3 | 12 ÷ 4 = 3 | 15 ÷ 5 = 3 |
| 8 ÷ 2 = 4 | 12 ÷ 3 = 4 | 16 ÷ 4 = 4 | 20 ÷ 5 = 4 |
| 10 ÷ 2 = 5 | 15 ÷ 3 = 5 | 20 ÷ 4 = 5 | 25 ÷ 5 = 5 |
| 12 ÷ 2 = 6 | 18 ÷ 3 = 6 | 24 ÷ 4 = 6 | 30 ÷ 5 = 6 |
| 14 ÷ 2 = 7 | 21 ÷ 3 = 7 | 28 ÷ 4 = 7 | 35 ÷ 5 = 7 |
| 16 ÷ 2 = 8 | 24 ÷ 3 = 8 | 32 ÷ 4 = 8 | 40 ÷ 5 = 8 |
| 18 ÷ 2 = 9 | 27 ÷ 3 = 9 | 36 ÷ 4 = 9 | 45 ÷ 5 = 9 |
| | | | |
| 6 ÷ 6 = 1 | 7 ÷ 7 = 1 | 8 ÷ 8 = 1 | 9 ÷ 9 = 1 |
| 12 ÷ 6 = 2 | 14 ÷ 7 = 2 | 16 ÷ 8 = 2 | 18 ÷ 9 = 2 |
| 18 ÷ 6 = 3 | 21 ÷ 7 = 3 | 24 ÷ 8 = 3 | 27 ÷ 9 = 3 |
| 24 ÷ 6 = 4 | 28 ÷ 7 = 4 | 32 ÷ 8 = 4 | 36 ÷ 9 = 4 |
| 30 ÷ 6 = 5 | 35 ÷ 7 = 5 | 40 ÷ 8 = 5 | 45 ÷ 9 = 5 |
| 36 ÷ 6 = 6 | 42 ÷ 7 = 6 | 48 ÷ 8 = 6 | 54 ÷ 9 = 6 |
| 42 ÷ 6 = 7 | 49 ÷ 7 = 7 | 56 ÷ 8 = 7 | 63 ÷ 9 = 6 |
| 48 ÷ 6 = 8 | 56 ÷ 7 = 8 | 64 ÷ 8 = 8 | 72 ÷ 9 = 8 |
| 54 ÷ 6 = 9 | 63 ÷ 7 = 9 | 72 ÷ 8 = 9 | 81 ÷ 9 = 9 |

Estimate 3 into 11 goes 3 times. However, $3 \times 37 = 111$, which is too large. Using 2 instead, multiply $2 \times 34 = 74$. Answer is 42, remainder 36, or 42 36/37.

Long division is an awkward process. Go over the examples above until you are thoroughly familiar with the method, then try these examples below:

$$37 \overline{)674}$$

(*Answer:* 18 rem. 8)

$$65 \overline{)1095}$$

(*Answer:* 16 rem. 55)

$$21 \overline{)5982}$$

(*Answer:* 284 rem. 18)

$$36 \overline{)8574}$$

(*Answer:* 238 rem. 6)

## How to Estimate Division Answers

Since long division can be tedious, estimating can save us a lot of time if all we need is an approximate answer. The easiest way is to round off the numbers in the problem so you can solve it in your head. Example:

$$
\begin{array}{r} 8 \\ 48\overline{)387} \\ 384 \\ \hline 3 \end{array}
\quad \text{rounded off to} \quad 50\overline{)400}
$$

*Answer:* 8

Note that the answer is within 3/48 of being exact.

Estimate the answers to the following division problems.

$$62\overline{)5248} \qquad 48\overline{)8029}$$

$$37\overline{)820} \qquad 52\overline{)9761}$$

## HOW TO UNDERSTAND AND USE COMMON FRACTIONS

Fractions are used when we need to express quantities less than 1. If, for example, a letter is more than one page long but less than two, we can express the part as ¼, ½ or ¾, depending on the exact length of the partial page.

If we say it is ¾ of a page, we are actually dividing the page into four equal parts and saying that the typing on the page covers 3 of those 4 parts.

¾ is a proper fraction. The 4 is called the denominator and it indicates the number of parts into which the whole is divided. The 3 is called the numerator and it tells how many of the equal parts we have measured or counted.

When the numerator equals the denominator we have a whole: ¼=1. When the numerator is smaller, we are dealing with a proper fraction. When the numerator is greater than the denominator we have an improper fraction: ⁵⁄₄. Since that fraction is ⁴⁄₄+¼, it can also be written 1¼.

Unusual things happen when fractions are added or subtracted, multiplied or divided. Let's start by multiplying the numerator of a fraction ¾ by 3 = ⁹⁄₄. Since ⁹⁄₄ can be written 2¼, we can see that the whole fraction is tripled in size. Thus, we can say: to multiply a fraction, multiply the numerator.

If we multiply the denominator of the same fraction by 2, we get $\frac{3}{4\times2}$ = ⅜, which is exactly ½ of ¾. Now we can say: multiplying the denominator of a fraction divides the fraction.

What happens if we multiply both top and bottom? ¾×½=⅜, which is the same size as ¾! Thus, we see that multiplying by the same number top and bottom really doesn't change anything. This shouldn't be surprising since ½ (the number we multiplied by) = 1.

If we divide the numerator, we divide the fraction:

$$\frac{4 \div 2}{5} = 2/5$$

Dividing the denominator, on the other hand, multiplies the fraction:

$$\frac{3}{8 \div 2} = 3/4$$

And, as we might suspect, dividing both top and bottom of a fraction by the same number changes nothing:

$$8/12 \div 4/4 = 2/3$$

## How to Add and Subtract Fractions

Fractions with the same denominator may be added and subracted by adding or subtracting the numerators:

$$5/5 + 3/5 = 8/5 = 1\text{-}3/5$$
$$7/8 - 5/8 = 2/8 = 1/4$$

However, if fractions have different denominators, it gets a little more complex. In the problem

$$3/8 + 1/4 = ?$$

we can see that by multiplying ¼×½ we get ⅔, an equivalent fraction. Now we can add ⅜+⅔=⅝.

| To subtract | $5/8 - 1/4 = ?$ |
|---|---|
| we multiply | $1/4 \times 2/2$ and get $2/8$ |
| | $5/8 - 2/8 = 3/8$ |

In another case

$$4/5 + 1/4 = ?$$

Here the only denominator that fits both fractions is 20 and it is necessary to change both fractions

$$4/5 = 16/20 \text{ (multiply top and bottom by 4), and}$$
$$1/4 = 5/20 \quad \text{(multiply by 5/5)}$$

then we have $^{16}/_{20} + ^{5}/_{20} = ^{21}/_{20} = 1^{1}/_{20}$. As you probably observed, 20 is the product of both denominators $(4 \times 5 = 20)$. Often this is the only way to obtain a common denominator to solve addition and subtraction problems.

Here is a common situation that illustrates the method: Gus Sondheim does part-time maintenance work for the Trumbull Company. Last week he worked 4 hours 20 minutes on Tuesday, 6 hours 30 minutes on Wednesday, and 5 hours 45 minutes on Friday. How many total hours did Gus work?

Here's how the problem can be expressed:

Tues. $4\frac{1}{3}$ hrs. (20 min. $= \frac{1}{3}$ hr.)
Wed. $6\frac{1}{2}$ hrs. (30 min. $= \frac{1}{2}$ hr.)
Fri.   $5\frac{3}{4}$ hrs. (45 min. $= \frac{3}{4}$ hr.)

There are several ways to add such mixed numbers, but adding integers and fractions separately is probably the simplest. Multiplying $3 \times 2 \times 6 = 36$, but inspection reveals that 12 is the smallest common denominator.

The addition goes as follows:

$$
\begin{array}{llll}
4 & 1/3 = & 4/12 & \text{(multiply by 4/4)} \\
6 & 1/2 = & 6/12 & \text{(multiply by 6/6)} \\
\underline{5} & 3/4 = & \underline{9/12} & \text{(multiply by 3/3)} \\
15 & & 19/12 = 1\text{-}7/12 \\
\underline{+\ 1\text{-}7/12} \\
16\text{-}7/12 & \text{hours Gus worked}
\end{array}
$$

## Taking the Mystery Out of Ratio and Proportion

These are terms often used in business and are commonly expressed as fractions. The ratio of one number to another is obtained by dividing one by another. For example, the ratio of 4 to 8 is $4 \div 8 = \frac{1}{2}$. And the ratio of 8 to 4 is 2. Since ratios often appear as fractions, problems involving ratios may generally be solved by using the principles of fractions that we have already reviewed.

Ratios often appear in the analysis of financial statements to compare one figure with another. The assets of a company for example must be compared to the liabilities in assessing the company's health. Accountants often refer to the current ratio in comparing current assets with current liabilities.

A proportion states that two ratios are equal. For example, the ratio of 4 to 6 is the same as 2 to 3. It may be written as

$$4/6 = 2/3$$

Proportions are useful for solving a number of common business problems. For example, if you can file 20 folders in 2 hours, how long will it take you to file 120 folders?

The ratio of the folders is bound to be the same as the ratio of the two times.

$$20/120 = 2/? \quad \text{If we divide 20 by 2 we get 10.}$$

We can also divide 120 by 10 without changing the fraction, so the time to file 120 folders must be 12 hours.

Another way to solve proportion problems is to multiply the numerator of the first ratio by the denominator of the second and equate it to the denominator of the first multiplied by the numerator of the second. Thus, $20/120 = 2/?$ becomes $20 \times ? = 120 \times 2$, or $2 \times ? = 24$ and $? = 12$.

Consider another problem: The shipping department at Ajax Company uses cartons at the rate of 80 per day. How long will it take to use up the current inventory of 480 cartons?

The ratio of cartons is 80/480. The ratios of days is 1/?. We can write

$$80/480 = 1/? \quad \text{or} \quad 8/48 = 1/?$$

Multiplying we get $? \times 8 = 1 \times 48$, which we can also write $? = 48/8 = 6$.

## Understanding and Using Decimal Fractions

Because common fractions are cumbersome to deal with at times (as we have just observed), decimal fractions are used more often—especially in business.

A decimal fraction is one whose denominator is 10 or an integral multiple of 10 (100, 1000, etc.). For example, the fractions 7/10, 45/100 and 275/1000 can also be written .07, .45, and .275. As noted before, such expressions are pure decimal fractions, but if you add whole numbers to them they become mixed decimals: 1.07, 3.45 and 57.275.

Now you can add these numbers as easily as you do simple whole numbers, except you have to keep track of the decimal point which separates the whole number from the fraction. To the left of the decimal point are the whole numbers starting with units going to tens, hundreds, thousands, etc., as we move left. To the right are tenths, hundredths, thousandths, etc., as we move right (see chart below).

| Hundreds | Tens | Units | | Tenths | Hundredths | Thousandths |
|----------|------|-------|---|--------|------------|-------------|
| 7 | 5 | 6 | . | 3 | 2 | 5 |

This number is read seven hundred fifty-six and three hundred twenty-five thousandths. The "and" locates the decimal point.

In performing decimal addition or subtraction, you'll want to keep the decimal points in column. For example:

$$
\begin{array}{r}
357.20 \\
821.35 \\
+465.14 \\
\hline
1643.69
\end{array}
\qquad
\begin{array}{r}
721.15 \\
-402.10 \\
\hline
319.05
\end{array}
$$

Multiplication is slightly more complicated. Multiply as if you were dealing with whole numbers. After you finish, count the places to the right of the decimal in both numbers being multiplied and put the decimal point an equal number of places to the left in the answer. Here's an example:

$$
\begin{array}{r}
45.23 \\
\times\ 3.5 \\
\hline
22615 \\
13569 \\
\hline
158.305
\end{array}
\qquad
\begin{array}{l}
2 \text{ decimal places} \\
+1 \text{ decimal place} \\
\hline
3 \text{ in the answer}
\end{array}
$$

Multiplying decimals by 10, 100, 1000 (or other multiples of 10) is easy. Just move the decimal point one, two, or three places to the right:

$$
\begin{array}{rcl}
35.245 \times 10 & = & 352.45 \\
35.245 \times 100 & = & 3524.5 \\
35.245 \times 1000 & = & 35245.
\end{array}
$$

In division problems, place the decimal point directly above the number being divided if you are dividing by a whole number.

$$
\begin{array}{r}
3.04 \\
12\overline{)\,36.48}
\end{array}
$$

If you're dividing by a decimal number, first make the divisor (the number you're dividing by) a whole number by moving the decimal point as many places to the right as needed. Move the decimal the same distance to the right in the number being divided and proceed as before. Here's how it works:

$$
1.2\overline{)\,36.48} \quad \text{becomes} \quad 12\overline{)\,364.8}^{\;30.4}
$$

If you're dividing by 10, 100, 1000, etc., simply move the decimal to the left one, two or three places as needed:

$$
\begin{aligned}
157.5 \div 10 &= 15.75 \\
157.5 \div 100 &= 1.575 \\
157.5 \div 1000 &= .1575
\end{aligned}
$$

In working with decimals, it's generally advisable to examine your answer to see if it appears reasonable. For example:

$$
3.2\overline{)\,35.52} \quad = \quad
\begin{array}{r}
11.1 \\
32\overline{)\,355.2} \\
32\phantom{5.2} \\
\hline
35\phantom{.2} \\
32\phantom{.2} \\
\hline
32 \\
32
\end{array}
$$

Since 35.52 is slightly more than ten times greater than 3.2, the answer is reasonable.

## How to Simplify Your Work By Converting to Decimal Fractions

Since decimal fractions are so much easier to work with than common fractions, it's handy to know how to change the latter to decimal form. To do this, simply divide the numerator into the denominator and the result is the decimal equivalent. For example, to change ⅜, divide—

$$
\begin{array}{r}
.375 \\
8\overline{)3.00} \\
\underline{2\,4} \\
60 \\
\underline{56} \\
40
\end{array}
$$

To save you time and trouble, a table of decimal equivalents for common fractions is included in the Appendix.

### How to Understand and Work Easily With Percentages

A percentage is one of the most convenient and commonly used arithmetic concepts, particularly in the business world. It is primarily a method of making comparisons. For instance, a business owner will compare profit with selling price of this year's business with last year's, and express the result as percentage. In addition, the amount of interest charged on a loan, the commission on the sales price, and the increase in costs over the previous season are all commonly given as percentages.

The problem given previously in decimal fractions will help you to understand percentages, since it is merely a different way of expressing decimal fractions.

The word PERCENT literally means hundredths. For example, 1% is one one-hundredth, or .01. 75% is the same as .75; 125% is 1.25, etc.

8% of a number is 8/100 or .08 multiplied by the number. As an example, 8% of 150 is .08 × 150 = 12.

The phrase "percent of" is obviously the same as "hundredths of." If we say that 50% of 24 is 12, we can also say that 50% = 50/100 or 1/2, and 1/2 of 24 = 12.

By the same method, 75% of 120 = 90. If we express 75% as 75/100, we can divide both parts of this fraction by 25 and get 3/4. And 3/4 of 120 = 90.

Now we're ready to find percentages. For example, what percent of 45 is 15? First we can say that it's 15/45. 15/45 = 1/3. To write 1/3 as a decimal fraction we divide—

$$
\begin{array}{r}
.333 \\
3\overline{)1.000}
\end{array}
\qquad \text{and } .333 = 33.3\%.
$$

(Note that we could have continued to divide 3 into 10 and gotten .33333 ... In such cases, we can round off the result and get as accurate an answer as we need.)

Figure the following percentages:

$$5 \text{ of } 25 =$$

$$(5/25 = 1/5 \quad 5 \overline{) \,\, 1.00}^{\,\,.20} \quad (\textit{Answer: } 20\%)$$

$$5 \text{ of } 48 = \qquad (\textit{Answer: } 10.4\%)$$

$$14 \text{ of } 35 = \qquad (\textit{Answer: } 40\%)$$

(Note that in converting decimal fractions to percentages, it is merely necessary to move the decimal point two places to the right.)

When we say 125% of 120 = 150, it will help us to know that

125% is called the rate
125   is the base and
150   is the percentage

If we know any two of these elements, we can find the third. So we have three kinds of problems:

1) What is 25% of 20 (percentage unknown)?
If we write 25% as 25/100 and divide both numbers by 25, the answer is 1/4. And 1/4 of 20 = 5.

2) 5 is 25% of what number (base unknown)?
25% can be written 25/100 = 1/4 (see above). Then $4 \times 5 = 20$.

3) 5 is what percent of 20 (rate unknown)?
5/20 is the equivalent fraction. 5/20 is 25/100 (multiply both numbers by 5). 25/100 = .25 = 25%.

## How Percentage Is Used in Business

The cost of a bank loan is often expressed as a percentage. If you go to a bank to borrow $1,000, you will be told that the cost of the loan (interest) will be 12% a year, or $120. (Later on we will see how banks compute interest and discounts using percentages.)

Most businesspeople express their profit on a sale as a percentage of the selling price. If, for instance, a jeweler sells a diamond ring for $2,000 and it cost him $1,200, his profit is $2000 - 1200 = \$800$ or $800/2000 = 2/5 = .40 = 40\%$.

Tax rates are frequently expressed as percentages. The state of New Jersey, for instance, charges 6% of the sale price on taxable merchandise. Other business applications include trade discounts offered to certain customer classes, depreciation on business property, and inventory turnover rates.

# CHAPTER 2

# How to Use the Electronic Calculator for Speed and Accuracy

Science has finally delivered us a tool to simplify our lives—at least as far as math is concerned. The handheld electronic calculator has been made so compact, inexpensive, and easy to operate that no home or office should be without one. When used in the right way, the calculator can save enormous amounts of time in figuring complex problems. Once you have learned to perform the calculations discussed in this book, the calculator will help you solve problems faster and more accurately. For that reason, we have devoted this section to help you become proficient with this electronic marvel and to show you how to take full advantage of your new knowledge.

## HOW TO SELECT A CALCULATOR THAT FITS YOUR NEEDS

With the tremendous variety and price range of calculators now available, selecting the right one can be a little difficult, particularly if you've never used one before. Here are some points to consider:

—Don't get carried away with the small sizes. Those calculators that fit on the barrel of a pen or the face of a watch are cute, but try using the keys quickly and accurately. You should press the keys a few times on the model you've chosen to see how easily they work and how many times you hit the wrong ones. You'll get more use out of your calculator if it's comfortable to handle.

—Be sure the number display is easy to read under various lighting conditions. Remember, if you can't read the numbers easily, it won't save time and accurately solve problems.

—Consider buying one of the newer solar-powered units. Battery-operated calculators can be a nuisance if the batteries have to be replaced, but with a solar-powered model, any kind of light will keep it working.

—Stay away from off-brands. In spite of their electronic capabilities, calculators do break down and you'll want a supplier to be able to repair it for you.

As far as capacity is concerned, stay away from models that perform more advanced calculations. These are more expensive and you probably won't need all their capabilities anyway. Most models have 8-digit capacity, which is more than enough for general work. In addition, it is desirable to select a unit with memory capability which stores numbers for later use.

Addition, subtraction, multiplication, and division are basic functions performed by even the simplest units. Other common and desirable features include error correction (when you push the wrong key), square-root computation, percentage indication, calculation with a constant and a floating decimal point.

## How to Use a Calculator for Best Results

Calculators vary in the way they work and key designation is not always uniform. In this section, we'll lead you through the common operations and also show you how to make use of the special features. However, before we start, make sure you're thoroughly familiar with the instrument—how to turn it on and off, and what each key means. The operating instructions should contain this information.

Some people forget to turn off the device when they've finished using it. This kind of neglect can wear down the batteries very quickly. For that reason, many newer models have an automatic turnoff feature. On most of these, the calculator simply turns itself off after 8 or 10 minutes if no key is pushed during that length of time.

Most models also have an error correction feature (usually labelled CE) that allows you to clear the number you've just entered without affecting any previous entries. Once you've solved a problem, it's necessary to clear the calculator completely before going on to the next. Use the C key for that purpose. If your unit has a memory, you'll have to press CM to clear stored data from the memory.

If the result of a calculation turns out to be a minus number (subtracting 5 from 4, for instance) a minus sign will appear in front of or behind the number. On most models, a small m or a dot will appear behind the display if a number is stored in the memory.

## How to Add and Subtract

To perform addition, enter the first number to be added, touch +, enter the second number, touch +, etc. When all numbers are entered, touch = and read the answer.

If you enter a decimal fraction, touch the decimal point key when you reach it (i.e., 12.95).

To check your work, add the column of figures a second time from the bottom up. If you're adding a long column, it's advisable to divide up the column into shorter, more manageable columns. If you want to show your cleverness, you can check your work by first writing down the indicated sum, then subtract each number in the column starting from the bottom. If your work was correct, the display should read zero.

Try these on your calculator and see if you get the same answers:

|  |  |  |  |
|---|---|---|---|
| 231 | 422 |  | 4572.96 |
| +589 | 657 |  | 8951.62 |
| 820 | 989 |  | 41.3 |
|  | 871 | 2068 | 655.01 |
| (Dividing column up | 125 |  | 14,220.89 |
| to avoid errors) | 764 | 1760 |  |
|  | 3828 |  |  |

Subtraction is equally as simple. Enter the top number, touch the − key, enter the bottom number and touch the = key. Read your answer on the display. Checking is easy. Without changing the display, touch the + key, enter the bottom and read the top number if your work is correct. Try these examples:

|  |  |  |  |
|---|---|---|---|
| 8,212 | 45,618 | 782.953 | 12.9763 |
| −4,057 | − 2,415 | − 47.002 | − 2.0506 |
| 4,155 | 43,203 | 735.951 | 10.9257 |

**How to Multiply**

Multiplication follows the same pattern. For instance, to multiply $2 \times 4$, touch 2, $\times$, and 4, and read the answer when you touch $=$. Use these examples to practice:

1. $45 \times 83 = 3735$
2. $62.1 \times 47.8 = 2968.38$
3. $22.356 \times 6.712 = 150.05347$

4. $49.8 \times 0.249 = 12.4002$
5. $0.857 \times 0.678 = 0.581046$

Since calculator operations are performed so quickly, you should get in the habit of checking your work. For multiplication, divide the product (result) by either of the multiplying figures. Your answer should be the other multiplier. Note, however, that in example 3, the product has exceeded the 8-digit capacity of the calculator, so the answer is rounded off. In checking, you will find the other multiplier to be slightly different than its true value.

Incidentally, if you multiply two large whole numbers and the capacity of the unit is exceeded, an E will appear alongside the display.

*EXAMPLE:*

$$65.720 \times 41.815 = 27.480818E$$

Depending on the calculator, there are various ways of handling overflow. Consult the instructions for detailed directions.

**How to Divide**

Division is handled like the other operations. To divide 375 by 3, for example, touch the 3, 7 and 5 keys, then $\div$, then 3. Touch $=$ to read the answer, 125.

To check division problems, multiply the answer by the divisor (the number divided by). The answer should be the number divided into. Try these examples and check their accuracy.

$2920 \div 31 = 94.193548$  
$424.3 \div 6.23 = 68.105939$  
$785,610 \div 3 = 261,870$

$48.922 \div .61 = 80.1$  
$728.28 \div 714 = 1.02$  
$0.9766 \div 1.04 = 0.9390384$

(You should have found one error.)

Your calculator can probably handle a chain of calculations like this one:

$$18.3 \times 15.6 \div 3 + 18 - 7 = 106.16$$

You can touch the numbers and the operational signs ($\times$, $\div$, $+$, $-$) in order and you should get the answer above.

If you run into a chain like this

$$3 + 10 - (3 \times 4 \div 6) = 11$$

you may have trouble. The problem must be solved by doing the multiplication and division first: $3 \times 4 \div 6 = 2$, then the addition and subtraction. Some calculators will sort this out automatically for you, others will not; so you'll have to consult your operating instructions. However, you can be sure of your results by always doing the multiplication and division first, then the addition and subtraction.

### How to Understand and Use Calculator Memory Functions

As outlined before, the calculator's memory will hold a number for you while you do an operation, then bring it back so you can use it again. Here's an example.

$$(12 + 15) \times (12 - 3) = 243$$

This means of course that you wish to multiply the sum of $12 + 15$ (27) by the difference between $12 - 3$ (9). On most calculators you can perform this operation as follows:

Touch $12 + 15 = 27$, next touch M+.   27 is now stored in the memory until you need it (this fact is generally indicated by a small m to the right of the display). Now touch $12 - 3 = 9$, then $\times$ and MR (which brings 27 back to the display). Now touch $=$ and 243 should appear.

*Note:* When you clear the display for the next problem, you must also clear the memory by touching MC. The small m will then disappear. Here are some examples to try:

$$270 \times (5 - 2) = 810$$
$$(45 - 22) \times (8 + 6) = 322$$
$$(7.5 + 8.6) \times (3 + 2) = 80.5$$

A division problem of the same kind requires slightly different handling:

$$(12 + 15) \div (12 - 3) = 3$$

Since the (12 + 15) factor is operated on by the (12 − 3), first subtract 12 − 3 = 9 and enter that into the memory (touch M+). Next, add (12 + 15) = 27, then touch ÷ and MR which brings back the stored 9, touch =, answer is 3.

The calculator may also have an M− key which subtracts the display number from the memory (if nothing is stored in the memory, it will store the number displayed with a minus sign).

## SIX CALCULATOR SHORTCUTS THAT WILL SIMPLIFY BUSINESS MATH

1. The percentage key (%) makes interest, markup, and discount problems easy and quick to solve. For example, if you borrow $6,000 at 8.5% interest, what's the annual interest?

*Answer:* Enter 6,000, touch ×, touch 8.5 and touch % key. Read $510.

2. If you buy a motorcycle for $850 and you want to resell it for a 16% gain, what's the resale price?

*Answer:* Enter 850 + 16 and touch %. Read $986.

3. If you decide to discount the $986 price 5%, what's the new price?

*Answer:* Enter 986 − 5 and touch %. Read $936.70, the discounted price.

4. If you wish to multiply a number by itself, i.e., $8 \times 8 = 64$, you can keep multiplying by touching the = key:

$8 \times 8 = 64$, or $8^2$          $8 \times 8 \times 8 = 512$, or $8^3$

$8 \times 8 \times 8 \times 8 = 4096$, or $8^4$          $8 \times 8 \times 8 \times 8 \times 8 = 32,768$, or $8^5$

5. These numbers are called the powers of 8 and are often used to avoid writing long numbers. For example: $10^2 = 100$, $10^3 = 1,000$, $10^4 = 10,000$, $10^6 = 1,000,000$.

Instead of writing 165,000,000, for instance, it is simpler to write 165 × $10^6$.

6. To calculate the reciprocal of a number—for example, the reciprocal of 8—enter 8, touch ÷, then =, and read 0.125. You'll remember this as the decimal fraction equivalent of 1/8.

## HOW TO USE A CONSTANT TO CUT YOUR MATH WORK IN HALF

Many calculations involve adding, subtracting, multiplying or dividing a single constant number in combination with a series of changing numbers. If, for example, you wish to increase all your prices by 15%, you must add 15% to every price in the store. Here is how it's done using the constant feature:

| Old Prices | New Prices |
|:---:|:---:|
| $1.25 | $1.44 |
| 2.75 | 3.16 |
| 3.20 | 3.68 |
| .85 | .98 |
| 4.90 | 5.64 |

First enter 1.15 (the constant), touch the × key, enter $1.25, touch the = key and read 1.4375 (round off to 1.44). Next, without changing the display, enter 2.75, touch the = key and read 3.1625 (round off to 3.16). Enter 3.20, touch =, read 3.68, and so on down the line.

Once the constant is entered, the calculator will make the multiplication automatically by entering the new number and touching the = key.

*Note:* Some calculators have a K key which you must touch after entering the constant. For example, in the pricing example above, the sequence would be: Enter 1.15, touch ×, then K, then 1.25. For subsequent operations, enter the variable number and touch the = and read the answer.

### How to Use a Constant to Solve Division Problems

For division, divide 2 (the constant) into 12, 10 and 8. First enter the variable, then ÷, then 2, and = 12÷2=6, enter 10, touch =, read 5. Enter 8, touch =, read 4.

With the K key, the sequence is: Enter 12, touch ÷, K and =.

For addition, the operation is: Enter variable number, touch +, enter constant, touch =. For example, add 12 to 6, 7 and 8: Enter 6, touch +, then 12 and =, read 18; enter 7, touch =, read 19; enter 8, touch =, read 20 (with the K key, enter 6, +, K, 12 and =).

### How to Use a Constant to Solve Subtraction Problems

For subtraction, follow the same procedure, except use − sign. For example, subtract 2 from 10, 11 and 12: Enter 10−2=8; enter 11, touch =, read 9; enter 12, touch =, read 10 (with the K key, enter, touch −, K, 2 and =).

As already noted, your calculator should have a key marked E or CE to clear errors. *Example:* Suppose you want to add 562 + 3412. After 562, touching +, you enter 3422 by mistake. The error key will allow you to clear the 3422 and enter 3412 without disturbing the other number (or numbers).

## PRACTICAL BUSINESS PROBLEMS YOU CAN SOLVE WITH YOUR CALCULATOR

There are many ways that you can use a calculator daily at home and at the office. That's why we've included a series of examples to demonstrate the abilities of the calculator and to lead you toward your own ideas for using it.

### Quick Ways to Convert From One Measurement to Another

The electronic calculator permits you to make conversions from metric to English systems as well as the reverse. Conversions within each system are also easily made. (In the section on measurement that follows, you will see how to calculate length, area, volume, speed, time, and temperature.)

To make these computations even quicker, a whole series of conversion factors from English to metric, metric to English, and conversion factors within the English system are listed on pages 217 through 220. One of the beauties of the metric system is that conversion between metric units is almost always an easy decimal transaction (divide or multiply by 10, 100, 1,000, etc.) so no conversion table is required.

### Practical Conversions You Can Do With a Calculator

1. If a building is 1,150 feet long, what is its length in meters? In rods?

*Solution:* First go to the conversion tables on page 208 in the Appendix. Note that 1 foot = 30.48 centimeters, or 0.3048 meters (multiply centimeters by 100 to get meters). On your calculator, enter

$$1150 \times 0.3048 = 350.52 \text{ meters}$$

To convert feet to rods, go to the conversion tables (page 210) and find that there are 16.5 feet in a rod. Enter

$$1150 \div 16.5 = 69.7 \text{ rods} \qquad \text{(rounded off)}$$

2. Cumberland Township comprises 542 square miles. How many square kilometers are contained? How many acres?

*Solution:* From the tables (page 216)

$$1 \text{ sq. mi.} = 2.59 \text{ sq. km., and}$$
$$640 \text{ acres} = 1 \text{ sq. mi.}$$

On your calculator enter

$$542 \times 2.59 = 1{,}403.78 \text{ sq. km., and}$$
$$542 \times 640 = 346{,}880 \text{ acres}$$

3. The Anderson Company has a 1,250 gallon fuel oil tank. How many liters does it contain? How many barrels?

*Solution:* From the tables:

$$1 \text{ gal.} = 3.785 \text{ liters, and}$$
$$31\text{-}1/2 \text{ gal.} = 1 \text{ barrel}$$

Enter on your calculator

$$1250 \times 3.785 = 4731.25 \text{ liters, and}$$
$$1250 \div 31.5 = 39.68$$

What if there is no conversion factor available for the conversion you want to make? Often you can make your own. Suppose you want to know how many acres there are in a square kilometer. From the tables, you know that:

$$1 \text{ sq. mi.} = 2.59 \text{ sq. km., and}$$
$$640 \text{ acres} = 1 \text{ sq. mi.}$$

If that is so, then

$$2.59 \text{ sq. km.} = 640 \text{ acres, and}$$
$$1 \text{ sq. km.} = \frac{640}{2.59} \text{ acres, and}$$
$$1 \text{ sq. km.} = 247.1 \text{ acres}$$

Here are some examples of conversion factors that you can compute yourself:

A. How many square inches are in a square meter? This is easy because of metric decimal relationships. From the table:

1 sq. in. = 6.452 sq. cm., or
1 sq. in. = .06452 sq. m. (since a sq. cm. = 0.01 sq. m.)

B. How many pints in a liter? From the table:

1 pint = 1/2 quart
1 quart = 0.9464 liter

Enter

1 pint = 1/2 × 0.9464
        = .47 liter

Here are several measurement conversion problems for you to solve:

|  | *Answers:* |
|---|---|
| 1) How many inches are in a kilometer? | 39,372 |
| 2) How many pounds in a metric ton? | 2,204.6 |
| 3) How many centimeters in a yard? | 91.44 |
| 4) How many cubic centimeters in a pint? | 473.2 |
| 5) How many rods in a kilometer? | 198.8 |
| 6) How many cubic inches in a liter? | 61.02 |
| 7) How many square yards in a square kilometer? | 1,195,988 |

## USING A CALCULATOR IN BUSINESS AND AT HOME

The sections that follow will show you time-saving ways for using a calculator in business and home situations.

### Figuring Depreciation

The subject of depreciation will be covered fully in Chapter 3. But because the calculator makes figuring constant percentage depreciation so simple, we thought you'd like to see an example:

Mr. Holden owns three cars used in his business. One car was bought in 1979, one in 1980, and one in 1981. The cars depreciate at the rate of 22% per year. Holden paid $8,210 for the first car, $9,750 for the second, and $11,450 for the third. What will the total book value of the cars be at the end of 1984?

*Solution:* As you learned earlier, you can multiply by 100− % rate rather than subtract the amount of depreciation. Thus, 100−22=78%. You can use the "multiplication by a constant technique" on your calculator to make this problem easy to solve:

Enter .78 (dec. equiv. of 78%) × cost of car 1 (8210) = 6404 (value at end of first year), touch = 4995 (value at end of second year), and so on through each year up to 1984 for all three cars. If you tabulate the results, the answer looks like this:

| | Car 1 | Car 2 | Car 3 | Book Value at End of Year |
|---|---|---|---|---|
| 1979 | 6404 | | | 6,404 |
| 1980 | 4995 | *9750 (new) | | 4,995 |
| 1981 | 3896 | 7605 | *11,450 (new) | 11,501 |
| 1982 | 3039 | 5932 | 8,931 | 17,902 |
| 1983 | 2370 | 4627 | 6,966 | 13,963 |
| 1984 | 1849 | 3609 | 5,434 | 10,892 |

*(Assume that the car was bought at the beginning of '80 and '81 respectively, thus not included in book value for previous year. Total book value at end of '84 is $10,892.)

This problem can also be solved another way almost as quickly using the % key. Take Car 1 as an example: Enter 8210−22, touch % key and answer appears as 6403.80 (rounded off in table). Touch −22 and % key and 4994.964 appears, etc.

## Three Sample Constant Percentage Depreciation Problems

1. Figure the book value at the end of five years for a truck bought in 1975 for $28,950, depreciated at 32% per year.

*Answer:* $4,209.14

2. Ed Raeburn is a farmer. He bought a new tractor in 1983 for $34,827, along with a cultivator for $2,760 and a plow for $3,721. Figure the combined book value of the equipment at the end of three years if the tractor is depreciated at 32%, the cultivator at 21%, and the plow at 17%.

*Answer:* $14,439.13

3. Walter Rohrschach buys a personal computer for his insurance business costing $8,750, plus an associated word processor for $6,725. Since computer equipment depreciates rapidly, he uses a figure of 36% per year. What is the book value of the equipment at the end of four years?

*Answer:* $2,596.27

## How to Find Areas, Make Linear Measurements, and Compute Volume

If your boss asks the maintenance man to repaint his office suite, you may be asked to figure how much paint to buy and what it will cost. The suite has two offices, his and yours. His is $8' \times 10'$ and yours is $6' \times 10'$, both with 8' ceilings. His office has two $3' \times 7'$ doors and yours has an equal number. Paint costs $12.50 per gallon, and one gallon covers 400 sq. ft.

*Solution:* First enter the following

> $2(8 \times 10) + 2(8 \times 8)$ (number of walls) = 288 sq. ft. (area of boss's office), then
>
> $3 \times 7 \times 2 = 42$ sq. ft. door area, then
> $2(8 \times 10) + 2(6 \times 8) = 256$ sq. ft. (your office), next
> $288 + 256 - 84$ (doors) = 460 sq. ft.
> *Answer:* 2 gals. required at $25.

Next, the boss decides to buy new drapes imported from Paris at $47 per linear meter. His office (a corner) has windows on two sides and yours has 6 feet of window. You are asked to figure the total length in feet and meters as well as the cost.

*Solution:* Enter these numbers:

$8 + 10 + 6 = 24'$, or 8 yds. (length of window in both offices), next

$8 \times 0.9144$ (yards in a meter from the table on page 210) = 7.32 meters, and

$7.32 \times 47 = \$344.04$ cost of drapes

Or you could solve it this way: $24' \times .3048$ (meters per ft.) = 7.32 m.

Since you've become so good with your calculator, your boss asks for help in solving another problem. He's importing two types of chemicals for a new process the company is experimenting with. He needs 250 gals. of chemical A and 560 gals. of chemical B. The importer has quoted a price of $65 per liter of A and $37 per liter of B. The boss wants to know how much the chemicals will cost.

*Solution:* Start with A. From the tables (page 208) 1 gal. = 3.785 liters. Enter 250 × 3.785 (no. of liters required) × 65 = $61,506.25 (price for 250 gals. of A), then 560 × 3.785 × 37 = $78,425.20 (cost of B). Total cost: $139,931.45

The boss now has another problem. He needs to know how large a tank to build to store the chemicals. Also he has a space 5 × 4 × 3 ft. to store the tanks. Is that enough space?

*Solution:* Again from the table:

1 cu. ft. = 7.48 gals.
Enter 250 ÷ 7.48 = 33.42 cu. ft. required to store A, and
     560 ÷ 7.48 = 74.87 cu. ft. required to store B
Total space = 108.29 cu. ft. required.
Next: space available = 5 × 4 × 3 = 60 cu. ft. Space is inadequate.

## Sample Problems in Linear Measurement, Area, and Volume

1. The Cohen Company has a triangular parking lot. It is a right triangle 60' at the base, 80' high, and 100' on the long side. The Company wants to pave it with asphalt that costs $3.50 a square yard. It also wants to put a fence around it. The fence costs $12.40 per linear yard. What are the total costs involved?

*Answer:* $1,925.33

2. Millard Brown wants to pave a driveway 100' long and 7' wide with concrete to a depth of 6". If concrete costs $27.70 a cubic yard, what will the driveway cost? (Note: this problem can be solved in one operation on the calculator.)

*Answer:* $359.07

3. Betty Compton has a foreign car. Its fuel consumption rating is 10.63 km./liter. What is that in miles per gallon?

*Answer:* 25.00 mi./gal.

4. Joan Thompson has a swimming pool 14' long, 9' wide, and 6' deep. How much water (in gals.) will it take to fill it? (Note: 7.48 gals. = 1 cu. ft.)

*Answer:* 5654.9 gals.

## Balancing Your Checkbook

Although balancing checkbooks will be discussed fully in Chapter 3, the calculator again makes the job easier. Here's an example:

Checks written during the statement period: $251.20, 18.90, 25.81, 6.75, 122.00, 652.00, 4.10, 51.55, 32.16 and 7.89.

Service charge: $2.71            Deposits: $475
Checkbook balance: $506.82    Checks written but not returned: $40.05
Bank balance: $544.16

Remember, balance is as follows: bank balance + deposits not credited − checks written but not returned = your balance − miscellaneous bank charges (service, checks, etc.).

*Solution:* First compute the left-hand side:

$$\text{Enter } 544.16 - 40.05 = 504.11$$

Next, do the right-hand side:

$$\text{Enter } 506.82 - 2.71 = 504.11$$

Checkbook is in balance.

## Handling a Series of Discounts

The calculator really speeds up the computation of discounts. Here's an example:

Roseanne Amalfi is buying dresses from the factory. As a distributor she receives a 30% discount. In addition, if she buys 100 dresses she earns a 7% quantity discount, and if she pays her bill in 10 days she earns a 2% cash discount. What is the net price on a $47 list dress if she earns all these discounts?

*Solution:* This operation can be done in one step. Enter 47 − 30, touch %, = 32.90 (this answer appears when you touch %) − 7% = 30.60 − 2% = 29.99, the net price. Note that you do not have to touch the = key during any step.

## Sample Discount Problems You Can Solve
## With Your Calculator

1. In his restaurant, Sid Rogers offers a 10% discount to his older patrons before 6 P.M. If a customer buys two meals costing $18.75 before 6 P.M. and uses a credit card (which costs Sid another 3%), what is his net income?

*Answer:* $16.37

2. The Acme Supply Company buys lumber at a 40% discount from the mill. It offers Bill Baker, a local carpenter, a 7% quantity discount and 3% for prompt payment. If Acme places a $13,500 order with the mill for delivery to Bill Baker, what is its price from the mill? What does Bill Baker pay for the lumber, and what is Acme's gross profit? (Caution: Baker's discounts come off the list price.)

*Answer:* Acme's price: $8,100
          Baker's cost: $12,178.35
          Acme's gross profit: $4,078.35

3. Jean Silver buys a new car at the factory. The price is $12,082 and she gets a 17% factory discount plus a 7% salesperson's discount. What is her cost?

*Answer:* $9,326.10

## How to Get Better Buys at the Supermarket

In today's economy, people take a sharp look at prices and will switch brands for a 10¢ price difference. The trouble is, most suppliers seem to be engaged in a conspiracy to avoid comparisons. Packages come in different sizes and weights so that they're hard to compare. And unit pricing (where it's used) is seldom complete enough to help. Here are a few ways to use your calculator:

1. Three different brands of sugar are priced as follows: Brand A $2.85 for 5 lbs.; brand B, 2½ lbs. for $1.50; and brand C, 2 lbs. for $1.30. Which is the best buy?

*Solution:* Compute the price per pound for each brand:

          Enter 2.85 ÷ 5 = 0.57/lb       Brand A
                1.50 ÷ 2.5 = 0.60/lb     Brand B
                1.30 ÷ 2 = 0.65/lb       Brand C

Obviously, brand A is the best buy.

2. A nationally advertised brand of tea is priced at $3.50 for 150 bags, another is $4.56 for 250 bags, and the store brand is 500 bags for $8.99. Which is the best buy?

*Solution:* Figure the cost per bag:

          Enter 3.5  ÷ 150 = 0.0233/bag
                4.56 ÷ 250 = 0.018/bag
                8.99 ÷ 500 = 0.01798/bag

Even though the store brand is slightly cheaper, you might want to buy the second brand unless you use a lot of tea.

If you go to the supermarket with a limited amount of money (or you're on a strict budget), your calculator can be a big help. Simply keep a running total of your purchases as you shop, and then eliminate unessential items as you approach your limit.

## How to Make the Most of Your Favorite Recipes

Recipes never seem to be written for the number of people you want to serve, i.e., if it will serve 6, you want to use it for 4, or 8 or 2. But the calculator will solve this problem easily and quickly. Use this recipe as an example:

### Oriental Beef

|  | 4 | 8 | 2 |
|---|---|---|---|
| 3 tablespoons salad oil | 2 | 4 | 1 |
| 1½ cups diced beef | 1 | 2 | 0.5 |
| 1⅓ cups rice | 0.89 | 1.8 | 0.45 |
| 2 cups hot water | 1.34 | 2.67 | 0.67 |
| 1½ cups shredded lettuce | 1 | 2 | 0.5 |
| 2 tablespoons soy sauce | 1.34 | 2.67 | 0.67 |
| Serves six | | | |

*Solution:* To adapt this recipe for 4, 8 or 2, use the appropriate multiplier. For 4, since ⁴⁄₆ = ⅔ = .667, enter .667 and multiply by each ingredient quantity. Since .667 is the constant, touch the = key after entering each quantity (see table above). For 8, ⁸⁄₆ = ⁴⁄₃ = 1⅓ = 1.334, and for 2, ²⁄₆ = ⅓ = 0.334.

As a practical matter, you can round off these quantities to one decimal place and use your judgment in measuring. For instance, 0.89 cup rice can be just a little less than a cup, etc.

## How to Figure Gas Mileage

Here's an easy way to figure gas mileage and see how well your car lives up to its EPA rating. You can save gas by driving slower and eliminating jack-rabbit starts.Try that on a tankful of gas and see how your mileage improves. Here's how it works:

1. Record your mileage reading the next time you fill your tank (be sure it's really full).

2. Then when you refill, record the mileage again and the quantity of gas you bought. If the tank was full each time you refilled, you can determine your gas mileage by subtracting the first reading from the second (= miles driven) and dividing that number by the quantity of gas purchased the second time. Let's try it out:

You filled your car with gas on March 10 and the odometer reading was 2,675. You refilled it with 13.7 gals. of gas on March 16 and the odometer reading was 3,096. What was your gas mileage?

*Solution:* Enter $3096 - 2675 = 421$ mileage driven. Next, enter $421 \div 13.7 = 30.73$ mi./gal.

Most of that mileage was a 375-mile trip. For the next 10 days you drove around town, then filled the tank with 11.7 gals. and an odometer reading of 3,385. What was your mileage in city driving?

*Solution:* Enter $3385 - 3096 = 289$ miles driven. Then $289 \div 11.7 = 24.7$ mi./gal. in city.

# CHAPTER 3

# How to Solve the Most Common Office Math Problems

Now it's time to apply some of the things you've learned in Chapters 1 and 2 to find the answers to the problems that you will encounter in your everyday business and personal life. First, we'll cover interest, a term you've heard if you've gone to your bank or credit union to borrow money or if your company lends or borrows. Then we'll look at a balance sheet and profit and loss statement, which come from the accounting department. You'll also get an overview of taxes and will become familiar with insurance terms. In addition, after you finish reading this section, you'll find out how to reconcile your checkbook.

## HOW TO COMPUTE SIMPLE INTEREST

Interest is the amount charged by the lender for using his money. The amount of money loaned is called the principal, and the percentage of the principal charged is called the rate. That rate determines the cost of the loan over a given period of time, usually a year. If, for example, a bank lends you $2,000 at the rate of 10% per year, the loan will cost you $200. You will have to repay the bank the principal plus interest, or $2,200.

Note that if you were to borrow the money for two years, the cost of the loan would increase to $400 (10% interest per year for two years) and you would have to repay the bank $2,400.

To put all this into a formula, let's call the principal P, the interest I, the rate r, and the period of the loan in years, t. Then we can say

$$I = P \times r \times t$$

Using the example above,

$$I = \$400, P = 2000, r = .10 \text{ and } t = 2$$
$$400 = 2000 \times .10 \times 2$$

It gets more complicated when the period of the loan does not equal one or more years. If, for example, the time is expressed in months, then it is a fraction of a year (for three months, $t = \frac{1}{3}$ or .33 year).

If the time is expressed in days, banks talk about two kinds of interest, ordinary and exact. Ordinary interest makes matters simple by assuming there are 12 months of 30 days each, or 360 days in a year. Exact interest, on the other hand, recognizes that there are uneven months and 365 days in a year. Computing the interest then takes a little more time.

For example, the ordinary interest on an $800 loan for 45 days at 8% is:

$$800 \times .08 \times \frac{45}{360} = 8.00$$

Note that ordinary interest is always more than exact interest since it's divided by 360 rather than 365.

### How to Compute Interest on a Promissory Note

Banks often take promissory notes from business firms or individuals to cover a short-term loan. As an example, Edward Bennett, a dentist, requires $5,000 to pay for equipment he's buying. His bank agrees to lend him the $5,000 at 9% interest for 6 months. He is required by the bank to sign a promissory note. In effect, this is a written promise by Bennett to repay the $5,000 with accumulated interest at the end of the 6 months.

Sometimes the period of the note is given in days between two dates. In that case, it becomes necessary to count out the number of days the note runs.

Two methods are used:

1. Exact time requires that the exact number of days between the note's beginning and end be computed. This method is usually employed for notes running for a short period of time.

2. Approximate time computations use the assumption that each month has 30 days and the year has 360 days.

## EXAMPLES:

Find the exact time from September 10 to December 12.

| | |
|---|---|
| Remaining days in Sept. | 20 |
| October | 31 |
| November | 30 |
| December | 12 |
| | 93 |

Banks often use precomputed tables to supply this kind of data (see page 206). Find the approximate time between the same dates.

| | |
|---|---|
| Remaining days in Sept. | 20 |
| October | 30 |
| November | 30 |
| December | 12 |
| | 92 |

(Note that exact time computations are generally longer than approximations.) By using these concepts, we can compute interest four different ways:

- Ordinary interest for exact *and* approximate time.
- Exact interest for exact *and* approximate time.

You might guess that bankers would prefer the first method since ordinary interest and exact time normally produce the greatest return.

Here is a group of problems with solutions provided:

—Compute the return on $25,000 @ 9% interest for the period from March 15 to June 10. Use all four methods.
1. Ordinary interest/exact time
   Time computation (exact)

|        |        |      |
|--------|--------|------|
| March  | 16     | days |
| April  | 30     |      |
| May    | 31     |      |
| June   | 10     |      |
|        | 87     |      |

Interest:

$$I = 25,000 \times .09 \times \frac{87}{360 \text{ ordinary}} = 543.75$$

2. Ordinary/approximate
   Time computation (approx.)

|        |        |      |
|--------|--------|------|
| March  | 16     | days |
| April  | 30     |      |
| May    | 30     |      |
| June   | 10     |      |
|        | 86     |      |

$$I = 25,000 \times .09 \times \frac{86}{360 \text{ approximate}} = 537.50$$

3. Exact/exact

$$I = 25,000 \times .09 \times \frac{87}{365} = 536.30$$

4. Exact/approximate

$$I = 25,000 \times .09 \times \frac{86}{365} = 530.14$$

(Note that Method 1 produces the highest return and produces $13.61 more interest than Method 4.)

—If a bank lends $45,000 at 8.5% ordinary interest and receives $1,912.50 when the loan is paid up, what was the period of the loan?

*Answer:*

$$\$45,000 \times .085 \times t = 1912.50$$

$$t = \frac{1912.50}{45,000 \times .085} = \frac{0.5 \text{ yr., or}}{\text{six months}}$$

—If the Hayward Company borrows $25,000 for exactly three months and the exact interest charge is $554.79, what is the interest rate? (Note: the loan runs from Jan. 1 to Mar. 31.)

*Answer:* January has 31 days, February 28 and March 31, for a total of 90 days. Thus:

$$25,000 \times I \times \frac{90}{365} = 554.79$$

$$I = \frac{554.79}{25,000 \times \frac{90}{365}} = .08999, \text{ or } 9\%$$

## HOW TO UNDERSTAND AND COMPUTE DISCOUNTS

Banks often make a practice of subtracting the interest charge in advance (particularly on consumer loans). This is called discounting the loan.

For instance, if you borrow $500 at 11% interest from a bank to be repaid in six months, the bank will probably subtract $27.50 (six months' interest) from the $500 and you will receive as the proceeds from the loan $472.50. Note that this is a more expensive loan, since you will not have full use of the money you're paying interest on for the period of the loan.

If the holder of a promissory note needs cash before the loan matures, he may go to a bank and sell the note at a discount. In effect, the bank buys the note from the holder (generally at a higher interest rate), subtracts the interest due for the remaining period of the loan, and pays the holder the balance.

**EXAMPLE:** The Bradley Company holds a six-month note for $10,000 at 11% payable by one of its customers, Crest Automotive Sales.

Bradley Company approaches its bank, the Summit Trust Company, to discount the note after one month. After checking Crest's credit rating, the bank offers to accept the note but charges Bradley 13%. As a result, Bradley receives $10,550 (maturity value) less 13% simple interest for five months or $571.46.

*Solved Problems:*

—Discount $7,500 at 8% for 7 months.
   *Answer:* $7,150 proceeds.
—Discount $12,000 at 14% for 2 years.
   *Answer:* $8,640 proceeds.

## HOW TO UNDERSTAND AND COMPUTE COMPOUND INTEREST

When money is loaned for extended periods of time or when savings are deposited in a long-term account, it is no longer adequate to charge simple interest.

For example, a savings and loan association offers depositors interest rates of 7% compounded annually. In effect, at the end of every year the money is left on deposit, the interest earned for that year is added to the principal, and the interest is computed for the whole amount next year.

Thus, if you deposit $500 on January 1, 1983 at 7%, your money will earn $35 in interest during 1983. In 1984, your money will earn 7% interest on $535.00, or $37.45. And in 1985, you will earn 7% on $572.45, or $40.07.

Some institutions offer rates compounded semiannually (every 6 months). Others go as high as monthly or daily compounding.

If you put $500 in a 7% savings account with semiannual compounding, here's how it would grow during the same two-year period:

$500.00 deposited Jan. 1, 1983
  17.50 interest to July 1, 1983
517.50
  18.11 interest to Jan. 1, 1984
535.61
  18.75 interest to July 1, 1984
554.36
  19.40 interest to Jan. 1, 1985
573.76

With semiannual compounding, your $500 will be worth $1.31 more than with annual compounding.

This kind of computation can become quite tedious, particularly with more frequent compounding and longer accumulations. To save time, see the table showing various interest rates and time periods below.

### TABLE SHOWING AMOUNT OF $1
### COMPOUNDED PERIODICALLY

| Period | 1½% | 2% | 2½% | 3% | 3½% | 4% | 5% | 6% |
|---|---|---|---|---|---|---|---|---|
| 1 | 1.0150 | 1.0200 | 1.0250 | 1.0300 | 1.0350 | 1.0400 | 1.0500 | 1.0600 |
| 2 | 1.0302 | 1.0404 | 1.0506 | 1.0609 | 1.0712 | 1.0816 | 1.1025 | 1.1236 |
| 3 | 1.0457 | 1.0612 | 1.0769 | 1.0927 | 1.1087 | 1.1249 | 1.1576 | 1.1910 |
| 4 | 1.0614 | 1.0824 | 1.1038 | 1.1255 | 1.1475 | 1.1699 | 1.2155 | 1.2625 |
| 5 | 1.0773 | 1.1041 | 1.1314 | 1.1592 | 1.1877 | 1.2167 | 1.2762 | 1.3382 |
| 6 | 1.0934 | 1.1262 | 1.1597 | 1.1941 | 1.2293 | 1.2653 | 1.3401 | 1.4185 |
| 7 | 1.1098 | 1.1487 | 1.1887 | 1.2298 | 1.2723 | 1.3159 | 1.4071 | 1.5036 |
| 8 | 1.1265 | 1.1717 | 1.2184 | 1.2668 | 1.3168 | 1.3685 | 1.4775 | 1.5938 |
| 9 | 1.1434 | 1.1951 | 1.2488 | 1.3048 | 1.3628 | 1.4233 | 1.5513 | 1.6895 |
| 10 | 1.1605 | 1.2190 | 1.2801 | 1.3433 | 1.4106 | 1.4802 | 1.6289 | 1.7908 |
| 11 | 1.1779 | 1.2434 | 1.3121 | 1.3842 | 1.4600 | 1.5395 | 1.7103 | 1.8983 |
| 12 | 1.1956 | 1.2682 | 1.3449 | 1.4258 | 1.5111 | 1.6010 | 1.7959 | 2.0122 |
| 13 | 1.2136 | 1.2936 | 1.3785 | 1.4685 | 1.5640 | 1.6651 | 1.8856 | 2.1329 |
| 14 | 1.2318 | 1.3195 | 1.4129 | 1.5126 | 1.6187 | 1.7317 | 1.9799 | 2.2609 |
| 15 | 1.2502 | 1.3459 | 1.4483 | 1.5580 | 1.6753 | 1.8009 | 2.0789 | 2.3966 |
| 16 | 1.2690 | 1.3728 | 1.4845 | 1.6047 | 1.7340 | 1.8730 | 2.1829 | 2.5404 |
| 17 | 1.2880 | 1.4002 | 1.5216 | 1.6528 | 1.7947 | 1.9479 | 2.2920 | 2.6928 |
| 18 | 1.3073 | 1.4282 | 1.5597 | 1.7024 | 1.8575 | 2.0258 | 2.4066 | 2.8543 |
| 19 | 1.3270 | 1.4568 | 1.5987 | 1.7535 | 1.9225 | 2.1068 | 2.5270 | 3.0256 |
| 20 | 1.3469 | 1.4859 | 1.6387 | 1.8061 | 1.9898 | 2.1911 | 2.6533 | 3.2071 |
| 21 | 1.3671 | 1.5157 | 1.6796 | 1.8603 | 2.0594 | 2.2788 | 2.7860 | 3.3996 |
| 22 | 1.3876 | 1.5460 | 1.7216 | 1.9161 | 2.1315 | 2.3699 | 2.9253 | 3.6035 |
| 23 | 1.4084 | 1.5769 | 1.7646 | 1.9736 | 2.2061 | 2.4647 | 3.0715 | 3.8197 |
| 24 | 1.4295 | 1.6084 | 1.8087 | 2.0328 | 2.2833 | 2.5633 | 3.2251 | 4.0489 |
| 25 | 1.4509 | 1.6406 | 1.8539 | 2.0938 | 2.3632 | 2.6658 | 3.3864 | 4.2919 |

**Problem:** Figure the value of $2,500 compounded quarterly for 18 months at 8%.

Number of periods on deposit: **6**

Rate per period: **8 ÷ 4 = 2**

From the table: Value of $1.00 deposited for 6 periods at 2% per period = $1.1262

**1.1262 × 2500 = $2815.50**

*Solved problems:*

—What is the value of $50,000 deposited for four years at 12% interest and compounded quarterly?

*Answer:* $80,235

—$20,000 for three years, compounded semiannually at 10%?

*Answer:* $26,802

—$150,000 for six years compounded quarterly at 12%?

*Answer:* $304,920

These examples clearly bring out the growth power of compound interest over long periods of time.

## Practical Examples of the Use of Interest

(1) John Daly owns a women's ready-to-wear shop. In August, he receives a shipment of sweaters and blouses. The invoice amounts to $5,270 and the terms are 2% discount for payment in 10 days or net 30 days.

John's cash on hand amounts to $2,500, but income during September will enable him to pay the invoice on time. However, he would like to take advantage of the 2% discount. The amount due less the cash discount is $5,270 − (.02 × 5270) or $5,164.60. If he can use $2,000 from cash on hand, he will still owe $3,164.60.

Calling his bank, John finds that it will lend him that amount for 30 days at 12% annual interest, or 1% per month. At that rate, $3,164.60 would cost $31.65 for one month. Since the savings from the discount would be $105.40, he can save $73.75 by borrowing the money.

(2) Barbara Evans has decided to buy a television set on the installment plan. The price of the set she wants is $300. The dealer has offered terms of $25 down and $25 per month for 12 months.

To determine the interest percentage, Barbara notes that she will owe:

| | |
|---|---|
| $275 for 1 month | $125 for 1 month |
| 250 for 1 month | 100 for 1 month |
| 225 for 1 month | 75 for 1 month |
| 200 for 1 month | 50 for 1 month |
| 175 for 1 month | 25 for 1 month |
| 150 for 1 month | $1,650 |

which is the equivalent of $1,650 for one month.

Assuming that the $25 down is the interest cost, then the interest equals 25/1650, or 1.5% per month. Under this assumption, the annual interest is 18%.

## HOW TO UNDERSTAND AND COMPUTE
## COMMERCIAL DISCOUNTS

We have already seen this term used in banking, but there are a number of other ways that discounts are used in business. For instance, invoices for merchandise sold contain the word several times. Sometimes the seller offers a prompt payment discount to induce his customers to pay their bills quickly. Payment terms are often stated as: 1%, 10, net 30 days (see previous example), which simply means that the buyer can reduce his payment by 1% if he pays within 10 days. Other typical terms of sale are 2% 10 net 30, or ½% 10 net 45, etc.

These percentages may seem small, but 1% 10 days is the equivalent of 3% per month, or 36% per year. Most merchants are keenly aware of the value of cash discounts and try to arrange their cash flow to take advantage of them.

Discounts are also used by manufacturers in selling to wholesalers and other manufacturers. As an example, a valve manufacturer may offer a 40% discount to a large distributor. In return, the manufacturer expects the distributor to carry a substantial stock of valves for the convenience of customers in his area.

The manufacturer may also offer quantity discounts to users, so the distributor may end up with less of a profit than the 40% discount would lead him to expect.

For instance, a valve that is priced at $25 list may carry a 10% quantity discount if ordered in lots of 100. The distributor buys valves at list less 40%.

Thus, if the distributor buys 100 valves at $25 each, the total list price is $2,500 and his discount is $40\% \times 2500 = \$1000$ and his cost is $\$2500 - \$1000 = \$1500$.

The customer buys 100 valves from the distributor at $25 each less 10%, or $22.50. His total cost is $2,250 and the distributor's profit is $\$2250 - \$1500 = \$750$. Since $750 is 30% of $2,500, the distributor earns appreciably less than 40%.

Most manufacturers publish list prices from which the discounts are taken. They not only can include special discounts to distributors and quantity buyers as we have seen, but also to other manufacturers that install these products for resale (original equipment manufacturer—OEM) and contractors.

To facilitate the computation of net prices, it is simpler to use multipliers. If the discount is converted to a decimal fraction and subtracted from 1.00, the result is a multiplier which will yield the net price directly.

For example, with a 40% discount, if the list price is $2,500, then from the example above we get $1,500 as the discounted price. The multiplier for 40% is .60, and $2500 \times .6 = 1500$. For a 35% discount, the multiplier is .65.

$$35\% \text{ of } 2500 = 875 \qquad 2500 - 875 = 1625$$
$$\text{or } .65 \times 2500 = 1625.$$

*Solved problems:*

1. The Grady Company manufactures electric motors. Its price list indicates that the #10 motor sells for $34. It also shows a quantity discount schedule as follows:

> **1-9** motors net
> **10-24** motors less **5%**
> **25-99** motors less **10%**
> **100** and up motors less **15%**

Grady's policy is to offer a flat 35% discount to its authorized distributors. In addition, it offers original equipment manufacturers (OEM) a 40% discount for purchases of 100 motors or more.

—If the Gordon Electrical Company, a distributor, buys 25 #10 motors, what is its net cost?

*Answer:* $552.50

—The Edwards Machine Tool Company (an original equipment manufacturer) buys 125 #10 motors to install in a line of small lathes. What is its cost?

*Answer:* $2,550.00

—John Thompson, a user, buys 18 motors from Gordon Electrical Company. What is Thompson's cost?

*Answer:* $581.40

What is Gordon's profit on the sale?

Gordon's cost/motor = **22.10 (552.50 ÷ 25)**
**22.10 × 18 = 397.80** cost of the 18 motors sold to Thompson
**581.40 − 397.80 = 183.60** Gordon's profit.


2. The Mill Supply Company, a distributor, buys rotary saw blades from the manufacturer at a list price of $3.00 each less 50% if it buys at least 1,000 blades. It in turn sells to jobbers in smaller quantities at list less 15%.

—What is the jobber's unit price?          *Answer:* $2.55
—What is Mill Supply's price?          *Answer:*  1.50
—What is Mill's unit profit?          *Answer:*  1.05

Mill Supply sells to OEM's at list less 15% and 10%. What is its profit?

—The OEM price is $3.00 × .85 × .90 = 2.295$
—MS's profit is $2.295 − 1.50 = .795$

(Note that 15 and 10 is much less of a discount than 25%.)


## UNDERSTANDING BALANCE SHEETS AND PROFIT AND LOSS STATEMENTS

These are the two ways that accountants use to measure the condition of a business. Understanding the information they convey will not only help you with your employer but also in your own business (if you have one), and in reading company annual reports (if you own stock).

## The Balance Sheet

The balance sheet is primarily a statement of ownership. Most businesses operate on a credit basis, that is, they extend credit to their customers and in turn have credit extended to them by their suppliers. In addition, they own the tools and equipment needed to operate the business. These credit amounts generally offset each other in a healthy business, and the positive difference is a measure of how much of the business is owned by the proprietors.

Consider the example of Ed Richardson who runs a small contracting business. On September 1, 1983 he owned a dump truck and front-end loader. Tony Amarillo owed him a final payment of $14,700, and he owed a note amounting to $3,500 held by the First National Bank, plus a balance of $800 due on a chattel mortgage covering the front-end loader. Furthermore, he owed $1,270 to the Garden Park Lumber Company.

He summarized the condition of his business this way:

| What the business *owned* | | What the business ownership *owed* | |
|---|---|---|---|
| Dump truck worth | $ 5,270 | Note First National Bank | $ 3,500 |
| Front loader worth | 7,700 | Chattel mortgage | 800 |
| Account receivable | 14,700 | Invoice Garden Park | 1,270 |
| (Tony Amarillo) | ——— | | ——— |
| | $27,670 | | $ 5,570 |
| | | Difference: | $22,100 |

This is a simplified form of the balance sheet. Items on the left are called "assets," items on the right "liabilities." And the amount owned is often called "net worth." In a corporation owned by stockholders, it is called "stockholders' equity."

The total amount due the company from customers who were sold on credit is called "accounts receivable," and the total amount due suppliers is called "accounts payable." Notes payable, mortgages, taxes and similar items are listed separately.

Since businesses operate under dynamic conditions, the balance sheet is only accurate on the day it's prepared. Most businesses prepare balance sheets on a quarterly or yearly basis, and by comparison, they can monitor the growth or decline of the company.

For manufacturers, wholesalers and retailers, one of the most important balance sheet items is the inventory. This is the stock of raw materials, parts, and finished goods the manufacturer has on hand when the balance sheet is prepared. For the wholesaler or retailer, it represents the amount of products on the shelves as of that day. The inventory is generally priced at cost and is listed as an asset.

*Solved problem:*

With the above information, prepare a balance sheet for the Cornell Hardware Company. At the top of your sheet write the company name, the date below it (June 30). List assets on the left, liabilities on the right. At the bottom of the right-hand column, show net worth (assets–liabilities). Add net worth to liabilities so that you have the same number in both columns, total assets to the left, liabilities plus net worth to the right.

Here are the conditions prevailing on June 30 at Cornell Hardware:

|     |     |     |
| --- | --- | --- |
| (1) | Cash on hand | $12,072 |
| (2) | Accounts receivable | 5,420 |
| (3) | Note payable State Bank | 2,120 |
| (4) | State taxes due | 851 |
| (5) | Merchandise inventory | 22,850 |
| (6) | Accounts payable | 15,801 |
| (7) | Furniture and fixtures | 6,122 |
| (8) | Mortgage on building | 7,500 |
| (9) | Cash in bank | 21,850 |

*Answers:* $68,314 assets, $26,272 liabilities, $42,042 net worth.

## The Profit and Loss Statement

The profit and loss statement measures how well the business has performed during the period under study. This period may vary from one day (for very dynamic businesses) to one year (to measure the year's performance in order to prepare tax returns, among other reasons).

The balance sheet, on the one hand, takes the business's pulse on a given day to measure its health. The profit and loss statement takes into account the business's activity during a measured period, and shows why its health has improved or declined.

For example, Dr. James Fisher, a dentist, received $3,800 in payment for his services during the month of April. His expenses for that month were as follows:

| | | | |
| --- | --- | --- | --- |
| Rent | $300 | Dental supplies | $720 |
| Utilities | 65 | Assistant's salary | 920 |
| Telephone | 35 | | |

Since these costs are necessary to Dr. Fisher's operation, they are called operating expenses. His accountant prepared a simple profit and loss statement as follows for the month of April.

Dr. James Fisher
**Profit & Loss Statement**
for April

| Income from patients | | $3,800 |
|---|---|---|
| Expenses | | |
| Rent | $300 | |
| Utilities | 65 | |
| Telephone | 35 | |
| Dental supplies | 720 | |
| Salary | 920 | |
| Total expenses | | $2,040 |
| Net profit | | $1,760 |

(Note that if Dr. Fisher's expenses for the month had run higher than his income, he would have had a loss for the month.) It should also be remembered that expenses may vary from month to month since taxes, professional fees for accounting and legal work, and other expenses may come into the picture. At the end of the year, Dr. Fisher's accountant will total up expenses and income to give the P&L statement for the whole year.

A P&L statement such as the one above is not adequate for a business that sells products from inventory, since an accounting of the cost of the merchandise sold must be made. The following is an example of such a business.

George Edwards owns a menswear shop. At the beginning of September, his inventory of salable merchandise amounted to $13,500 at cost. During the month he received an additional $7,250 in new merchandise. At the end of September, he took inventory and found that he had $9,250 still on hand.

He then computed the cost of goods sold for September as follows:

| Inventory on hand, Sept. 1 | $13,500 |
|---|---|
| Purchases in Sept. | 7,250 |
| Cost of inventory for sale | 20,750 |
| Inventory on hand, Sept. 30 | 9,250 |
| Cost of goods sold | $11,500 |

Since George knew that his income from sales for September was $17,251, he was now ready to compute his P&L statement for September. First, he computed his gross profit. It is called that because it does not take operating expenses into account:

### Edwards Men's Store
### Profit & Loss Statement
### for the month ending September 30

| | | |
|---|---:|---:|
| Income from retail sales | | $17,251 |
| Cost of goods sold | | |
| Inventory as of Sept. 1 | $13,500 | |
| Purchases in Sept. | 7,250 | |
| Cost of inventory for sale | 20,750 | |
| Inventory on hand Sept. 30 | 9,250 | |
| | | 11,500 |
| Gross profit | | $ 5,751 |

Now, by adding operating expense, the statement is complete:

| | | |
|---|---:|---:|
| Rent | $ 1,100 | |
| Telephone | 176 | |
| Salaries | 2,200 | |
| Miscellaneous expense | 571 | |
| | | 4,047 |
| Net profit | | $ 1,704 |

Manufacturing companies that convert raw materials, purchased parts, and direct labor into finished products use more complex methods to compute cost of goods sold. Nevertheless, the process is the same as we have followed here. Understanding the purpose and derivation of the balance sheet and profit and loss statement will help you read annual reports and other financial statements with greater ease.

### Solved problem:

The Reading Materials Company is a wholesaler that supplies building materials to contractors and homeowners. Its sales in October amounted to $65,301. Its inventory on October 1 amounted to $43,502 at cost.

During October the company bought 250 bags of cement for $720, assorted sizes of lumber for $4,708, 2,500 cinder blocks for $2,350, and 25 pallets of roofing for $5,250. On October 31, its closing inventory was calculated at $28,401.

Reading had the following operating expenses during October:

| | |
|---|---:|
| Building rent | $ 4,700 |
| Utilities | 822 |
| Telephone | 671 |
| Payroll | 16,000 |
| Office supplies | 127 |
| Miscellaneous | 425 |
| Taxes | 927 |
| | $23,672 |

Prepare a complete profit and loss statement for October.

*Answer:* Cost of goods sold $28,129, Gross profit $37,172, Net Profit $13,500.

### Understanding and Computing Appreciation and Depreciation

A company's balance sheet is designed to present as accurate a picture of the company's net worth as possible. Yet the value of some of the assets carried on the books (particularly such assets as furniture and fixtures, machine tools, cars and trucks, etc.) vary in value from year to year.

Fixed assets such as these tend to lose value from one year to the next. They wear out, become less efficient in operation, their appearance deteriorates, and they lose value in comparison to new equipment of more advanced design. In order to account for this loss of value and to provide funds for replacement of obsolete equipment, the concept of depreciation is used.

As an example, a car purchased in 1985 at a price of $10,500 loses value at such a rate that by 1994, it is only worth $900. The simplest way to figure depreciation on the car is to assume that it loses an equal amount in value each year. In that case, the yearly depreciation is:

$10,500 (purchase price) − 900 (value in 10 years)
divided by 10 = $960 per year

On the balance sheet then, $960 is subtracted from the value of the car every year. Or, more properly, a depreciation charge of $960 per year is entered on the liability side of the balance sheet. Thus, money is deducted every year from net worth to purchase a replacement vehicle when necessary.

The value of the car at any time during the ten-year period is equal to the original cost less accumulated depreciation, and is called "book value."

The computation used above is called the "straight-line method." Since all equipment does not lose value at the same rate, various methods of figuring depreciation are used. Since a car, for instance, depreciates faster actually during the first few years of its useful life, the constant percentage method of depreciation might be used. Here a constant percentage of the book value at the beginning of the year is figured as the depreciation charge.

The car in the previous example, for instance, might be depreciated at the rate of 20% per year as follows:

| | |
|---|---|
| 1985 — $10,500 | 1990 — $3,441 |
| 1986 —   8,400 | 1991 —  2,753 |
| 1987 —   6,720 | 1992 —  2,202 |
| 1988 —   5,376 | 1993 —  1,762 |
| 1989 —   4,301 | 1994 —  1,410 |

There are a number of other, more complex methods of computing depreciation, but those above will suffice to demonstrate the principle.

Under certain circumstances, assets can also appreciate in value. During the high inflation periods of recent years, certain assets such as land and buildings have appreciated substantially in value. Even certain types of machinery have become more valuable. Other objects such as antiques, paintings, and other works of art also appreciate in value.

Most companies with property which has increased in value prefer to keep it on their books at its current book value, unless they are forced to reassess it for tax purposes or in case of a sale. Then the services of an expert appraiser are used to make a judgment.

There is no accepted accounting method (as with depreciation) to keep track of increased value.

### Solved problems:

1. The Laidlaw Company has three trucks. One was purchased in 1984 for $10,550. The other two were bought in 1985 for $12,275 each.

If these trucks depreciate at a rate of 30% per year, what is the combined depreciation charge for 1986?

*Answer:*

| Truck 1 | $10,550.00 new | Trucks 2 & 3 | $24,550.00 |
|---|---|---|---|
| less 30% in '84 | 7,385.00 | less 30% in '85 | 17,185.00 |
| less 30% in '85 | 5,169.50 | Depr. chg. '86 | 5,155.50 |
| Depr. chg. '86 | 1,550.85 | | |

Combined depr. chg. = $6,706.35

2. John Silvester owns a real estate and insurance business. In 1983, he purchased a small computer to handle insurance and real estate records for $7,900. He estimates that the computer will be worth $300 in five years. Using straight-line depreciation, what will the book value be in 1985?

*Answer:*

$7,900 − $300 = $7,600 total depreciation

Annual depr. = $7,600 ÷ 5 = $1,520

1985 book value = $7,900 − (2 × 1520) = $4,860

3. Ray White owns a small machine shop. In 1981, he bought a new drill press for $7,520. In 1984, he bought an engine lathe for $15,600. What will be the total depreciation charge at the end of 1985 if the drill press depreciates at 25% a year and the lathe at 30%? What will be the book value of each machine?

*Answer:*          $13,097 total depr. chg. 1985

Book value of drill press $2,379

Book value of lathe $7,644

## UNDERSTANDING THE MATH OF TAXES

Taxes of various kinds affect you as an individual, if you own your own business, or if you're an employee. In this section, you'll learn about the most common forms of taxation in order to make the form of taxation clear, as well as to assist you in computing the amount of tax.

### Sales Tax

At present, 46 of the 50 states charge their residents a sales tax. The tax varies from 3% to 7% of the sale, and there are a number of exclusions for food and clothing in certain states. Other states do not charge tax on small dollar amounts. In New Jersey, for instance, the sales tax is currently 6%, but purchases of food and clothing are tax exempt.

### Solved problems:

—Lois Edwards made the following purchases in New Jersey stores during the month of October.

| New dress | $72.00 | Paint and varnish | $19.80 |
|-----------|--------|-------------------|--------|
| Gas for car | 28.00 | Clock radio | 14.25 |
| Card table | 21.50 | Records | 8.85 |
| Chairs | 40.10 | Baked goods | 4.45 |
| Groceries | 92.20 | Gloves | 6.50 |
| Blankets | 14.10 | Tennis racquet | 48.00 |

What was the total sales tax due?

*Answer:* $11.68

Also in New Jersey (and in many other states), merchandise purchased for resale is not taxable.

—Johnson's Hardware Store made the following purchases during the week of October 1, 1985:

| | |
|---|---|
| 50 lbs. of nails | $ 82.50 |
| 25 table saws | 560.00 |
| 20 steel hammers | 81.50 |
| 60 boxes assorted wood screws | 122.00 |
| *25 gals. gas for truck | 34.20 |
| *1 box typewriter ribbons | 15.50 |
| *500 invoice forms | 21.60 |
| *500 window envelopes | 8.00 |

(The starred items are for use in the store and are thus subject to tax.)

What did Johnson's owe in sales tax?

*Answer:* $4.76

## Property Taxes

Property taxes are generally collected by municipalities to cover the cost of local government including schools, libraries, police and fire services, administration, etc.

Such taxes are levied on real property owned by the residents and businesses. They are based on an assessed valuation of the property and are expressed in cents per $100 dollars. The total tax due may include local or regional school taxes, municipal, and county taxes.

### Solved problem:

George Lincoln operates a printing business. He has just received his 1985 tax bill. The assessed valuation is: land $27,800, improvements $42,500, for a total of $70,300.

The tax rate is broken down as follows: local government $.847, local school $2.06, and county government $.562—all per $100 assessed value.

What are his taxes for each element? What are his total taxes? If they are payable quarterly, what is each payment?

*Answers:* $595.44, $1,448.18, and $395.09—total $2,438.71. $609.68 quarterly payment.

## Social Security Taxes

If you're currently employed or have been in the past, and unless you work for the government or the railroads, you're certainly familiar with social security. In addition to your contribution, your employer contributes a matching amount. The proceeds flow into a trust fund administered by the Social Security Administration to be repaid to you as a retirement fund.

Upon retirement at age 65, you will receive a monthly check, the amount of which is partially determined by your total contributions during the time you've been employed. If you decide to retire at 62, you will receive a smaller amount; and if you have a dependent spouse 62 or over, you will receive 50% more. At this time, the contribution is 6.7% of your annual salary up to a maximum $35,700. Be sure to use current rates and limits.

If you work for two employers during a given year, it is possible that between them they will deduct more than the maximum $2,391.90. In that case, you may either apply for the return of the excess or you may apply it toward payment of your income tax.

### *Solved problem:*

Employees of the Mayfair Company earned the following salaries during 1985. Compute each employee's contribution per paycheck and the total for the year 1985 (answers as shown):

| | | |
|---|---|---|
| Elizabeth Dickinson | (paid weekly) | $ 9,250 |
| Rose Orwell | (paid weekly) | 12,400 |
| John Daly | (paid monthly) | 21,500 |
| Ed Stimson | (paid monthly) | 26,950 |
| George Orloff | (paid monthly) | 39,150 |
| Robert Mayfair | (paid monthly) | 61,700 |

| Contribution per paycheck | Annual Contribution |
|---|---|
| $ 11.92 | $ 619.75 |
| 15.98 | 830.80 |
| 120.04 | 1,440.50 |
| 150.47 | 1,805.65 |
| 218.59 | 2,391.90* |
| 344.49 | 2,391.90* |

*Weekly contribution is paid until maximum amount of $2,391.90 is reached. No further payments are made.

Elizabeth Dickinson and Rose Orwell each received a 15% salary increase on July 1. What was the additional weekly deduction? What was the additional annual contribution?

*Answer:* Elizabeth Dickinson—weekly $1.78, annual $46.48; Rose Orwell—weekly $2.40, annual $62.31.

## Federal and State Income Taxes

These are the taxes that take the biggest bite out of your own paycheck as well as those of your fellow employees. The Federal government and some states require employers to withhold a portion of each paycheck to cover the estimated amount of tax due for the period covered by the paycheck.

At year end, the total amount collected by your employer is compared with the total income tax due for the year. You are then required to pay any additional amount you owe when you submit your tax return. By the same token, if you have overpaid, the Internal Revenue Service will reimburse you.

You are required to file a tax return if you are single (and under 65) and if you earned $3,300 a year or more, even if you owe no tax. If you are married, the figure is $5,400. (Note: the numbers used here apply specifically to 1984. There may be slight changes in later years.) Even when you owe no tax, you will have to file a return to collect a refund on money withheld from your pay for tax purposes.

The government tries to make it easy for taxpayers who are single with no dependents. If that's your situation, you can use Form 1040EZ (which is easy to fill out) provided your income was all from salary.

Tax deductions are available to those who own mortgaged property, or who have extensive medical expenses, charitable contributions, or casualty losses. To claim them you will need to submit Form 1040. Form 1040A can be used by those who do not itemize their deductions but have dependents or income from outside sources.

### Solved problem:

At the Judd Machine Company, the salaried payroll is listed below. Given the annual salary of each employee, what is the weekly or monthly gross pay, the federal tax withheld, the federal tax due, and the refund or additional payment required?

| Name | Annual Salary | Weekly Salary | Monthly Salary | No. of Dependents | No. of Exemptions* | Tax Withheld | Taxable Income (less 10% deduction & exempt.*) | Tax Due | Over- or Under- Payment |
|---|---|---|---|---|---|---|---|---|---|
| Liz Rogers | $10,500 | $201.92 | — | 0 | 1 | $17 | $ 8,450 | $ 956 | −$ 72 |
| Ed Morino | 12,100 | 232.69 | — | 1 | 2 | 18 | 8,890 | 1,028 | − 92 |
| Ray Filipo | 11,600 | 223.08 | — | 2 | 3 | 14 | 7,440 | 779 | − 51 |
| Linda Terhune | 14,200 | 273.08 | — | 4 | 5 | 16 | 7,780 | 835 | − 3 |
| Marie Sandoz | 13,500 | 259.62 | — | 1 | 2 | 21 | 10,150 | 1,265 | − 173 |
| Rod Phillips | 16,700 | 321.15 | — | 3 | 4 | 26 | 11,030 | 1,452 | − 100 |
| Bernie Hauser | 19,900 | 382.69 | — | 3 | 4 | 36 | 13,910 | 2,139 | − 267 |

*In addition, each employee may claim a $1,000 exemption for each family member.

Use Table 1 on page 80 to determine withholding tax. Assume that all employees are married and use Form 1040A with a standard 10% deduction, and that each file separate returns.

**EXAMPLE:** Liz Rogers has a weekly salary of $10,500 ÷ 52 = $201.92. From Table 1, the amount withheld is $17 (0 dep.). Liz's total payment is 52 × $17 = $884. Using Form 1040A, Liz's taxable income is $10,500 − $1,050 − $1,000 (exemption) = $8,450 (gross income less 10% standard deduction).

From tax Table 2 (page 81), the tax on $8,450 is $956. The difference between $884 and $956 is $72. Liz owes $72.

## HOW TO FIGURE A PAYROLL

If you're employed by a small business, you may be assigned to prepare the weekly payroll. Although many larger companies now use computers for this task, it is still done manually in many retail businesses and smaller manufacturing companies. Accuracy is the fundamental requirement in computing payrolls, particularly since employees are very sensitive to any discrepancies, even minor ones, when their paycheck is affected.

People who perform direct labor are generally paid on an hourly basis, although this practice is changing. This means that their rate of pay is figured on an hourly basis and that their wages are paid only for those hours worked. Federal wage and hour regulations require that overtime be paid for work performed on Saturdays, Sundays, and holidays.

Office and clerical workers are generally paid weekly salaries rather than hourly wages. All employees are assessed deductions for income tax withholding, social security, and other charges such as hospitalization, workmen's compensation, and United Way contributions.

The payroll clerk compiles all these figures into shop and office payrolls from which employees are paid. Here is the procedure followed for the hourly payroll.

1. Add the hours worked by each employee each day of the week. (Note: To compute overtime, multiply overtime hours by the applicable factor.) Generally, employees who work on Saturdays are paid time and a half, and work done on Sundays and holidays are paid double time. The time-and-a-half rate is also paid to employees who work more than eight hours on any one weekday.

2. Multiply each employee's hourly pay rate by the total number of hours worked, to obtain the weekly gross pay.

3. Compute the Social Security tax by multiplying gross pay by 6.7%.

4. Find the withholding tax due by using Table 1 on page 80.
5. Add in any additional deductions indicated.
6. Add all deductions to compute the total.
7. Subtract total deductions from gross pay to determine net pay.

### Solved problem:

The Clinton Printing Company has ten employees. Seven work in the shop, the others are office workers. The company deducts a flat $3.10 for hospital and medical insurance. All employees are married. Here are the time records for the shop employees.

(Week ending December 11):

| Name | Mon | Tu | Wed | Th | Fri | Sat | Sun | Straight Time | O' Time | Total |
|---|---|---|---|---|---|---|---|---|---|---|
| Claude Godell | 8 | 8 | 10 | 8 | 8 | 8 | | 40 | 10 | 55 |
| Tom Mancini | 7½ | 8 | 10 | 8 | 8 | 8 | | 39½ | 10 | 54½ |
| Robin Towson | 10 | 8 | 8 | 8 | 8 | | | 40 | 2 | 43 |
| Gene Hood | 8 | 8 | 10 | 8 | 8 | | | 40 | 2 | 43 |
| Ron Fellows | 8 | 8 | 4 | 8 | 8 | | | 36 | — | 36 |
| Ray Hudek | 8 | 8 | 8 | 8 | 10 | | | 40 | 2 | 43 |
| Warren Chavez | 8 | 8 | 8 | 6 | 8 | | | 38 | — | 38 |

Here is the complete company payroll:

| | Hrs. Worked | Rate | Gross Pay | No. Dep. | With- holding | Soc. Sec. | Hosp. | Net Pay |
|---|---|---|---|---|---|---|---|---|
| Claude Godell | 55 | 6.50 | 357.50 | 3 | 34.00 | 23.95 | 3.10 | 296.45 |
| Tom Mancini | 54½ | 6.25 | 340.63 | 2 | 36.00 | 22.82 | 3.10 | 278.71 |
| Robin Towson | 43 | 6.25 | 268.75 | 1 | 26.00 | 18.01 | 3.10 | 221.64 |
| Gene Hood | 43 | 6.75 | 290.25 | 4 | 21.00 | 19.45 | 3.10 | 246.70 |
| Ron Fellows | 36 | 6.25 | 225.00 | 1 | 20.00 | 15.08 | 3.10 | 186.82 |
| Ray Hudek | 43 | 6.50 | 279.50 | 2 | 24.00 | 18.73 | 3.10 | 233.67 |
| Warren Chavez | 38 | 6.25 | 237.50 | 3 | 16.00 | 15.91 | 3.10 | 202.49 |
| Ed Young | Sal. | — | 400.00 | 3 | 43.00 | 26.80 | 3.10 | 327.10 |
| Cynthia Evans | Sal. | — | 220.00 | 1 | 20.00 | 14.74 | 3.10 | 182.16 |
| Tom Jones | Sal. | — | 225.00 | 1 | 20.00 | 15.08 | 3.10 | 186.82 |
| | | | Totals | | 260.00 | 190.57 | | $2362.56 |

Here is one of the payroll lines worked out: Claude Godell worked 8 hours on 5 days. He had a total of 10 hours of overtime (Wed. and Sat.) which ×1.5=15. Thus, his total hours were 40+15=55.

His hourly rate was $6.50×55=$357.50 gross pay. From the withholding table (Table 1), his tax was $34.00 (3 dep). Subtracting $23.95 (6.7% of $357.50) for social security and $3.10 for hospitalization insurance, leaves a net of $296.45. Note that the total amount of the payroll $2,362.56 must be given to the bookkeeper so that sufficient funds are deposited in the payroll account at the company's bank.

In addition, the company is required to forward promptly the income tax withheld ($260.00), plus the employees' social security tax, and the company's equal contribution to a depository designated by the Internal Revenue Service. There are severe penalties for failure to deposit these sums according to IRS regulations, since it is money held in trust on the employees' behalf.

## HOW TO FIGURE INSURANCE COSTS

Insurance is a key expense in most businesses. It protects the firm against financial loss due to unforeseen events. Fire insurance, for instance, protects against the loss of the company's building, machinery, office equipment, records and vehicles.

The cost of the insurance (the premium) varies considerably depending on the business's location, the type of building it's housed in, and the type of merchandise stored and sold on the premises.

A lumber company and a paint manufacturer for instance pay extremely high premiums for their insurance coverage due to the volatile and flammable nature of their products and the chemicals used in the manufacturing process.

The type of fire protection available also plays a hand in the cost. Companies located in urban areas with professional firefighting organizations buy their insurance cheaper than similar businesses in rural areas with poor protection.

Fire insurance is grouped under the general category of property insurance. This insurance protects owners from various types of hazards including burglary, theft, floods, hurricanes, breakage, and collision of vehicles.

The company that sells the insurance is called the "underwriter." The buyer is called the "insured," and the contract between the underwriter and the insured is called the "insurance policy."

To reduce the cost of the insurance, the property owner may cover only a portion of the business—from 20% to 80% of its appraised value, for instance—or he may buy a policy that covers a longer period of time than one year.

Property owners may also save money on the premium for fire insurance by accepting a coinsurance clause in the policy. With the coinsurance, the owner agrees to accept payment for damage to his property equal to the percent of its value stated in the policy. That figure is generally 80%. Here is an example of the use of the 80% clause:

Mr. Johnson's stationery store is valued at $60,000 and his fire insurance policy (which contains the 80% clause) has a face value of $45,000 (the specified amount of coverage). The 80% clause means, in effect, that the insurance company expects Johnson to buy insurance that covers at least 80% of the property's value.

The store suffered $12,000 worth of fire damage. Since the insurance coverage amounted to only 75% of the property's value (45,000 ÷ 60,000), the insurance company's liability is limited to an amount no greater than the proportion of the coverage (45,000) to 80% of the property's value.

80% of 60,000 = 48,000

Insurance coverage = 45,000

$$\frac{45,000}{48,000} = \frac{15}{16}$$ of the damage will be paid by the company, or

$$12,000 \times \frac{15}{16} = \$11,250$$

## Life Insurance

Life insurance is available for people who wish to protect their families or businesses from the financial consequences of their deaths. Thus, a young man with a wife and two small children might need a substantial life insurance policy to help that family cope with the loss of his salary in the event of his death. Even a couple with no children and each partner working might want to protect each other against the loss of either income if one of them dies.

## Term and Ordinary Life Policies

In recent years, insurance companies have begun to offer their customers a greater and greater variety of new types of life insurance. Rather than discuss this broad variety, the two basic types of insurance policies from which the new offerings have been derived will be covered.

The simplest form of insurance is the *term* policy which provides a certain amount of insurance in return for an annual premium. For example, a man or woman in his or her early thirties might buy 10-year term insurance for $35 annual premium per $1,000 of coverage. Under such a policy, the insurance would expire at the end of 10 years, because presumably the need for coverage would no longer exist.

On the other hand, an *ordinary life* policy carries a higher premium because a portion of the premium is set aside by the insurance company to accumulate toward the policy's cash surrender value. Under the terms of such a policy, the policy owner, after a period of time, may cancel his policy and receive a specified amount of cash in return. The policy owner may also borrow a portion of the value of the policy from the insurance company without losing his coverage.

The cost of life insurance varies greatly depending on the age of the purchaser when he buys his policy. This variation is due to the life expectancy of the policyholder. For example, a 20-year-old person has a much greater life expectancy than a 40-year-old. The insurance company anticipates collecting premiums from the younger person for a longer period of time.

Here is a typical table of annual rates for ordinary life and 10-year term insurance per $1,000 of coverage:

| Age | Ordinary Life | 10-year Term |
|-----|---------------|--------------|
| 20 | 32.50 | 18.10 |
| 30 | 37.20 | 21.40 |
| 40 | 44.80 | 32.70 |
| 50 | 57.25 | 43.15 |
| 60 | 71.10 | 61.20 |

*Solved problems:* (use tables above)

1. What does a $7,500 insurance policy cost for a woman aged 20?
                    A. ordinary life?        B. term?

*Answer:*
A. ordinary life premium age 20: $32.50.   $32.50 \times 7.5 = \$243.75$
B. term premium age 20: $18.10.   $18.10 \times 7.5 = \$135.75$

2. A 40-year-old doctor buys two life insurance policies: one, $75,000 of ordinary life; the other, $100,000 of 10-year term. What is his total premium?

*Answer:*

$$\begin{array}{lll} \text{Ordinary life} - 44.80 \times 75 & = & \$3360 \\ \text{Term} \quad\quad - 32.70 \times 100 & = & \underline{3270} \\ & & \$6630 \end{array}$$

3. A young man buys a $15,000 ordinary life policy at age 30. He dies at age 62. What is the total cost of the policy at the time of his death and what was the net value of his insurance?

*Answer:*

Premium $= 37.20 \times 15 = \$558$
Number of years paid $= 62 - 30 = 32$
Total cost $= 32 \times 558 = \$17,856$
Net value $= -\$2,856$

4. At age 30, a man buys a $50,000 10-year term policy. Each year of the policy, he invests the difference between the cost of ordinary life and term in a savings account that pays a 10% annual dividend. At the end of two years, how much money does he have in the savings account?

*Answer:*

Annual premium difference
37.20 × 50 = 1860
21.40 × 50 = 1070
‾‾‾‾
790

Amount in savings account:
End of first year: 790 + 79 = $869
End of second year: 869 + 86.90 = $955.90 + 790 (2nd year) = $1745.90

## HOW TO RECONCILE YOUR CHECKBOOK WITH THE BANK STATEMENT

This nasty little problem confronts you every month when you receive your statement from the bank. If you yield to the temptation to leave it until next month, the job eventually becomes impossible.

Here is a simple way to do the reconciliation quickly:

1. If your bank returns your checks with the statement, match them to the entries in your checkbook. Be sure that the amounts on the checks match your check stubs. Mark off all those checks the bank has returned.

2. Note the closing date on the bank statement. Record the balance in your checkbook as of that date (or a date following the bank's date as closely as possible).

3. Since the length of time required for the banks to receive your checks varies, some of the checks you've written (as of your balance date) may not appear in the bank's balance yet.

On the other hand, a check may clear so quickly that it may appear in the bank's balance but shows in your checkbook at a date later than your balance date.

4. Using the form shown below, record these checks as follows:

- Your balance as of _____(Date)_____                    $ _____
- Plus checks you have written as of this date but that the bank has not returned
- Less checks included in the bank's statement that you have written after the balance date above
- Corrected balance should match the bank's                    $ _____

If your bank does not return cancelled checks, you will have to use the amounts and dates listed on its balance sheet. This is more cumbersome since the amounts do not show your check numbers, and the dates are recorded when the bank receives the check and not the date in your checkbook.

Remember, if you have trouble identifying the amount shown in the statement, the bank is obligated to send you a photocopy of the check if you so request.

*Solved problems:*

1. Mary Furillo receives her bank statement for June, and notes that it is dated June 21. After matching the checks enclosed with the statement, she finds first that four checks written as of June 21 have not been returned. They are: London Dry Cleaners $14.50, Tiffany Restaurant $27.21, Rogers & Co. (rent) $275, and Vanity Fair $37.80. She also finds that two checks dated June 23 are included in the statement. One check was for $8.25, the other for $11.79. The bank's balance as of June 21 was $823.41 including a $4.50 service charge. Mary's checkbook balance as of June 21 was $493.44. Reconcile the two figures.

*Answer:*

| | | |
|---|---:|---:|
| Mary's balance on 6/21 | | $493.44 |
| Plus checks written but not shown in the bank's balance | $ 14.50 | |
| | 27.21 | |
| | 275.00 | |
| | 37.80 | |
| | | 847.95 |
| Less checks written after 6/21 | 8.25 | |
| | 11.79 | |
| | | 827.91 |

Since the $4.50 service charge has been subtracted from the bank's balance but not from hers, Mary subtracts $827.91 − $4.50 = $823.41.

2. On February 21, the Community Cleaners received its monthly statement from the bank. It read as follows:

Date: February 21, 19___

| Date | Checks | | Date | Deposits | Balance |
|---|---|---|---|---|---|
| Jan. 28 | 45.00 | | | | 462.50 |
| Jan. 30 | 75.50 | 18.10 | | | 368.90 |
| Feb. 1 | 275.00 | 14.62 | Feb. 1 | 4,022.50 | 4,101.78 |
| Feb. 6 | 812.00 | | | | 3,289.78 |
| Feb. 8 | 352.00 | 41.71 | Feb. 8 | 3,721.00 | 6,617.07 |
| Feb. 13 | 88.91 | 1562.00 | | | 4,966.16 |
| Feb. 18 | 1465.27 | | Feb. 15 | 1,222.40 | 4,732.29 |
| Feb. 19 | 22.40 | | | | 4,700.89 |
| Feb. 19 | 4.50* | | | | 4,696.39 |

*Service charge

Mr. Childs, the store manager, showed a balance of $2,725.14. On February 18 he had written two checks, one for $200 and the other for $1,775.75. Neither of these checks had been returned. Reconcile the bank's February 19 balance of $4,696.39 with Mr. Childs' balance.

|  |  |  |
|---|---|---|
| Child's balance 2/19/__ |  | $2725.14 |
| Plus checks not returned | $200.00 |  |
|  | 1775.75 | 1975.75 |
|  |  | 4700.89 |
| Less bank service charge |  | − 4.50 |
|  |  | $4696.39 |

## REVIEW PROBLEMS FOR YOU TO SOLVE

This is a series of problems covering the subjects we have discussed in this section. Solving them will give you an opportunity to see how well you understand these topics. The answers to these problems are listed in the back of the chapter, so that you can check yourself for accuracy. (See pages 77 through 79.)

### Simple Interest

1. Figure the return on a $75,000 loan at 12% interest using all four methods for the period from June 1 through September 15.
2. Compute the return on $360 invested at simple interest of 8% for a 4-month and an 18-month period.
(*Note:* The next three problems can be solved by use of the formula: I (interest) = P (principal) × r (rate) × t (time). Where I and P are expressed in dollars, r is a decimal fraction (8% = .08) and t is in years if r is the annual interest rate.)
3. If Ed Jennings deposits $700 in a savings account and receives $84 in interest at the end of 18 months, what is the rate of interest?
4. Robert Mellon puts $1,200 in a money market account that earns 9.5% interest. How long will it have to remain in the account to earn $142.50?
5. Richard Altobelli has money in a money market fund. His latest report shows that he has earned $962.50 during the last year and that the current interest rate is 8.75%. How much money did he have in his account at the beginning of the year?

## Discount

1. Mary Ellen Williams borrowed $750 at 11% interest from her bank to purchase hi-fi equipment. If the money was borrowed for six months and the bank discounted the note, how much money did Mary Ellen receive to buy the equipment?

2. The Summit Bank holds a six-month note with an interest rate of 14% and a face amount of $20,000. After one month the bank discounts the note at a rate of 16%. How much money does the bank receive?

3. Discount $7,500 at 12% for 8 months. What are the proceeds?

4. Discount $150,000 at 15% for 18 months. Give the proceeds.

## Compound Interest

(*Note:* Use compound interest table, page 49, to solve these problems.)

1. Compute the compound interest on $35,000 placed on deposit for 5 years at 12% and compounded quarterly.

2. Compute the value of $400 deposited for 6 years at 8% interest compounded quarterly.

3. If George Johnson leaves $1,200 on deposit for 4 years at 16% compounded quarterly, what will his money be worth at the end of the first, the second, and the fourth year?

4. What amount of money must be deposited at 10%, compounded semiannually, to have $15,920 at the end of 10 years?

## Discounts (Commercial)

1. The Foster Company sells industrial electric switches. They offer a 50% distributor discount and the following quantity discounts:

|         |         |
|---------|---------|
| 1– 99   | 10%     |
| 100–499 | 15%     |
| 500 and up | 20%  |

Their discount to original equipment manufacturers (OEM) is 15% plus quantity discount.

Eagle Electric Company, a distributor, buys an assortment of switches for $22,520. What is its net cost?

Monarch Electric Products is an OEM. If it buys 250 switches at $35 each, what is its total cost?

What would Eagle Electric's profit have been if they had sold the switches to Monarch?.

John Reynolds owns an electrical repair shop. He buys 110 switches at $19.50 each. What is his cost? What is Eagle's profit on the sale?

2. Eagle Electric's terms of sale are 2% 10 net 30.

How much would Monarch and Reynolds have saved by taking Eagle's discount?

## Balance Sheets and Profit and Loss Statements

1. The Key Stationery Company is closing its books as of June 30. Here are the pertinent facts:

| | |
|---|---|
| 1. Cash on hand | $3,200 |
| 2. Cash in bank | 7,150 |
| 3. Income tax payable | 752 |
| 4. Accounts receivable | 4,152.50 |
| 5. Furniture and fixtures | 3,158 |
| 6. Bank loan | 2,150 |
| 7. Accounts payable | 2,791 |
| 8. Mortgage on store | 2,500 |
| 9. Inventory | 7,800 |

First, identify assets and liabilities, then prepare a balance sheet.

For the month of June, Key had the following activities:

| | |
|---|---|
| 1. Opening inventory | $ 8,145 |
| 2. Sales | 10,722 |
| 3. Purchases | 3,570 |
| 4. Salaries | 4,125 |
| 5. Phone | 227 |
| 6. Utilities | 181 |
| 7. Miscell. expense | 322 |
| 8. Closing inventory | 7,800 |

Make up a profit and loss statement for Key Stationery.

2. The Georgetown Music Company ends its fiscal year on June 30. Its inventory as of that date showed: records and tapes $1,650; sheet music, $250; hi-fi and stereo equipment amounting to $11,500. Cash on hand is $1,121.43, and in the bank is $1,585. Furniture and fixtures add up to $1,600. Accounts payable are $12,500. Prepare a June 30 balance sheet.

3. At the end of the year (December 31), Georgetown Music has records and tapes amounting to $1,048, sheet music at $120, and hi-fi and stereo equipment at $7,850. Cash on hand is $722, and in the bank is $2,312. Accounts payable are $8,922 and year-end taxes amount to $2,250. What does the December 31 balance sheet look like?

4. On September 1, the inventory at White City Electronics was: TV sets $8,221, hi-fi and stereo equipment $7,815, computers and accessories $11,992.

At the end of September, the combined inventory was $25,021. During the month, purchases amounted to $4,575 and sales were $12,022. Operating expenses for the month were as follows: rent $850, salaries $2,575, office supplies $77.50, telephone $122, utilities $217, insurance $45, and miscellaneous expense $110. Prepare a complete profit and loss statement as of September 30.

5. On February 1, Coleman Brothers Jewelry Store had an inventory of $7,852 in jewelry, silverware and watches. During February, purchases amounted to $5,630 and sales were $9,921. At the end of February, inventory was $6,220.

Operating expenses for the month included: rent $650, salaries $1,525, office supplies $129.75, telephone $67.50, utilities $142.60, insurance $91.00, and miscellaneous expense $82.20. Make up a P&L statement for February.


## Depreciation

1. The office furniture at the Highland Realty Company was bought in 1983 at a price of $4,150. It is being depreciated on the straight-line method and the scrap value in 1993 will be $100. What is the annual depreciation charge and what will be the book value at the end of 1985?

2. The Rowland Company has two office copiers, one bought in 1980 for $3,220. Its useful life is 7 years, and it will be worth $200 at that time. The other was bought in 1982 for $1,250. At the end of 10 years, it will have a scrap value of $50. What is the combined annual depreciation charge and book value at the end of 1985?

3. The Eagle Drug Store owns two delivery vehicles. One, a van, was bought in 1981 for $12,220; it depreciates 15% per year. The other, a station wagon, was bought in 1982 for $9,850; it depreciates 20% per year. What is the 1985 depreciation charge for both vehicles and their book value at the end of the year?

4. Meyers & Lavin, a law firm, owns two word processors. One, bought in 1982, depreciates at 25% per year. The second, bought in early 1985, depreciates at 20% per year. If the first cost $11,700 and the second $12,450, compute depreciation charge and book value at the end of '85.

## Taxes

1. The Richmond Stationery Store made the following purchases in February, 1985:

| | | | |
|---|---|---|---|
| Greeting cards | $227.50 | Cash register | $8,520 |
| Candy | 571.00 | Display counters | 1,410 |
| #10 envelopes | 49.00 | | |
| typewriter ribbons | 29.50 | | |

The store is located in New Jersey and the tax is 6%. How much sales tax did Richmond pay?

2. Rosalie Travell bought the following items in a New Jersey supermarket: meat $8.22, bread $1.25, fresh vegetables $5.40, milk $2.50, light bulbs $4.50, ice cream $2.75, orange juice $1.20, saucepan $6.25. How much sales tax did she pay?

3. Ray and Marie Ponsell own a home with an assessed value of $87,500. Their tax rate is as follows: local government $.92, local schools $2.21 and county government .639, all per $100 assessed value. What are their taxes for local government, schools and county government? What are the total taxes and the quarterly payments?

## Payroll

Below are the time records for Johnson's Auto Body Shop:

| Name | Mon | Tu | Wed | Th | Fri | Sat | Straight Time | O' Time | Total |
|---|---|---|---|---|---|---|---|---|---|
| R. Silvio | 9 | 9 | 8 | 4 | 8 | 8 | 36 | 10 | 51 |
| G. Butts | 10 | 9 | 7 | 8 | 8 | | 39 | 3 | 43½ |
| W. Feller | 9 | 9 | 8 | 8 | 8 | 8 | 40 | 10 | 55 |
| A. Vasquez | 9 | 9 | 8 | 8 | 8 | | 40 | 2 | 43 |

Compute the payroll, withholding tax, and social security if each worker makes $8.00/hour. Use the withholding table on page 80. Dependents are as follows: Silvio 2, Butts 1, Feller 3, Vasquez 4.

## Insurance

1. Figure what proportion of the damage will be paid under the following fire insurance policies containing the 80% clause.

        Policy A—Property value $105,000       Face Value $120,000
        Policy B—Property value  250,000       Face Value  275,000
        Policy C—Property value  60,000       Face Value    85,000

2. Walter Jones' house valued at $340,000 suffers $42,000 worth of damage. The face value of his insurance policy is (with an 80% clause) $250,000. How much will the policy pay of the $42,000 damage?

3. Figure the cost of a $250,000 life insurance policy for a man aged 50, both for a 10-year term and an ordinary life policy (use table on page 68).

4. Which is cheaper over the first 5 years for a man aged 30, a $75,000 10-year term policy or a $50,000 ordinary life policy?

5. If a man buys $50,000 of 10-year term at age 20 and $25,000 of ordinary life at age 40, what is the total cost of his insurance at age 50? (Note: he does not renew the term insurance.)

## SOLUTIONS TO BUSINESS MATH PROBLEMS

### Simple Interest (page 71):

1. Ordinary-exact          $2,675
   Ordinary-approx.        $2,625
   Exact-exact            $2,638.36
   Exact-approx.          $2,589.04
2. $9.60 and $43.20
3. 8%
4. 15 mos.
5. $11,000

### Discount (page 72):

1. $708.75
2. $19,973.33
3. $6,900
4. $116,250

### Compound Interest (page 72):

1. $63,213.50
2. $643.36
3. First year: $1,403.88; second year: $1,642.20; fourth year: $2,247.60
4. $6,000.08

### Discounts (Commercial) (page 72):

1. Eagle Electric's cost:       $11,260
   Monarch's cost:            $ 6,321.88
   Eagle Electric's profit:   $ 1,946.88
   Reynold's cost:            $ 1,823.25
   Eagle's profit:            $   750.75
2. Monarch's savings:         $   126.44
   Reynold's savings:         $    36.47

*Balance Sheet and Profit and Loss Statements (page 73):*

1. Balance sheet—
   Assets:       $25,460.50
   Liabilities:   8,193.00
   Net worth:    17,267.50

   P & L Statement—
   Cost of goods sold:   $ 3,915
   Gross profit:          6,807
   Operating expense:     4,855
   Net profit:            1,952

2. Assets:       $17,706.43
   Liabilities:   12,500.00
   Net worth:      5,206.43

3. Assets:       $12,052
   Liabilities:   11,172
   Net worth:        880

4. Cost of Sales:
   $28,028 Opening inventory
   __4,575__ Purchases
    32,603
   __−25,021__ Closing inventory
   $ 7,582 Cost of sales

   Sales:
   $12,022
   __− 7,582__
     4,440     Gross profit
   __− 3,996.50__ Operating expenses
   $    443.50 Net profit

5. Sales                          $9,921
      Cost of sales:   $ 7,852
                       __5,630__
                       $13,482
                       __− 6,220__
                                      __7,262__
                                      $2,659    Gross profit
                                      __− 2,688.05__ Operating expenses
                                      __−    29.05__ Net loss

*Depreciation (page 74):*

1. $405 Annual depreciation charge
   $3,340 Book value end 1985
2. $551.43 Combined annual depreciation charge
   $1,952.85 Combined book value end 1985
3. $2,387 Depreciation charge
   #1—$6,379; #2—$5,043 end 1985 book value
4. $4,135 Depreciation charge
   $14,896 Book value

*Taxes (page 75):*

1. $614.16
2. $0.65
3. Local government: $805; schools: $1,933.75; county: $559.13
   Total taxes: $3,297.88; Quarterly payments: $824.47

*Payroll (page 75):*

|         | Hours | Gross    | Soc. Sec. | Withhld. | Net        |
|---------|-------|----------|-----------|----------|------------|
| Silvio  | 51    | $  408   | $ 27.34   | $ 47     | $  333.66  |
| Butts   | 43.5  | 348      | 23.32     | 39       | 285.68     |
| Feller  | 55    | 440      | 29.48     | 50       | 360.52     |
| Vasquez | 43    | 344      | 23.05     | 29       | 291.95     |
| Totals  | 192.5 | $1,540   | $103.19   | $165     | $1,271.81  |

*Insurance (page 76):*

1. Policy A — In full
   Policy B — In full
   Policy C — 88% of damage
2. $38,603
3. 10-year term:     $10,787.50
   Ordinary life:    $14,312.50
4. 10-year term:     $ 8,025
   Ordinary life:    $ 9,300
5. $20,250

## MARRIED Persons–WEEKLY Payroll Period
### (For Wages Paid After December 1984)

| And the wages are— | | And the number of withholding allowances claimed is— | | | | | | | | | | |
|---|---|---|---|---|---|---|---|---|---|---|---|---|
| At least | But less than | 0 | 1 | 2 | 3 | 4 | 5 | 6 | 7 | 8 | 9 | 10 |
| | | The amount of income tax to be withheld shall be— | | | | | | | | | | |
| $0 | $52 | $0 | $0 | $0 | $0 | $0 | $0 | $0 | $0 | $0 | $0 | $0 |
| 52 | 54 | 1 | 0 | 0 | 0 | 0 | 0 | 0 | 0 | 0 | 0 | 0 |
| 54 | 56 | 1 | 0 | 0 | 0 | 0 | 0 | 0 | 0 | 0 | 0 | 0 |
| 56 | 58 | 1 | 0 | 0 | 0 | 0 | 0 | 0 | 0 | 0 | 0 | 0 |
| 58 | 60 | 1 | 0 | 0 | 0 | 0 | 0 | 0 | 0 | 0 | 0 | 0 |
| 60 | 62 | 1 | 0 | 0 | 0 | 0 | 0 | 0 | 0 | 0 | 0 | 0 |
| 62 | 64 | 2 | 0 | 0 | 0 | 0 | 0 | 0 | 0 | 0 | 0 | 0 |
| 64 | 66 | 2 | 0 | 0 | 0 | 0 | 0 | 0 | 0 | 0 | 0 | 0 |
| 66 | 68 | 2 | 0 | 0 | 0 | 0 | 0 | 0 | 0 | 0 | 0 | 0 |
| 68 | 70 | 2 | 0 | 0 | 0 | 0 | 0 | 0 | 0 | 0 | 0 | 0 |
| 70 | 72 | 3 | 0 | 0 | 0 | 0 | 0 | 0 | 0 | 0 | 0 | 0 |
| 72 | 74 | 3 | 1 | 0 | 0 | 0 | 0 | 0 | 0 | 0 | 0 | 0 |
| 74 | 76 | 3 | 1 | 0 | 0 | 0 | 0 | 0 | 0 | 0 | 0 | 0 |
| 76 | 78 | 3 | 1 | 0 | 0 | 0 | 0 | 0 | 0 | 0 | 0 | 0 |
| 78 | 80 | 3 | 1 | 0 | 0 | 0 | 0 | 0 | 0 | 0 | 0 | 0 |
| 80 | 82 | 4 | 1 | 0 | 0 | 0 | 0 | 0 | 0 | 0 | 0 | 0 |
| 82 | 84 | 4 | 2 | 0 | 0 | 0 | 0 | 0 | 0 | 0 | 0 | 0 |
| 84 | 86 | 4 | 2 | 0 | 0 | 0 | 0 | 0 | 0 | 0 | 0 | 0 |
| 86 | 88 | 4 | 2 | 0 | 0 | 0 | 0 | 0 | 0 | 0 | 0 | 0 |
| 88 | 90 | 5 | 2 | 0 | 0 | 0 | 0 | 0 | 0 | 0 | 0 | 0 |
| 90 | 92 | 5 | 3 | 1 | 0 | 0 | 0 | 0 | 0 | 0 | 0 | 0 |
| 92 | 94 | 5 | 3 | 1 | 0 | 0 | 0 | 0 | 0 | 0 | 0 | 0 |
| 94 | 96 | 5 | 3 | 1 | 0 | 0 | 0 | 0 | 0 | 0 | 0 | 0 |
| 96 | 98 | 5 | 3 | 1 | 0 | 0 | 0 | 0 | 0 | 0 | 0 | 0 |
| 98 | 100 | 6 | 3 | 1 | 0 | 0 | 0 | 0 | 0 | 0 | 0 | 0 |
| 100 | 105 | 6 | 4 | 2 | 0 | 0 | 0 | 0 | 0 | 0 | 0 | 0 |
| 105 | 110 | 7 | 4 | 2 | 0 | 0 | 0 | 0 | 0 | 0 | 0 | 0 |
| 110 | 115 | 7 | 5 | 3 | 0 | 0 | 0 | 0 | 0 | 0 | 0 | 0 |
| 115 | 120 | 8 | 6 | 3 | 1 | 0 | 0 | 0 | 0 | 0 | 0 | 0 |
| 120 | 125 | 9 | 6 | 4 | 2 | 0 | 0 | 0 | 0 | 0 | 0 | 0 |
| 125 | 130 | 9 | 7 | 4 | 2 | 0 | 0 | 0 | 0 | 0 | 0 | 0 |
| 130 | 135 | 10 | 7 | 5 | 3 | 0 | 0 | 0 | 0 | 0 | 0 | 0 |
| 135 | 140 | 10 | 8 | 6 | 3 | 1 | 0 | 0 | 0 | 0 | 0 | 0 |
| 140 | 145 | 11 | 9 | 6 | 4 | 2 | 0 | 0 | 0 | 0 | 0 | 0 |
| 145 | 150 | 12 | 9 | 7 | 4 | 2 | 0 | 0 | 0 | 0 | 0 | 0 |
| 150 | 160 | 13 | 10 | 8 | 5 | 3 | 1 | 0 | 0 | 0 | 0 | 0 |
| 160 | 170 | 14 | 11 | 9 | 6 | 4 | 2 | 0 | 0 | 0 | 0 | 0 |
| 170 | 180 | 16 | 13 | 10 | 8 | 5 | 3 | 1 | 0 | 0 | 0 | 0 |
| 180 | 190 | 17 | 14 | 11 | 9 | 6 | 4 | 2 | 0 | 0 | 0 | 0 |
| 190 | 200 | 18 | 16 | 13 | 10 | 8 | 5 | 3 | 1 | 0 | 0 | 0 |
| 200 | 210 | 20 | 17 | 14 | 11 | 9 | 6 | 4 | 2 | 0 | 0 | 0 |
| 210 | 220 | 21 | 18 | 16 | 13 | 10 | 8 | 5 | 3 | 1 | 0 | 0 |
| 220 | 230 | 23 | 20 | 17 | 14 | 11 | 9 | 6 | 4 | 2 | 0 | 0 |
| 230 | 240 | 24 | 21 | 18 | 16 | 13 | 10 | 8 | 5 | 3 | 1 | 0 |
| 240 | 250 | 26 | 23 | 20 | 17 | 14 | 11 | 9 | 6 | 4 | 2 | 0 |
| 250 | 260 | 28 | 24 | 21 | 18 | 16 | 13 | 10 | 8 | 5 | 3 | 1 |
| 260 | 270 | 29 | 26 | 23 | 20 | 17 | 14 | 11 | 9 | 6 | 4 | 2 |
| 270 | 280 | 31 | 28 | 24 | 21 | 18 | 16 | 13 | 10 | 8 | 5 | 3 |
| 280 | 290 | 32 | 29 | 26 | 23 | 20 | 17 | 14 | 11 | 9 | 6 | 4 |
| 290 | 300 | 34 | 31 | 28 | 24 | 21 | 18 | 16 | 13 | 10 | 8 | 5 |
| 300 | 310 | 36 | 32 | 29 | 26 | 23 | 20 | 17 | 14 | 11 | 9 | 6 |
| 310 | 320 | 38 | 34 | 31 | 28 | 24 | 21 | 18 | 16 | 13 | 10 | 8 |
| 320 | 330 | 39 | 36 | 32 | 29 | 26 | 23 | 20 | 17 | 14 | 11 | 9 |
| 330 | 340 | 41 | 38 | 34 | 31 | 28 | 24 | 21 | 18 | 16 | 13 | 10 |
| 340 | 350 | 43 | 39 | 36 | 32 | 29 | 26 | 23 | 20 | 17 | 14 | 11 |
| 350 | 360 | 45 | 41 | 38 | 34 | 31 | 28 | 24 | 21 | 18 | 16 | 13 |
| 360 | 370 | 47 | 43 | 39 | 36 | 32 | 29 | 26 | 23 | 20 | 17 | 14 |
| 370 | 380 | 48 | 45 | 41 | 38 | 34 | 31 | 28 | 24 | 21 | 18 | 16 |
| 380 | 390 | 50 | 47 | 43 | 39 | 36 | 32 | 29 | 26 | 23 | 20 | 17 |
| 390 | 400 | 52 | 48 | 45 | 41 | 38 | 34 | 31 | 28 | 24 | 21 | 18 |
| 400 | 410 | 55 | 50 | 47 | 43 | 39 | 36 | 32 | 29 | 26 | 23 | 20 |
| 410 | 420 | 57 | 52 | 48 | 45 | 41 | 38 | 34 | 31 | 28 | 24 | 21 |
| 420 | 430 | 59 | 55 | 50 | 47 | 43 | 39 | 36 | 32 | 29 | 26 | 23 |
| 430 | 440 | 61 | 57 | 52 | 48 | 45 | 41 | 38 | 34 | 31 | 28 | 24 |
| 440 | 450 | 63 | 59 | 55 | 50 | 47 | 43 | 39 | 36 | 32 | 29 | 26 |
| 450 | 460 | 66 | 61 | 57 | 52 | 48 | 45 | 41 | 38 | 34 | 31 | 28 |
| 460 | 470 | 68 | 63 | 59 | 55 | 50 | 47 | 43 | 39 | 36 | 32 | 29 |
| 470 | 480 | 70 | 66 | 61 | 57 | 52 | 48 | 45 | 41 | 38 | 34 | 31 |
| 480 | 490 | 73 | 68 | 63 | 59 | 55 | 50 | 47 | 43 | 39 | 36 | 32 |

**TABLE 1**

**1984 Tax Table**

| If line 37 (taxable income) is— At least | But less than | And you are— Single | Married filing jointly * | Married filing separately | Head of a household |
|---|---|---|---|---|---|
| | | | Your tax is— | | |
| **5,000** | | | | | |
| 5,000 | 5,050 | 329 | 179 | 413 | 306 |
| 5,050 | 5,100 | 336 | 184 | 420 | 312 |
| 5,100 | 5,150 | 343 | 190 | 427 | 318 |
| 5,150 | 5,200 | 350 | 195 | 434 | 324 |
| 5,200 | 5,250 | 357 | 201 | 441 | 330 |
| 5,250 | 5,300 | 364 | 206 | 448 | 336 |
| 5,300 | 5,350 | 371 | 212 | 455 | 342 |
| 5,350 | 5,400 | 378 | 217 | 462 | 348 |
| 5,400 | 5,450 | 385 | 223 | 469 | 354 |
| 5,450 | 5,500 | 392 | 228 | 476 | 360 |
| 5,500 | 5,550 | 399 | 234 | 483 | 366 |
| 5,550 | 5,600 | 406 | 240 | 490 | 372 |
| 5,600 | 5,650 | 413 | 246 | 497 | 378 |
| 5,650 | 5,700 | 420 | 252 | 504 | 384 |
| 5,700 | 5,750 | 427 | 258 | 511 | 390 |
| 5,750 | 5,800 | 434 | 264 | 518 | 396 |
| 5,800 | 5,850 | 441 | 270 | 525 | 402 |
| 5,850 | 5,900 | 448 | 276 | 532 | 408 |
| 5,900 | 5,950 | 455 | 282 | 539 | 414 |
| 5,950 | 6,000 | 462 | 288 | 547 | 420 |
| **6,000** | | | | | |
| 6,000 | 6,050 | 469 | 294 | 555 | 426 |
| 6,050 | 6,100 | 476 | 300 | 563 | 432 |
| 6,100 | 6,150 | 483 | 306 | 571 | 438 |
| 6,150 | 6,200 | 490 | 312 | 579 | 444 |
| 6,200 | 6,250 | 497 | 318 | 587 | 450 |
| 6,250 | 6,300 | 504 | 324 | 595 | 456 |
| 6,300 | 6,350 | 511 | 330 | 603 | 462 |
| 6,350 | 6,400 | 518 | 336 | 611 | 468 |
| 6,400 | 6,450 | 525 | 342 | 619 | 474 |
| 6,450 | 6,500 | 532 | 348 | 627 | 480 |
| 6,500 | 6,550 | 539 | 354 | 635 | 487 |
| 6,550 | 6,600 | 546 | 360 | 643 | 494 |
| 6,600 | 6,650 | 554 | 366 | 651 | 501 |
| 6,650 | 6,700 | 561 | 372 | 659 | 508 |
| 6,700 | 6,750 | 569 | 378 | 667 | 515 |
| 6,750 | 6,800 | 576 | 384 | 675 | 522 |
| 6,800 | 6,850 | 584 | 390 | 683 | 529 |
| 6,850 | 6,900 | 591 | 396 | 691 | 536 |
| 6,900 | 6,950 | 599 | 402 | 699 | 543 |
| 6,950 | 7,000 | 606 | 408 | 707 | 550 |
| **7,000** | | | | | |
| 7,000 | 7,050 | 614 | 414 | 715 | 557 |
| 7,050 | 7,100 | 621 | 420 | 723 | 564 |
| 7,100 | 7,150 | 629 | 426 | 731 | 571 |
| 7,150 | 7,200 | 636 | 432 | 739 | 578 |
| 7,200 | 7,250 | 644 | 438 | 747 | 585 |
| 7,250 | 7,300 | 651 | 444 | 755 | 592 |
| 7,300 | 7,350 | 659 | 450 | 763 | 599 |
| 7,350 | 7,400 | 666 | 456 | 771 | 606 |
| 7,400 | 7,450 | 674 | 462 | 779 | 613 |
| 7,450 | 7,500 | 681 | 468 | 787 | 620 |
| 7,500 | 7,550 | 689 | 474 | 795 | 627 |
| 7,550 | 7,600 | 696 | 480 | 803 | 634 |
| 7,600 | 7,650 | 704 | 487 | 811 | 641 |
| 7,650 | 7,700 | 711 | 494 | 819 | 648 |
| 7,700 | 7,750 | 719 | 501 | 827 | 655 |
| 7,750 | 7,800 | 726 | 508 | 835 | 662 |
| 7,800 | 7,850 | 734 | 515 | 843 | 669 |
| 7,850 | 7,900 | 741 | 522 | 851 | 676 |
| 7,900 | 7,950 | 749 | 529 | 859 | 683 |
| 7,950 | 8,000 | 756 | 536 | 867 | 690 |

| If line 37 (taxable income) is— At least | But less than | And you are— Single | Married filing jointly * | Married filing separately | Head of a household |
|---|---|---|---|---|---|
| | | | Your tax is— | | |
| **8,000** | | | | | |
| 8,000 | 8,050 | 764 | 543 | 875 | 697 |
| 8,050 | 8,100 | 771 | 550 | 884 | 704 |
| 8,100 | 8,150 | 779 | 557 | 893 | 711 |
| 8,150 | 8,200 | 786 | 564 | 902 | 718 |
| 8,200 | 8,250 | 794 | 571 | 911 | 725 |
| 8,250 | 8,300 | 801 | 578 | 920 | 732 |
| 8,300 | 8,350 | 809 | 585 | 929 | 739 |
| 8,350 | 8,400 | 816 | 592 | 938 | 746 |
| 8,400 | 8,450 | 824 | 599 | 947 | 753 |
| 8,450 | 8,500 | 831 | 606 | 956 | 760 |
| 8,500 | 8,550 | 839 | 613 | 965 | 767 |
| 8,550 | 8,600 | 847 | 620 | 974 | 774 |
| 8,600 | 8,650 | 855 | 627 | 983 | 781 |
| 8,650 | 8,700 | 863 | 634 | 992 | 788 |
| 8,700 | 8,750 | 871 | 641 | 1,001 | 795 |
| 8,750 | 8,800 | 879 | 648 | 1,010 | 804 |
| 8,800 | 8,850 | 887 | 655 | 1,019 | 812 |
| 8,850 | 8,900 | 895 | 662 | 1,028 | 821 |
| 8,900 | 8,950 | 903 | 669 | 1,037 | 829 |
| 8,950 | 9,000 | 911 | 676 | 1,046 | 838 |
| **9,000** | | | | | |
| 9,000 | 9,050 | 919 | 683 | 1,055 | 846 |
| 9,050 | 9,100 | 927 | 690 | 1,064 | 855 |
| 9,100 | 9,150 | 935 | 697 | 1,073 | 863 |
| 9,150 | 9,200 | 943 | 704 | 1,082 | 872 |
| 9,200 | 9,250 | 951 | 711 | 1,091 | 880 |
| 9,250 | 9,300 | 959 | 718 | 1,100 | 889 |
| 9,300 | 9,350 | 967 | 725 | 1,109 | 897 |
| 9,350 | 9,400 | 975 | 732 | 1,118 | 906 |
| 9,400 | 9,450 | 983 | 739 | 1,127 | 914 |
| 9,450 | 9,500 | 991 | 746 | 1,136 | 923 |
| 9,500 | 9,550 | 999 | 753 | 1,145 | 931 |
| 9,550 | 9,600 | 1,007 | 760 | 1,154 | 940 |
| 9,600 | 9,650 | 1,015 | 767 | 1,163 | 948 |
| 9,650 | 9,700 | 1,023 | 774 | 1,172 | 957 |
| 9,700 | 9,750 | 1,031 | 781 | 1,181 | 965 |
| 9,750 | 9,800 | 1,039 | 788 | 1,190 | 974 |
| 9,800 | 9,850 | 1,047 | 795 | 1,199 | 982 |
| 9,850 | 9,900 | 1,055 | 802 | 1,208 | 991 |
| 9,900 | 9,950 | 1,063 | 809 | 1,217 | 999 |
| 9,950 | 10,000 | 1,071 | 816 | 1,226 | 1,008 |
| **10,000** | | | | | |
| 10,000 | 10,050 | 1,079 | 823 | 1,235 | 1,016 |
| 10,050 | 10,100 | 1,087 | 830 | 1,244 | 1,025 |
| 10,100 | 10,150 | 1,095 | 837 | 1,254 | 1,033 |
| 10,150 | 10,200 | 1,103 | 844 | 1,265 | 1,042 |
| 10,200 | 10,250 | 1,111 | 851 | 1,276 | 1,050 |
| 10,250 | 10,300 | 1,119 | 858 | 1,287 | 1,059 |
| 10,300 | 10,350 | 1,127 | 865 | 1,298 | 1,067 |
| 10,350 | 10,400 | 1,135 | 872 | 1,309 | 1,076 |
| 10,400 | 10,450 | 1,143 | 879 | 1,320 | 1,084 |
| 10,450 | 10,500 | 1,151 | 886 | 1,331 | 1,093 |
| 10,500 | 10,550 | 1,159 | 893 | 1,342 | 1,101 |
| 10,550 | 10,600 | 1,167 | 900 | 1,353 | 1,110 |
| 10,600 | 10,650 | 1,175 | 907 | 1,364 | 1,118 |
| 10,650 | 10,700 | 1,183 | 914 | 1,375 | 1,127 |
| 10,700 | 10,750 | 1,191 | 921 | 1,386 | 1,135 |
| 10,750 | 10,800 | 1,199 | 928 | 1,397 | 1,144 |
| 10,800 | 10,850 | 1,208 | 935 | 1,408 | 1,152 |
| 10,850 | 10,900 | 1,217 | 942 | 1,419 | 1,161 |
| 10,900 | 10,950 | 1,226 | 949 | 1,430 | 1,169 |
| 10,950 | 11,000 | 1,235 | 956 | 1,441 | 1,178 |

| If line 37 (taxable income) is— At least | But less than | And you are— Single | Married filing jointly * | Married filing separately | Head of a household |
|---|---|---|---|---|---|
| | | | Your tax is— | | |
| **11,000** | | | | | |
| 11,000 | 11,050 | 1,244 | 963 | 1,452 | 1,186 |
| 11,050 | 11,100 | 1,253 | 970 | 1,463 | 1,195 |
| 11,100 | 11,150 | 1,262 | 977 | 1,474 | 1,203 |
| 11,150 | 11,200 | 1,271 | 984 | 1,485 | 1,212 |
| 11,200 | 11,250 | 1,280 | 991 | 1,496 | 1,220 |
| 11,250 | 11,300 | 1,289 | 998 | 1,507 | 1,229 |
| 11,300 | 11,350 | 1,298 | 1,005 | 1,518 | 1,237 |
| 11,350 | 11,400 | 1,307 | 1,012 | 1,529 | 1,246 |
| 11,400 | 11,450 | 1,316 | 1,019 | 1,540 | 1,254 |
| 11,450 | 11,500 | 1,325 | 1,026 | 1,551 | 1,263 |
| 11,500 | 11,550 | 1,334 | 1,033 | 1,562 | 1,271 |
| 11,550 | 11,600 | 1,343 | 1,040 | 1,573 | 1,280 |
| 11,600 | 11,650 | 1,352 | 1,047 | 1,584 | 1,288 |
| 11,650 | 11,700 | 1,361 | 1,054 | 1,595 | 1,297 |
| 11,700 | 11,750 | 1,370 | 1,061 | 1,606 | 1,305 |
| 11,750 | 11,800 | 1,379 | 1,068 | 1,617 | 1,314 |
| 11,800 | 11,850 | 1,388 | 1,075 | 1,628 | 1,323 |
| 11,850 | 11,900 | 1,397 | 1,082 | 1,639 | 1,332 |
| 11,900 | 11,950 | 1,406 | 1,089 | 1,650 | 1,341 |
| 11,950 | 12,000 | 1,415 | 1,097 | 1,661 | 1,350 |
| **12,000** | | | | | |
| 12,000 | 12,050 | 1,424 | 1,105 | 1,672 | 1,359 |
| 12,050 | 12,100 | 1,433 | 1,113 | 1,683 | 1,368 |
| 12,100 | 12,150 | 1,442 | 1,121 | 1,694 | 1,377 |
| 12,150 | 12,200 | 1,451 | 1,129 | 1,705 | 1,386 |
| 12,200 | 12,250 | 1,460 | 1,137 | 1,716 | 1,395 |
| 12,250 | 12,300 | 1,469 | 1,145 | 1,727 | 1,404 |
| 12,300 | 12,350 | 1,478 | 1,153 | 1,739 | 1,413 |
| 12,350 | 12,400 | 1,487 | 1,161 | 1,751 | 1,422 |
| 12,400 | 12,450 | 1,496 | 1,169 | 1,764 | 1,431 |
| 12,450 | 12,500 | 1,505 | 1,177 | 1,776 | 1,440 |
| 12,500 | 12,550 | 1,514 | 1,185 | 1,789 | 1,449 |
| 12,550 | 12,600 | 1,523 | 1,193 | 1,801 | 1,458 |
| 12,600 | 12,650 | 1,532 | 1,201 | 1,814 | 1,467 |
| 12,650 | 12,700 | 1,541 | 1,209 | 1,826 | 1,476 |
| 12,700 | 12,750 | 1,550 | 1,217 | 1,839 | 1,485 |
| 12,750 | 12,800 | 1,559 | 1,225 | 1,851 | 1,494 |
| 12,800 | 12,850 | 1,568 | 1,233 | 1,864 | 1,503 |
| 12,850 | 12,900 | 1,577 | 1,241 | 1,876 | 1,512 |
| 12,900 | 12,950 | 1,586 | 1,249 | 1,889 | 1,521 |
| 12,950 | 13,000 | 1,596 | 1,257 | 1,901 | 1,530 |
| **13,000** | | | | | |
| 13,000 | 13,050 | 1,606 | 1,265 | 1,914 | 1,539 |
| 13,050 | 13,100 | 1,616 | 1,273 | 1,926 | 1,548 |
| 13,100 | 13,150 | 1,626 | 1,281 | 1,939 | 1,557 |
| 13,150 | 13,200 | 1,636 | 1,289 | 1,951 | 1,566 |
| 13,200 | 13,250 | 1,646 | 1,297 | 1,964 | 1,575 |
| 13,250 | 13,300 | 1,656 | 1,305 | 1,976 | 1,584 |
| 13,300 | 13,350 | 1,666 | 1,313 | 1,989 | 1,593 |
| 13,350 | 13,400 | 1,676 | 1,321 | 2,001 | 1,602 |
| 13,400 | 13,450 | 1,686 | 1,329 | 2,014 | 1,611 |
| 13,450 | 13,500 | 1,696 | 1,337 | 2,026 | 1,620 |
| 13,500 | 13,550 | 1,706 | 1,345 | 2,039 | 1,629 |
| 13,550 | 13,600 | 1,716 | 1,353 | 2,051 | 1,638 |
| 13,600 | 13,650 | 1,726 | 1,361 | 2,064 | 1,647 |
| 13,650 | 13,700 | 1,736 | 1,369 | 2,076 | 1,656 |
| 13,700 | 13,750 | 1,746 | 1,377 | 2,089 | 1,665 |
| 13,750 | 13,800 | 1,756 | 1,385 | 2,101 | 1,674 |
| 13,800 | 13,850 | 1,766 | 1,393 | 2,114 | 1,683 |
| 13,850 | 13,900 | 1,776 | 1,401 | 2,126 | 1,692 |
| 13,900 | 13,950 | 1,786 | 1,409 | 2,139 | 1,701 |
| 13,950 | 14,000 | 1,796 | 1,417 | 2,151 | 1,710 |

*This column must also be used by a qualifying widow(er).

**TABLE 2**

# CHAPTER 4

# How to Present Information for Maximum Clarity and Impact

In your work, you may already have observed how much your company depends on information that is expressed in numbers. As computers take a greater role in business, that dependence will grow even further. For that reason, it's important for you to know how to compile the numbers used and to present them clearly and in a way that conveys the information quickly and simply.

Today, most computers can take stored data and convert it into charts, graphs, and tables on the screen. However, the art of presenting such information in reports and letters still demands secretarial skill.

You may be called on to gather this type of information from available data, combine it with other figures, and organize it so it will be comprehensible to others in the company. For example, you might be asked to obtain prices and specifications on various types of electronic calculators in connection with a plan to supply clerical workers in the accounting department. Such additional information as desk space required, convenience in use, service contracts available, and length of guarantee would all be combined into a final recommendation for presentation to management.

Graphs, tables and charts are generally used to dramatize numerical information, to make specific aspects of the data stand out, and to subordinate unimportant details. In this chapter, you will see examples of these techniques in use and learn how to plan and execute these figures yourself.

## HOW TO LOCATE AND CLASSIFY INFORMATION

You may be asked to research data from widely different sources including government reports, newspaper and magazine articles, corporate annual reports, and standard reference works. However, in most cases, your data source will be the company itself. If your company does not have a reference library, you can often find what you need in the business section of your local public library.

In most cases, you will have to extract the information pertinent to your situation from a larger mass of raw data. It is this process of distilling the important facts from the surrounding mass that distinguishes well-prepared reports.

As you compile the data, it must be classified so that the reader can make comparisons, draw conclusions, and discern trends. Although there are many ways of classifying data, the most common are by size, type, place, by alphabetic or numerical order, and by time.

For example, if you list the ten largest cities in the U.S., you would probably use size to place them in order: the largest first and the smallest last. And if you were listing the cars a dealer had in stock, you might divide them into types: sedan, wagon, coupe, etc. If you were classifying material in a large stockroom, you would probably want to designate the location of each item. Other examples are your telephone book, which is a typical alphabetical listing, and the Federal Government, which lists working citizens by social security numbers.

Time is used in many ways to classify data, most frequently variable and repetitive quantities such as daily temperature readings, daily, weekly or monthly stock averages, etc.

After the information has been compiled, it may be desirable to highlight certain aspects. If you want to emphasize that the data collected shows common characteristics in spite of variations, it may help to use averages. The math of statistics makes frequent usage of averages to demonstrate common behavior characteristics. Although statistics are beyond the scope of this book, we can borrow some of their tools.

### How to Use the Mode, the Simplest Average

**Typical problem:** A real estate office has a nine-person sales team. These are the number of houses sold by each sales person during a one-year period:

$$5, 8, 5, 8, 7, 5, 5, 7, 4$$

The manager is interested in finding the average number of houses sold by the team. The mode is one average that can be used. The mode is defined as the number which appears most frequently in a group of numbers. In this case, the mode is 5; it appears 4 times.

As you can see, the mode requires no computation to locate. It's simply a matter of counting the number of times each number appears in a group. It's the statistic most often used when you are concerned with a popular choice.

*Solved Problems:*

1. Your office staff has the following sick-day record. Find the mode, the number of days taken off by most employees.

$$2, 3, 7, 3, 4, 6, 3, 9, 3, 4, 2$$

*Answer:* 3

2. Each division of your company has a rejection rate, a figure that describes the number of products each makes that fails to pass inspection. Find the mode from this list of each division's rejection record.

$$17, 22, 21, 16, 14, 18, 19, 22$$

*Answer:* 22

**Typical Problem:** In the previous examples, only one number appeared frequently enough to qualify as the mode. That is, the modal number appeared more often than any other number. Suppose that two numbers appear the same number of times, as in the following example:

$$2, 3, 5, 5, 3, 7, 6, 9$$

The numbers 3 and 5 appear twice. Can there be a mode? The answer is "yes," and the distribution is called bimodal.

*Solved Problem:*

As part of a plan to improve office efficiency, you are required to record the number of times your telephone rings each hour in an eight-hour day. What is the mode in the following record?

$$2, 4, 5, 2, 3, 4, 6, 7$$

*Answer:* 2 and 4

**Typical Problem:** In the previous examples, one or more numbers appeared more than other numbers in the list. Suppose that no number appears more than once, as in the following example:

$$1, 2, 3, 4, 5, 6, 7, 8, 9$$

Since no number appears more than once, there simply isn't a mode. When this occurs, other statistics must be used to describe the average. One such statistic is the median, which is the next topic of discussion.

### Using the Median to Find the Midpoint

If we arrange a series of measurements in order of their size, the median is defined as the exact midpoint between the highest and the lowest in the series. For example, if a group of job applicants made the following scores on a qualification test:

$$18, 24, 36, 41, 45, 50, 57$$

41 is the median, since there are an equal number of scores above it and below it. In other words, the median is the midpoint score.

How do we find the median if the number of measurements is an even number? For example:

$$18, 24, 36, 41, 45, 50, 57, 62$$

In this case, take the number of measurements, add one to it and divide by 2:

$$8 \text{ (no. measurements)} + 1 = 9 \div 2 = 4\tfrac{1}{2}$$

The median is found to be 4½ numbers from either the top or the bottom, that is halfway between 41 and 45, or 43. Even though 43 is not one of the scores, it is still accepted as the median in this group.

### Solved Problems:

1. The ages of the women in a stenographic pool are;

$$22, 24, 25, 27, 28, 31, 33$$

What is the median age?

*Answer:* 27

2. The weights of a group of high school football players are as follows:

### 130, 136, 141, 145, 152, 154, 156, 161

What is the median weight?

*Answer:* Since there is an even number of weights (8), add 1 to it and divide by 2 = 4.5. Thus, the median is between 145 and 152. Since there are 7 pounds difference between the two, the median weight is 148.5.

## Using the Mean

The arithmetic mean or average is the third way of representing a group of numbers. It is the statistic most people think of when they use the word average.

The mean is determined by adding up the quantities in a series and dividing by the number. It is the method most frequently used, and thus is probably most familiar to you.

**EXAMPLE:** If the salaries of five clerks in an office are $170, $185, $160, $165 and $172, what is the average? The total of all salaries is $852 which divided by 5 = $170.40, the mean or average salary of all five clerks.

A weighted average is one which takes into account the fact that certain numbers have more importance than others. For example, in the table below, a series of ages is given together with the number of people of that age in the group being measured:

| Number of Persons | Age in Years | |
|---|---|---|
| 2 | 9 | 18 |
| 1 | 10 | 10 |
| 1 | 11 | 11 |
| 3 | 12 | 36 |
| 4 | 15 | 60 |
| | | 135 |

Find the weighted average age.

First, the age must be multiplied by the number of people of that age (see Col. 3 above), then the total is divided by the number of persons (11), and the weighted average is 12.27.

## Solved Problems:

1. A high school science class had the following test grades:

| No. of Persons | Grade | |
|---|---|---|
| 3 | 100 | 300 |
| 4 | 96 | 384 |
| 3 | 90 | 270 |
| 4 | 85 | 340 |
| 2 | 83 | 166 |
| 3 | 78 | 234 |
| 1 | 75 | 75 |
| | | 1,769 |

What are the weighted average, median and mode grades?

*Answers:* The total grades = 1769 ÷ 20 (students) = 88.45 weighted average. Median = 87.5, mode = 96 and 85.

2. A meatpacker bought several lots of hogs at these prices:

| | |
|---|---|
| 6 at $70 each | $ 420 |
| 8 at $84 each | 672 |
| 10 at $92 each | 920 |
| 4 at $105 each | 420 |
| | $2432 |

Compute the average and median price per head.

*Answers:* average = $86.86, median = $88.

3. Typing tests in the office stenographic pool showed the following results (in words per minute):

| Score | No. of Tests | |
|---|---|---|
| 22 | 2 | 44 |
| 26 | 4 | 104 |
| 27 | 1 | 27 |
| 30 | 3 | 90 |
| 31 | 5 | 155 |
| 34 | 3 | 102 |
| 36 | 1 | 36 |
| 37 | 2 | 74 |
| | | 632 |

What are the mean, median and mode scores?

*Answer:* 30.1 mean, 31 median, and 31 mode.

Occasionally in business it is useful to find a trend in a series of measurements. For instance, you or your boss may be watching the market price of a certain stock. Often, the day-to-day prices move so erratically that it's difficult to spot trends.

One of the techniques used to smooth out day-to-day fluctuations and clarify trends in such figures is the progressive or moving average. Such an average is arrived at by changing the average as the data changes. For example, below are the closing prices for Federal Telephone Company for the first ten trading days in September:

| Day | Closing Price | Moving Average |
|-----|---------------|----------------|
| 1 | 51½ | — |
| 2 | 51¼ | 51.375 |
| 3 | 51 | 51.25 |
| 4 | 49¾ | 50.875 |
| 5 | 51 | 50.9 |
| 6 | 49½ | 50.67 |
| 7 | 50 | 50.57 |
| 8 | 49¼ | 50.41 |
| 9 | 50¼ | 50.39 |
| 10 | 50 | 50.35 |

The moving average is obtained by adding in the new closing price every day and dividing by the number of prices accumulated to date. Thus, the second day moving average is 51½ + 51¼ = 102¾ divided by 2 = 51.375. Note that the moving average shows the stock's downward trend very clearly while day-to-day variations confuse the real extent of the loss.

### Solved problems:

1. The Maxwell Company's daily closing prices were as follows in June 1985:

| Date | Closing Price | Moving Average |
|------|---------------|----------------|
| June 3 | 18½ | — |
| June 4 | 19 | 18.75 |
| June 5 | 19¼ | 18.92 |
| June 6 | 19½ | 19.06 |
| June 7 | 19½ | 19.15 |

| Day | Closing Price | Moving Average |
|-----|---------------|----------------|
| June 10 | 19 | 19.13 |
| June 11 | 18¾ | 19.07 |
| June 12 | 18¼ | 18.97 |
| June 13 | 17¾ | 18.83 |
| June 14 | 18 | 18.75 |
| June 17 | 18¼ | 18.70 |
| June 18 | 17¾ | 18.63 |
| June 19 | 18 | 18.58 |
| June 20 | 17¾ | 18.52 |

Compute the moving average from June 2 to June 17. Based on the moving average, what does the trend show?

*Answer:* (For moving averages, see Col. 3 above.) The average shows that the stock was moving up in price until June 6 when it started to fall, and continued to fall until the end of the period measured.

2. Airways Corporation showed the following closing prices during August 1985.

| Date | Closing Price | Moving Average |
|------|---------------|----------------|
| Aug. 12 | 8⅛ | — |
| Aug. 13 | 9½ | 8.81 |
| Aug. 14 | 9 | 8.88 |
| Aug. 15 | 7½ | 8.53 |
| Aug. 16 | 8 | 8.43 |
| Aug. 19 | 9¾ | 8.65 |
| Aug. 20 | 7¾ | 8.52 |
| Aug. 21 | 8¼ | 8.48 |
| Aug. 22 | 8 | 8.43 |
| Aug. 23 | 7 | 8.29 |

Figure the moving average and describe the trend (if any).

*Answer:* (See Col. 3 above for MA.) The price trend is down by over half a point in two weeks.

## How to Use Percentages to Highlight Data

Percentages (discussed in Chapter 1) are an excellent way to highlight data and to make differences and comparisons stand out. Here is a table of stock prices over a five-year period at six-month intervals:

### Price/Share General Carton Co.

|            |       | Increase/Decrease | % Diff. |
|------------|-------|-------------------|---------|
| Jan. 1980  | 27.50 | —                 | —       |
| June 1980  | 21.25 | − 6.25            | − 22.7  |
| Jan. 1981  | 18.00 | − 3.25            | − 15.3  |
| June 1981  | 19.25 | + 1.25            | + 6.9   |
| Jan. 1982  | 24.50 | + 5.25            | + 27.3  |
| June 1982  | 29.75 | + 5.25            | + 21.4  |
| Jan. 1983  | 36.00 | + 6.25            | + 21.0  |
| June 1983  | 40.50 | + 4.50            | + 12.5  |
| Jan. 1984  | 47.00 | + 6.50            | + 16.0  |
| June 1984  | 44.75 | − 2.25            | − 4.8   |
| Cumulative change |  | + 17.25       | + 62.7  |

Note how easy it is to compare the month-to-month price changes as well as the overall change using the percentage figures.

## HOW TO PRESENT INFORMATION FOR MAXIMUM EFFECT

There are several ways to present data in a report for ready visibility and easy understanding. The most commonly used are tables. They are preferred for completeness and exactness. On the other hand, graphic representation is useful to highlight important portions of the information, to illustrate conclusions, or separate certain items from the mass of data. We will discuss all forms, so you can choose the most useful for your specific purpose.

### How to Organize and Use Tabular Information

In reading business reports, magazines and books, you will find reference tables which are generally intended for continuous use, such as those in the Appendix of this book (tables of weights and measures or decimal/fraction equivalents). Other tables are designed to illustrate some special topic, perhaps the subject of a report or to demonstrate historic trends, or even to project future events.

Regardless of purpose, tables should be easy to read and understand. Column headings or line descriptions should be comprehensible at a glance, and the information to be highlighted must be easy to find. Avoid including irrelevant or insignificant items.

Careful planning goes into the preparation of a neat and professional-looking table. If the table is to be typed, a pencil rough draft is advisable to insure proper spacing and margins. A word processor is ideal for planning a table since lines and spacing can be visualized on the screen and adjusted by eye for best appearance before printing.

Here are some tips for preparing professional-looking tables:

- Titles—should contain everything necessary to identify the subject matter, purpose, and time. Ideally, the title makes the table stand alone without need for further explanation. If the report contains a group of tables, number them for easy reference.

- Columns—in many cases, it is desirable to number the columns, particularly if the report refers to them specifically. Abbreviations can be used to condense column headings. If the headings require clarification or qualification, use footnotes.

- Figures—in writing dollar amounts, indicate the dollar sign at the top of the column and in totals only.

$$
\begin{array}{ll}
\textit{Example:} & \$4{,}223.50 \\
& \phantom{\$}687.20 \\
& \underline{\phantom{\$}496.80} \\
& \$5{,}407.50
\end{array}
$$

When entering large numbers in columns, space can be saved and readability improved by dropping the last digits in each number and calling attention to that fact in a footnote:

| Examples: | $3,627,450 | becomes | $3,627 |
|---|---|---|---|
| | 4,850,021 | | 4,850 |
| | 5,027,512 | | 5,028 |

Footnote: (Figures in millions of dollars)

Note that 5 or more in the first number to be dropped is rounded off to the next higher number, otherwise the number is simply dropped.

*Example:* 5,027,512 becomes 5,028

Here is an example of a well-designed table:

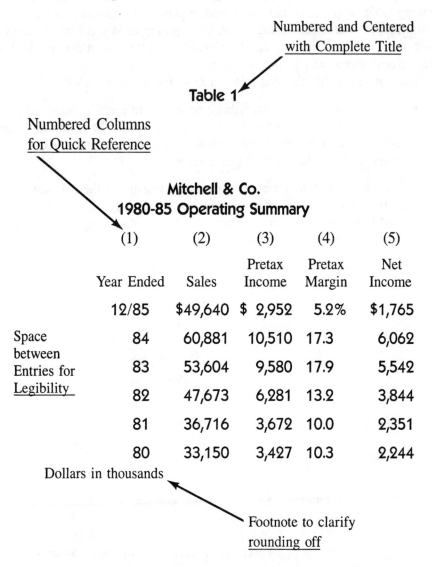

Numbered and Centered
with Complete Title

Table 1

Numbered Columns
for Quick Reference

**Mitchell & Co.**
**1980-85 Operating Summary**

| | (1) | (2) | (3) | (4) | (5) |
|---|---|---|---|---|---|
| | | | Pretax | Pretax | Net |
| | Year Ended | Sales | Income | Margin | Income |
| | 12/85 | $49,640 | $ 2,952 | 5.2% | $1,765 |
| | 84 | 60,881 | 10,510 | 17.3 | 6,062 |
| | 83 | 53,604 | 9,580 | 17.9 | 5,542 |
| | 82 | 47,673 | 6,281 | 13.2 | 3,844 |
| | 81 | 36,716 | 3,672 | 10.0 | 2,351 |
| | 80 | 33,150 | 3,427 | 10.3 | 2,244 |

Space
between
Entries for
Legibility

Dollars in thousands

Footnote to clarify
rounding off

*Note:* Either leave plenty of white space between columns and lines or use lines between entries to make table easy to read.

If the table is long with large amounts of information, it is helpful to break it into blocks by leaving a line blank every five to ten lines.

## HOW TO PRESENT FIGURES GRAPHICALLY
## FOR CLARITY AND IMPACT

Graphs and charts are used in business to display statistics and numbers in an easily understood and dramatic form. When we want to compare pieces of information, for instance, the comparison can be shown clearly in graphic form. Growth, decline, high and low points, and even lack of change are all easily depicted with the use of graphs.

This clarity of view is particularly important in dealing with large numbers or a great quantity of data. In meetings, conferences, seminars and classrooms, business people use graphs to sell their ideas, make sales presentations, or defend ideas. So it will pay you to become familiar with these pictorial concepts and how to prepare them.

Here are some of the specific ways that you can use graphs to good effect:

1. To compare quantities (or groups of numbers), with particular regard for common identities.

2. To show the rate of growth of a business, its sales or investment, stocks, prices or losses, etc.

3. To demonstrate a change in percentage increase or decrease.

4. To depict how one number depends on another.

5. To record changes over a period of time.

6. To make clear how the parts of a whole relate to each other and to the whole.

### Types of Graphs You Can Use

There are a number of ways to display graphic concepts and some are more suitable than others, depending on what's being presented. The simple one-bar graph is used to demonstrate how a whole subject is broken down into parts. For example, if the owner of a hardware store breaks down his inventory as: tools 15%, lawn mowers 25%, consumable items 50%, and electrical items 10%, a bar graph might look like the one in Figure 1.

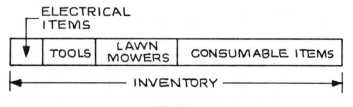

**FIGURE 1**

Circle graphs are also frequently used for such breakdowns. A circle graph of the inventory would look like the one in Figure 2.
Circle graphs are sometimes called pie charts for obvious reasons.

Picture graphs are similar to bar graphs except that pictures of different sizes are used to demonstrate the relationship. If, for example, you wished to show that the U.S. imports 40% of its oil and produces 60% domestically, you might use two oil wells sized to show the relationship. (See Figure 3.)

Line graphs are often used to demonstrate continuing trends over a period of time. You will see line graphs in *The Wall Street Journal,* for instance, showing how the stock market is rising, falling, or remaining steady. Graphs can also be used in mathematics to demonstrate how an algebraic formula behaves as one quantity changes with respect to others in the formula.

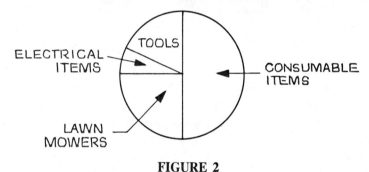

**FIGURE 2**

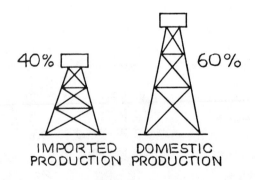

**FIGURE 3**

### How to Prepare Accurate Graphs

Since you may be called on to prepare graphs as part of your work, a few tips on how to make a neat graph that expresses its message clearly, might be useful.

The accuracy of your graph is the most important consideration. Be sure it is to exact scale, that the picture reflects precisely the quantities measured, and that the data is clearly labelled.

Obviously, the graph must be neat and attractive. Select measurement scales to make reading and comparison easy. Graph paper is available from stationery suppliers. It is marked off in squares of various sizes depending on the paper you choose. Select the paper that will show off your data best and make the job of locating points on the graph easiest.

Select colors, the size of the bars or lines, and paper type to make an effective presentation. The purpose of a graph is to present data in picture form so the comparisons and judgments can be made at a glance.

Be sure that labels are complete and easy to read, and that all the data is identified and the title included. By the same token, keep the graph as simple as possible. Don't use too many numbers on the scale lines and don't put too much information on one graph.

Above all, don't exaggerate the story you're presenting for the sake of drama. Newspapers, for instance, often suppress the zero on a graph so that a 2% to 3% change in conditions appears much larger than it really is. However, the picture presented is inaccurate and distorted.

And finally, be sure to use conventional forms of presentation so your graph is easily understood. The horizontal scale on a bar or line graph should be at the bottom (or center if your graph includes minus numbers) of the page and read from left to right. The vertical axis (or scale) is placed at the left (or center if you use minus numbers) and reads from the bottom of the page up.

### Single Bar Graphs Tell a Story Instantly

Generally speaking, such a graph is used to divide a whole quantity into its component parts. The total length of the bar is equal to the sum of the components. The width of the bar is not important except for visibility or if you wish to label the parts inside the bar.

Select a length to fill most of the page. If you pick a figure of 10″ or 10 centimeters, it will be easy to divide into the appropriate percentages.

**EXAMPLE:** The Reeves Company wishes to show its P&L statement in graphic form. The figures break down as follows:

| | |
|---|---|
| Sales | $75,220 |
| Cost of Sales | 54,800 |
| Gross Profit | 20,420 |
| Operating Exp. | 14,850 |
| Net Profit | 5,570 |

In presenting these figures, note that cost of sales, operating expenses, and net profits add up to total sales so the graph should read:

$$\text{Sales} \qquad = 100\%$$

$$\text{Cost of Sales} \quad = \frac{54{,}800}{75{,}220} = 72.9\%$$

$$\text{Operating Exp.} = \frac{14{,}850}{75{,}220} = 19.7\%$$

$$\text{Net Profit} \qquad = \frac{5{,}570}{75{,}220} = 7.4\%$$

Next, we need to select a line long enough to display our information. Since 10 inches is too wide for the page, we can use 5 and divide the results by 2.

Thus, 72.9% would be 7.29" on a 10" line but 3.64" on a 5" line, or approximately 3⅝". 19.7% is 1.97" ÷ 2 = .985, approximately 1", and 7.4% is .74" ÷ 2 = .37 or roughly ⅜". The graph will look like the one in Figure 4.

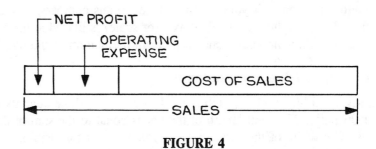

**FIGURE 4**

We can also graph the relationship of gross profit and cost of sales to sales as follows:

$$\text{Sales} \qquad = 75{,}220 = 100\%$$

$$\text{Gross Profit} \quad = \frac{20{,}420}{75{,}220} = 27.1\%$$

$$\text{Cost of Sales} = \frac{54{,}800}{75{,}220} = 72.9\%$$

If we use the same scale (5″):

$$\text{Gross profit} = \frac{2.71}{2} = 1.35″ \text{ approx. } 1\frac{3}{8}″ \text{ as before}$$

$$\text{Cost of Sales} = \frac{7.29}{2} = 3.61″ \text{ approx. } 3\frac{5}{8}″$$

The graph looks like this:

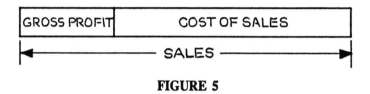

**FIGURE 5**

### How to Tell a Complex Story with Circle Graphs

Circle graphs are used for the same kind of information as the single bar graph. In constructing them, however, it is necessary to divide the circle into the number of degrees corresponding to the percentages indicated by the data.

**EXAMPLE:** Using the same data presented in the previous graph, sales = 100% or 360° (number of degrees in a full circle), cost of sales = 72.9% = 262° (72% of 360°), operating expense = 19.7% or 71°, and net profit = 7.4% or 27°. (See Figure 6.)

To measure off the angles exactly, it is necessary to use a protractor. However, if we remember that 90° is a quarter circle, 180° a half, 270° three quarters, and that 45° is one-eighth of a circle, the angles can often be estimated with reasonable accuracy.

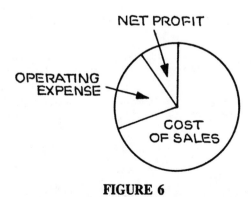

**FIGURE 6**

*Solved Problem:*

The Reynolds family budgets its expenditures as follows:

$$
\begin{array}{rl}
\text{Salary :} & \$32,000 \\
\text{Food :} & 9,600 \\
\text{Home Mortgage :} & 6,400 \\
\text{Clothing :} & 4,800 \\
\text{Utilities \& Maintenance :} & 3,840 \\
\text{Taxes :} & 3,200 \\
\text{Savings \& Miscellaneous :} & 4,160
\end{array}
$$

Construct single bar and circle graphs of the budget:

*Answer:* Calculating the percentages first—

$$
\begin{array}{rll}
\text{Salary} = & 32,000 = & 100\% \\
\text{Food} = & 9,600 = & 30\% \\
\text{Home Mortgage} = & 6,400 = & 20\% \\
\text{Clothing} = & 4,800 = & 15\% \\
\text{Utilities \& Maintenance} = & 3,840 = & 12\% \\
\text{Taxes} = & 3,200 = & 10\% \\
\text{Savings \& Miscellaneous} = & 4,160 = & 13\%
\end{array}
$$

Using a 5″ bar, lengths are: food 1.5″, mortgage 1″, clothing .75″, utilities and maintenance .6″, taxes .5″, savings and miscellaneous .65″, and the graph looks like Figure 7 below:

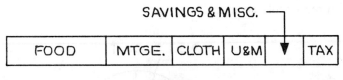

**FIGURE 7**

The circle graph looks like the one in Figure 8 on page 99:

| | | | | |
|---|---|---|---|---|
| Food | = 108° | | U&M | = 43.2 |
| Mtge. | = 72 | | Taxes | = 36 |
| Clothes | = 54 | | S&M | = 46.8 |

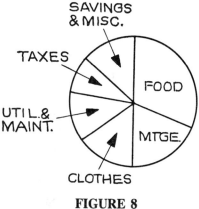

**FIGURE 8**

## Multiple Bar Graphs

This type of graph is most useful for making comparisons or showing growth or decline. The bars can be horizontal or vertical. Conventionally, the time scale is laid out horizontally. If you are comparing two or three numbers, horizontal bars are more striking.

**EXAMPLE:** These three airlines fly the following number of passenger miles per year:

|  |  |
|---|---|
| People Express | 3,700,000 |
| New York Air | 657,000 |
| Midway | 648,000 |

If we graph their performance for comparison, it will look like the one in Figure 9. (Using a scale of 1″=1,000,000 miles.)

PEOPLE EXPRESS 3,700,000

NEW YORK AIR 658,000

MIDWAY 648,000

**FIGURE 9**

*Solved problem:*

The sales of General Corporation were as follows over the six-year period 1979-1984:

| Year | Sales in millions of dollars |
|------|------------------------------|
| 1979 | 12.6 |
| 1980 | 14.7 |
| 1981 | 16.5 |
| 1982 | 16.2 |
| 1983 | 14.8 |
| 1984 | 16.4 |

Since time is involved, it will be the horizontal scale and the vertical scale will be $\frac{1}{4}'' = \$1$ million. See the graph in Figure 10. Note that it goes from left to right.

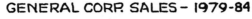

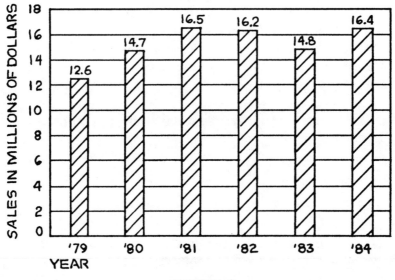

**FIGURE 10**

*Notes:*

1. The width of the bars is insignificant. Make them as wide as necessary to stand out clearly.

2. Bars are shaded to make them stand out clearly.

3. Both axes are clearly labelled and the graph is titled.

4. Numerical figures are shown over each bar.

5. See how the recession year of 1983 contrasts with other years.

### How to Use a Line Graph to Simplify Information

Line graphs are similar to bar graphs in the way they are laid out. However, instead of making a bar for each piece of information, the points indicating the height of the bar are joined in a continuous line. If we use a line graph for the General Corporation's sales, it will look like the one in Figure 11.

If you look at the top of the bar graph, you will note that it conforms to the shape of the line graph.

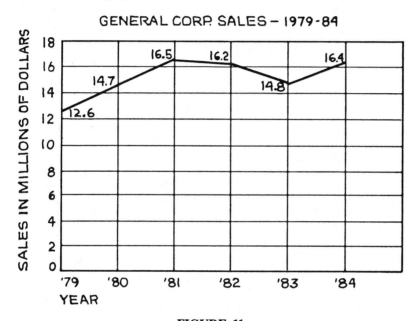

**FIGURE 11**

*Solved problem:*

Here are the temperature readings taken at the Capital City Airport on December 21, 1984 from 6 P.M. until 12 midnight. Make a line graph of the data:

| Temperature | Time |
|---|---|
| 42° | 6 P.M. |
| 39° | 7 |
| 37° | 8 |
| 36° | 9 |
| 31° | 10 |
| 28° | 11 |
| 26° | 12 |

In constructing this graph, we need a temperature of 0 to 42°. Therefore, we'll pick a scale of 5° = ½″ so the graph will be just under 4½″ high to accommodate the high reading. Again, we'll make time the horizontal axis from left to right. It is almost imperative to make line graphs on graph paper so we can locate the points by following the lines across and down from each axis. (See Figure 12.)

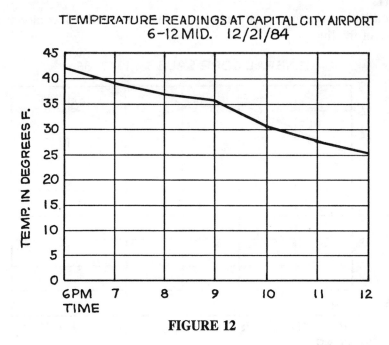

**FIGURE 12**

Since we are interested in comparative temperature readings at each hour, we could have started the horizontal axis at 25° instead of zero. However, care should be used in constructing such suppressed zero graphs to avoid giving mistaken impressions to the reader.

We can construct line graphs to contain several sets of related information. For instance, if General Corporation's yearly sales data included cost of sales information like this:

| Year | Sales* | Cost of Sales* |
|------|--------|----------------|
| 1979 | 12.6   | 9.5            |
| 1980 | 14.7   | 11.3           |
| 1981 | 16.5   | 13.0           |
| 1982 | 16.2   | 12.8           |
| 1983 | 14.8   | 11.5           |
| 1984 | 16.4   | 13.3           |

*Millions of dollars

We can make the same line graph, but adding cost of sales makes it look like the one in Figure 13.

This type of graph can be quite informative. The distance between the two curves is gross profit, for instance, and it shows too that cost of sales does not decline as fast as sales in a recession.

Operating costs and net profits could have been shown on the same graph revealing additional information about the company's operations as sales first increased and then declined.

Some of the new small computers now being used in many businesses have the capability of constructing graphs from tabular data. In this way, owners and managers can review past performance and plan future changes. Seeing the results in graphic form on a computer screen often facilitates planning and decision making.

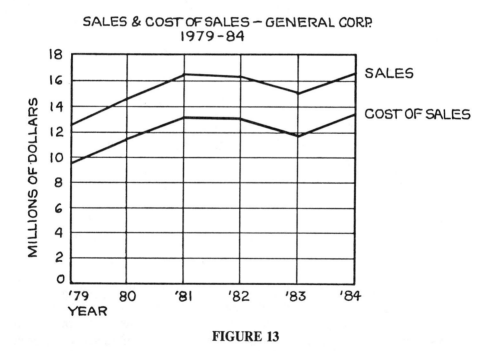

**FIGURE 13**

# CHAPTER 5

# How to Calculate the Most Common Business Measurements

In this chapter, we will deal with the most common measurements used in business, so you can be comfortable with the concepts and numbers involved.

## UNDERSTANDING AND USING MEASURES OF LENGTH

We use measures of length when we say it's a quarter-mile walk from the bus to the office or it's a 10-mile drive to the ocean. An 8½ × 11 sheet of paper is 11 inches long in one direction and 8½ inches in the other (at right angles to the first).

Length is one of the three basic measurements, the others being time and mass (weight). All the other common mechanical quantities including area, volume, density, velocity, acceleration, force, pressure, energy, and power can be expressed in terms of the three basics: length, mass, and time. Nonmechanical quantities used in measurement include temperature, electric current, and intensity of light.

The English system of measurement used in the United States expresses lengths in inches, feet, yards, rods, and miles. These units are derived from early methods of measurement: the inch from the length of the first joint of the thumb to the tip; the foot from an obvious source, and the yard from the length of a man's arm.

Thus, the relationships between the units are nondecimal numbers. For example,

$$
\begin{array}{rll}
12 & \text{inches} & = 1 \text{ foot} \\
3 & \text{feet} & = 1 \text{ yard} \\
5\tfrac{1}{2} & \text{yards} & = 1 \text{ rod} \\
320 & \text{rods} & = 1 \text{ mile} \\
1760 & \text{yards} & = 1 \text{ mile} \\
5280 & \text{feet} & = 1 \text{ mile}
\end{array}
$$

These odd numbers made conversions and computations somewhat awkward.

In 1875, the French, in an effort to simplify measurements, introduced the metric system. Here, the basic unit of length is the meter which equals 39.37 inches, or 1.0936 yards. For longer distances, the unit of measurement is the kilometer which equals 1,000 meters, or 0.62 miles. For smaller measurements, the centimeter is used. It is equal to .01 meters, or .3937 inches. The millimeter is .001 meters.

Note each unit is expressed as a decimal fraction of another, making conversion an easy matter. For instance, the centimeter's relationship to the kilometer is 0.00001 by simple observation.

The metric system has replaced the English system in every scientifically advanced country in the world, including Great Britain and Canada, excepting the United States. In addition, it is universally used by scientists, including Americans. For these reasons, it is important to be able to work in both systems and translate quantities back and forth readily.

### Solved problems:

1. The runway at Colonial Airport is 0.7 mile long. Translate that into feet, then yards, and then inches. Use the table on page 209.

*Answers:*

$$
\begin{aligned}
1 \text{ mile} &= 5{,}280 \text{ ft.} \times 0.7 = 3{,}696 \text{ ft.} \\
3696 \times 12 &= 44{,}352 \text{ in.} \\
3696 \div 3 &= 1{,}232 \text{ yds.}
\end{aligned}
$$

2. A crate arrived from Europe at the Diamond Corporation. Its dimensions were marked on the packing list as 1.8m high by .9m by .6m. What are the dimensions in inches? Translate those dimensions into feet.

*Answers:* The dimensions in centimeters are $180 \times 90 \times 60$. Since 1 cm = 0.394 in.—

$$
\begin{aligned}
180 \times 0.394 &= 70.92 \text{ in.} = 5.91 \text{ ft.} \\
90 \times 0.394 &= 35.46 \text{ in.} = 2.96 \text{ ft.} \\
60 \times 0.394 &= 23.64 \text{ in.} = 1.97 \text{ ft.}
\end{aligned}
$$

3. The town of Hawthorne is 2.1 miles from Midland Park, 6.5 miles from Oakland, and 1.8 miles from Paterson. What are those distances in kilometers?

*Answers:* From the table on page 208, 1 Km = 0.6 mi.—

$$2.1 \div 0.6 = 3.5 \text{ Km}, \ 6.5 \div 0.6 = 10.83 \text{ Km},$$
$$\text{and } 1.8 \div 0.6 = 3 \text{ Km}$$

4. John Reilly is a salesman. He has a choice of three accounts to call on. One is 7.8 miles away, the second is 12.6 Km away, and the third is 12,320 yards distant. Which account is closest?

*Answer:*

$$12.6 \text{ Km} \times .6 = 7.56 \text{ mi. dist. to Account 2.}$$
$$12,320 \div 1760 \text{ (yards in a mile)} = 7 \text{ mi. to Account 3.}$$

Account 3 is closest.

## MEASURES OF AREA

Since area and volume are expressed in terms of length, we'll discuss those next. Area is the way we define two-dimensional space; for example, the size of floor space in a room, the size of a rug or tablecloth, or even the size of a sheet of paper.

A standard 8½ × 11 sheet of paper covers 93.5 sq. in. That number is arrived at by multiplying the length (8½″) by the width (11″). The answer signifies that the area of a sheet of paper contains 93.5 blocks of space 1 in. wide by 1 in. high.

Larger areas can be expressed in terms of square feet, square yards, and square miles. An 8 ft. × 10 ft. rug, for example, covers 80 sq. ft. of floor space.

An area of park land 12 miles long and 3 miles wide covers 36 square miles. To convert square inches to square feet, consider the diagram below:

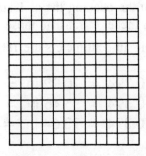

If the diagram is 1 ft. wide and 1 ft. high, it has an area of 1 sq. ft. It is also 12 in. high and 12 in. wide. If we multiply $12 \times 12 = 144$, we find that to be the number of square inches in one square foot.

Similarly, one square yard is 3 ft. high and 3 ft. wide and contains 9 sq. ft. The same square yard is 36 in. high and 36 in. wide and contains 1,296 sq. in.

If there are 5,280 ft. in a mile, then a square mile contains 27,878,400 sq. ft ($5,280 \times 5,280$). And if 1,760 yards equal a mile, then $1760 \times 1760 = 3,097,600$ sq. yds. are in a square mile.

The metric system also uses linear units to measure area. But look how easy the conversion is:

1 sq. meter is 100 cm. $\times$ 100 cm., or 10,000 sq. cm.

1 sq. kilometer is 1000 meters $\times$ 1000 meters, or 1,000,000 sq. m.

From the above information, it should be easy to see that we can compute any rectangular area if we know its length and width. For example, a room $12' \times 10'$ has an area of 120 sq. ft.

### Solved Problems in Area Measurement:

We can compute other areas as well. Look at the L-shaped area in Figure 1 below. We can figure this area by dividing it into two rectangles—$5' \times 10'$ and $8' \times 10'$, or 130 sq. ft.

Even some types of triangular areas are easily handled. (See Figure 2.)

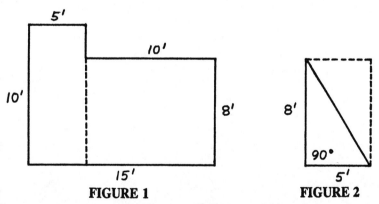

|           |           |
|:---------:|:---------:|
| FIGURE 1  | FIGURE 2  |

A right triangle with a square corner can be converted to a rectangle as shown by the dotted lines. Since that rectangle is exactly twice as big as our triangle, the area of the triangle must be $8' \times 5' = 40 \div 2 = 20$ sq. ft.

1. An office space is $20' \times 25'$. How many 50 sq. ft. office cubicles will it contain?

*Answer:* Total available area is $20 \times 25 = 500$ sq. ft. and $500 \div 50 = 10$ cubicles.

2. A letter received from France mentions an office area $10 \times 12$ meters. What is the equivalent area in sq. ft.?

*Answer:* 1 meter = 3.281 ft. (from table, page 209). Area is then 32.81 ft. × 39.37 ft. Area is $32.81 \times 39.37 = 1291.73$ sq. ft.

3. Compute the area shown below in sq. ft.:

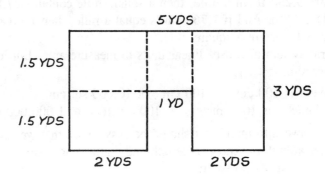

*Answer:* Divide area into three rectangles as shown by dotted lines. The two larger rectangles are equal in size. The small rectangle is $1 \times 1.5$ yds., or $3 \times 4.5 = 13.5$ sq. ft. The other rectangles are $2 \times 3$ yds., or $6 \times 9 = 54$ sq. ft. Together they are 108 sq. ft. + 13.5 = 121.5 sq. ft. total area.

4. Compute the following areas:

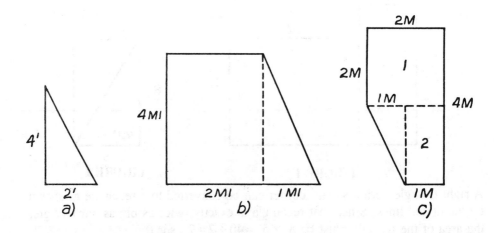

*Answers:*
    a. $4 \times 2 = 8$ sq. ft. (rectangle)
      $8 \div 2 = 4$ sq. ft. (triangle is half of rectangle)

  b. Rectangle is $4 \times 2 = 8$ sq. mi.
   Triangle is $4 \times 1 \div 2 = 2$ sq. mi.
   Total area is 10 sq. mi.
  c. Break up figure as shown by dotted lines. Rectangle 1 is 2m × 2m
   or 4 sq. meters. Rectangle 2 is $2m \times 1m = 2$ and the triangle is
   $1 \times 2 = 2/2 = 1$ sq.m. Total area is $4 + 2 + 1 = 7$ sq. meters.

  5. Translate the areas of the first two figures in problem 4 to the metric
system. Translate the area in the third figure to the English system.

  *Answers:* From the Tables of Equivalents on page 216:
Figure a: 1 sq.m = 1.196 sq. yds., and since there are 9 sq. ft. in 1 sq. yd:

$$\text{1 sq.m.} = 1.196 \times 9 = 10.764 \text{ sq. ft. in 1 sq. m.}$$
$$\frac{4}{10.764} = 0.37 \text{ sq. m area of Figure a}$$

Figure b: Again from the tables, 1 sq. km. = .386 sq. mi:

$$\text{1 sq. mi.} = \frac{1}{.386} = 2.59 \text{ sq. km.}$$

then the area of Figure 5 is $10 \times 2.59 = 25.9$ sq. km.
Figure c: Since 1 sq. m. contains 10.764 sq. ft. (see above), the area of Figure
c is:

$$10.764 \times 7 = 75.348 \text{ sq. ft.}$$

## UNDERSTANDING AND MEASURING THE VOLUME OF ANYTHING

  Linear units are also used in measuring volume. If area was the way we
measured the floor space in a room, then volume is the way we measure the
whole space taken up by the room including the floor-to-ceiling dimension.
  Look at the cube below. It is 1 ft. wide, 1 ft. high, and 1 ft. long.

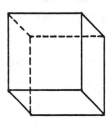

Imagine that we have taken a cube $1'' \times 1'' \times 1''$ out of the corner of the big cube. If we divided the cube up completely in smaller $1''$ cubes, how many would there be? Since each dimension is $12''$, there would be $12 \times 12 \times 12 = 1728$, which simply means there are 1,728 cubic inches in 1 cubic foot.

In the United States, separate measures of volume are used for liquid and dry measurement. The ounce, pint, quart, and gallon are liquid measures; and cubic inches, cubic yards and bushels are dry measures.

In the metric system, the liter is the basic unit of measurement for both liquid and dry applications. See page 217 for the relationships between U.S. and metric volume units.

### Solved Problems:

1. Calculate the volume in cu. ft. of a room 4 yards wide by 3 yards deep and 2⅔ yards high.

*Answer:* Change dimensions to feet before solving: 12 ft. wide × 9 ft. deep and 8 ft. high. Total volume = 864 sq. ft.

2. What is the volume of the room in cubic yards?

*Answer:* Problem can be solved two ways:
A. Volume in cubic yards $= 4 \times 3 \times 2.667 = 32.004$ cu. yds.
B. Divide volume in cubic ft. by 27 (number of cubic feet in a cubic yard):

$$864 \div 27 = 32$$

(Note: Error in A. comes from converting 2⅔ to 2.667 and rounding off.)

3. Three cubic yards of sand are to be deposited in a bin 5′ wide and 4′ deep and 8′ high. How much space will be left over in the bin after filling?

*Answer:* First calculate volume of bin in cu. ft.—

$5' \times 4' \times 8' = 160$ cu. ft., or $160 \div 27 = 5.93$ cu. yds.
$5.93 - 3 = 2.93$ cu. yds. left over.

4. In the previous problem, calculate the volume of the bin, the sand, and the leftover space in cubic meters. (See page 217 for conversion factor.)

*Answer:*

> Bin vol. = 5.93 cu. yds. or 5.93 ÷ 1.308 = 4.53 cu. m.
> Sand vol. = 3 ÷ 1.308 = 2.29 cu. m.
> Space vol. = 2.93 ÷ 1.308 = 2.24 cu. m.

5. Elizabeth needs a closet to store her trunk which is 4 ft. high × 2 ft. × 3 ft. Which of these closets will the trunk fit into: A. 2′ × 2′ × 8′; B. 1.5′ × 2′ × 8′; C. 3′ × 4′ × 8′?

*Answer:* This is a little tricky. The volume of the trunk is 4 × 2 × 3 = 24 cu. ft. The volumes of the closets are: A. 32 cu. ft; B. 24 cu. ft.; C. 96 cu. ft. So the volume of the trunk will fit in any one, and the height of the trunk is only half the height of each closet, but the area taken up by the trunk is 2 × 3 = 6 sq. ft. on the floor. A and B are thus too small and the trunk won't fit in either. C is the only closet that fits.

## HOW TO COMPUTE WEIGHT

Having dealt with those measurements expressed in units of length, we can now turn to the second fundamental measurement, weight. Physics demonstrates that weight is actually the force exerted on a mass of material by gravity. On earth, the weight of a body is constant, but if we weigh the same body in an orbiting spaceship, it appears to have no weight at all since the pull of gravity (which makes the body have weight) is offset by the centrifugal force of the spaceship in orbital motion.

In the English system, weight is measured in units of ounces, pounds, and tons. In the metric system, the basic unit of weight measurement is the gram which equals .035 ounce. The kilogram (or kilo) (1000 gms.) equals 2.205 lbs. The metric ton is equal to 1000 kilograms or 1.102 U.S. tons.

*Solved problems:*

1. The Jepson Company received a shipment from France. The packing list showed a net weight of .97 metric ton. Jepson had ordered 1 U.S. ton of the material. Was their order filled?

*Answer:* Since 1 metric ton = 1.102 U.S. tons, .97 × 1.102 = 1.07 U.S. tons. The shipment was satisfactory.

2. A truck of Johnson Lines was detained at a state highway weighing station. It weighed 112,000 lbs. and the legal limit was 105,000 lbs. The Johnson dispatcher had loaded it with merchandise weighing 92,000 lbs. The empty truck and trailer weighed 10½ tons. What was the actual loaded weight of the truck when it left the shipping dock?

*Answer:*

**Cargo weight = 92,000 lbs.**
**Truck weight = 10½ tons or 21,000 lbs.**
**Total weight = 113,000 lbs.**

The weighing station underweighed the truck by 1,000 lbs.

3. Charles Jones was a shipping clerk at Johnson Lines. His union contract specified that a clerk was not required to carry loads weighing more than 75 lbs. and no more than 400 lbs. on a single shift.

On Oct. 18, Jones lifted 6 boxes weighing 35 kilograms, 37 kg, 29 kg, 33 kg, 32 kg, 28 kg. At this point, Jones balked saying some of the loads were too heavy and he was over his shift limit anyway. Was he right?

*Answer:* The boxes weighed (2.2 × kg weight) 77 lbs., 81.4 lbs., 63.8 lbs., 72.6 lbs., 70.4 lbs., and 61.6 lbs. Total weight 426.8 lbs. Jones was right, 2 boxes were overweight and the total was over 400 lbs.

## HOW TO UNDERSTAND AND MEASURE TIME

Time is the third fundamental measurement. Techniques for its measurement have advanced as the need for more accuracy has grown.

Starting with sundials, we have now progressed to the point where inexpensive battery-powered watches driven by the oscillations of a quartz crystal allow us to measure time with errors of less than a minute per month. The time of day is measured in seconds, minutes, and hours. Beyond a day, we simply count the days and use calendars to keep track of weeks, months, and years. And time measurement is universal. The same system is followed worldwide.

We keep track of the motion of the sun in the sky by changing time zones so that the sun is at its zenith in the center of each zone at 12 noon zone time. Greenwich (England) Mean Time is where it all starts, and hours are subtracted when we travel westward toward the U.S. and added when we travel eastward.

Halfway around the world is the International Date Line where to keep the system in synch, we gain a day traveling west and lose a day traveling east.

## HOW TO MEASURE THE SPEED OF THINGS

One of the most important ways of using time in measurement is to calculate speed, or velocity.

In our current civilization, speed has become an important quantity. Corporations pay sizable premiums, for example, to have important packages delivered overnight. Planes have replaced buses and trains almost completely for long-distance travel, primarily because of their speed.

So how do we measure such an important quantity? Fundamentally, it's simple. We measure the length of time it takes to travel a certain distance. For example, if it takes two hours to walk six miles, we express it as:

$$\text{speed} = \frac{\text{distance}}{\text{time}}, \text{ or as we walked}$$

$$\frac{\text{six miles}}{\text{two hours}} = \frac{6}{2} = \frac{3}{1}, \text{ or 3 miles per hour.}$$

If we travel 60 miles in one hour in a car, our speed is 60 miles per hour. This is a rate of speed, and you don't necessarily have to travel for an hour to go that fast. For example, at the rate of 60 mph, it will take us one minute to go a mile or 10 minutes to go 10 miles. Slower speeds can be expressed in miles per day and very high speeds in feet per second, or if you're an astronaut in orbit, in miles per second.

*Solved problems:*

1. A hiker walks 4.25 miles in the first hour, 3.5 miles in the second hour, and as he grows tired, 3 miles in the third hour. After a short rest, he covers 4.8 miles in the next hour and 4.2 in the last. What was his average speed in the five miles traveled?

*Answer:*

$$\text{Total mileage traveled} = 4.25 + 3.5 + 3 + 4.8 + 4.2 = 19.75$$

$$\text{Average speed} = \frac{19.75}{5} = 3.95 \text{ miles/hour.}$$

2. If a car travels 85 miles per hour, what is its speed in feet/second?

*Answer:*

$$\frac{85 \text{ miles} \times 5280 \text{ (ft/mile)}}{\text{hour} \times 60 \times 60} = \frac{448{,}800}{3600}$$

$$= 124.667 \text{ ft/sec.}$$

3. Two delivery trucks leave the warehouse at 9 A.M. One driver travels 47 miles at an average speed of 24 miles/hour and the second driver covers 56 miles at an average speed of 25.5 miles/hr. Which driver gets back to the warehouse first?

*Answer:*

$$\text{If speed} = \frac{\text{distance}}{\text{time}}, \text{ then time} = \frac{\text{distance}}{\text{speed}}$$

$$\text{For Driver \#1, } t_1 = \frac{47}{24} = 1.96 \text{ hrs.}$$

$$\text{For Driver \#2, } t_2 = \frac{56}{25.5} = 2.196 \text{ hrs.}$$

#1 returns first.

4. Two messengers cover the inner city and the suburbs. The first uses a bicycle which travels 12 miles/hr. He travels 49 miles. The second uses a car to cover 148 miles at a speed of 23 miles/hr. How long does each messenger take to cover his route?

*Answer:*

$$\text{\#1–time} = \frac{49}{12} = 4.08 \text{ hrs.}$$

$$\text{\#2–time} = \frac{148}{23} = 6.43 \text{ hrs.}$$

5. A mailman covers his route on foot. He travels 13 miles at an average speed of 2.3 miles/hr. A second uses a truck, but he has to cover 124 miles at an average speed of 16.7 miles/hr. Which route would you rather have? Why?

*Answer:*

$$\text{Foot route: } t_1 = \frac{13}{2.3} = 5.65 \text{ hours}$$

$$\text{Truck route: } t_2 = \frac{124}{16.7} = 7.43 \text{ hours}$$

The foot route is best because the mailman gets off work almost 2 hours earlier.

## HOW TO UNDERSTAND AND MEASURE TEMPERATURE

Temperature is measured by thermometers in atmospheric conditions. Instruments like pyrometers or thermocouples are used to measure high temperatures in steel mills and ceramic ovens. In this country, temperature levels are measured in Fahrenheit degrees, and in metric system countries, the centigrade scale is used.

The centigrade scale starts to measure temperature at the freezing point of water which is called 0°C. Since 32° is the Fahrenheit point where water freezes, 0°C = 32°F. On the other end of the scale, 100°C is the temperature at which water boils, so 100°C = 212°F.

Unfortunately, one degree C. is a larger quantity than 1 degree F., so a rather complicated formula is required to convert from one to another. To convert Fahrenheit degrees to centigrade, first subtract 32, then multiply the remainder by 5/9. To convert centigrade to Fahrenheit, first multiply by 9/5, then add 32.

*Solved problems:*

1. Convert these Fahrenheit readings to centigrade: +10°, 50°, 75°.

*Answer:*

```
10°F:   10 − 32 =  −22* × 5/9 =  −12.22°C
50°F:   50 − 32 =   18 × 5/9 =    10°C
75°F:   75 − 32 =   43 × 5/9 =  23.89°C
```

(*This is a below freezing reading, so centigrade reading is minus.)

2. Convert these centigrade temperatures to Fahrenheit: 5°, 105°, 61°.

*Answer:*

```
  5°C:   5 × 9/5 =    9   + 32 = 41°F
105°C: 105 × 9/5 = 189   + 32 = 221°F
 61°C:  61 × 9/5 = 109.8 + 32 = 141.8°F
```

## PROBLEMS ON MEASUREMENT FOR YOU TO SOLVE

(The answers to the following problems are on page 118.)

1. Using a yardstick, Tom measured the size of a crate to be 3½ yards wide, 2 yards high, and 4⅔ yards long. What are the dimensions in feet? In inches?

2. Janet ran 3 laps around a track 440 yds. long. How many feet did she run? What part of a mile?

3. Williams & Company added a room 10′ long × 12′ high and 8′ wide to its office space. Compute the floor area in sq. feet and sq. yards. Compute the area of each wall, noting that one 10′ × 12′ wall has a door space in it 7′ × 3′. What area will be covered by paint (omit floor)?

A. Compute the volume of the room in cubic feet and cubic yards.

B. Convert the answer in (A) to metric volume.

4. Walter Adams has an open area in his building which is 3 yards long and 6 yards wide. How many 6×9 ft. offices can he fit in the area?

5. Compute the area of these figures:

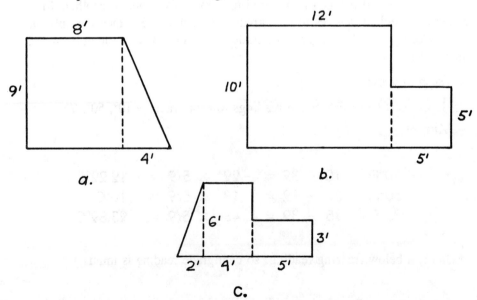

a.

b.

c.

6. Edward Rollins bought 3 cu. yds. of concrete to fill a foundation which is 3' wide × 9' long. How deep will his foundation be if he pours and levels all the concrete?

7. Bill and Jack are digging a hole to bury 2.37 cubic yards of trash. The hole can be no more than 2' wide and 4' long. How deep does it have to be to hold all the trash?

8. Ed Johnson is pouring an area 20' wide and 30' long with gravel. One cubic yard of gravel will pave 15 sq. ft. Ed's truck can carry 3,000 lbs. The gravel weighs 300 lbs. per cubic yard.

A. How much gravel is required to pave the area?

B. How much gravel can Ed carry in one load?

C. How many trips will he have to make to complete the job?

9. The elevator at the Hinkley Co. has a capacity of 1,500 lbs. John Harvey has to move 250 crates each weighing 50 lbs. to the fourth floor. Each crate is 2' × 4' × 4'. The elevator is 10' wide and 8' high and 6' deep. How many trips will John have to make?

10. The dispatcher at Johnson Lines has 15 cartons to ship. Five cartons weigh 50 lbs. each. Three cartons weigh 200 lbs. each. Four cartons weigh 150 lbs. each, and three cartons weigh 400 lbs. each. He has three vans available, each with a capacity of 900 lbs. How can he divide the load so each van has only one trip to make?

11. Roger Edwards has 10 gals. of gas in his car's tank. At an average speed of 40 miles/hr. he gets 27 mi./gal. How far can he travel at that speed before he runs out of gas?

12. Willard Thompson has to reach his home by 12 midnight. How fast will he have to drive if his home is 480 miles away and he leaves at six o'clock?

13. Roy Allen's milk route is 22 miles long. If it takes him four hours to cover it, what's his average speed?

14. Ken Williams is a truck driver. If he drives at an average speed of 40 mi./hr. and leaves the terminal at 6 A.M., when will he arrive at his destination, 320 miles away?

## SOLUTIONS TO BUSINESS MATH PROBLEMS

1. In feet: $10\frac{1}{2} \times 6 \times 14$. In inches: $126 \times 72 \times 168$
2. 3,960 ft., or ¾ mile
3. Area: 80 sq. ft., or 8.89 sq. yds.
   One wall: 120 sq. ft.
   Two walls: 96 sq. ft.
   Fourth wall: 99 sq. ft.
      411 sq. ft. to be painted
   A. 960 cu. ft., or 35.56 cu. yds.
   B. 46.51 kiloliters (cubic meters)
4. 3
5. A. 90 sq. ft.   B. 145 sq. ft.   C. 45 sq. ft.
6. 3 feet
7. 8 feet
8. A. 40 cu. yds. B. 10 cu. yds. C. 4 trips
9. Elevator will support 30 crates, but no more than 14 will fit. 18 trips required.
10. Van 1: 1-400 lbs., 1-200 lbs., 2-150 lbs.
    Van 2: 1-400 lbs., 2-200 lbs., 2-50  lbs.
    Van 3: 3-50  lbs., 2-150 lbs., 1-400 lbs.
11. 270 miles
12. 80 mi./hr.
13. 5.5 mi./hr.
14. 2 P.M.

# CHAPTER 6

# Everything You Need to Know About Banking Business

Although checking accounts and banking were covered briefly in Chapter 3, you may well be called on to handle a wide variety of banking transactions in your work as a secretary. The amount of detail involved will vary depending on the size office in which you work. However, the contents of this chapter will give you the background to handle *any* type of banking work that crosses your desk.

*Checking Accounts*—In a small office, you may be asked to handle the company's checking account; in a large company, your boss may want you to perform routine banking transactions for his personal account. If you are asked to write checks or to deposit them, you must first be authorized to use your signature. To do this, the person responsible for the account must sign a bank authorization on your behalf so you can either sign checks yourself or in combination with someone else. The bank will also request a signature card from you.

*Receiving Checks*—Incoming checks in payment of merchandise sold or services rendered must be verified to insure that the correct amount has been paid and that the check is properly filled out and dated.

Before deposit, the check must also be endorsed. And finally, a record of the check's receipt and deposit must be made.

To speed up the receipt of cash, some companies now use a lock-box system. Payers are instructed to send their checks to the numbered lock box under the bank's control. Checks are thus received directly by the bank, saving a day or two in the deposit transaction. The bank, of course, forwards a record of the deposits to the company. It's important, of course, to verify the deposit record to insure that proper payment has been made.

*The Deposit*—If the company receives and deposits its own checks, duplicate deposit slips are generally made out in advance (one for the bank, one for the company) as often as checks are received. All checks are listed on the slip, and in the case of retail businesses, cash is listed as well. If cash is deposited, bills should be separated by denomination and wrapped. Your bank will supply you with wrappers for the bills and rolls for coins. Be sure to identify the packages with your company name to avoid mistakes in banks where large amounts of money are handled.

A typical deposit slip is shown below as filled out for a mixed deposit of checks and cash.

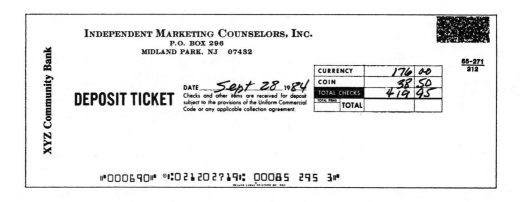

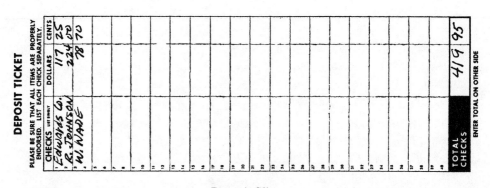

Deposit Slip

Checks must be properly endorsed before deposit. For personal accounts, the payee generally endorses the checks by signing his name. However, you may endorse such checks for deposit by so marking them and the bank will accept them for deposit but not for cash. Company checks are generally endorsed by a rubber stamp with the legend "For Deposit Only" plus the company name and bank account number.

It should be noted that personal checks endorsed by the payee with his signature only can be cashed by anyone in possession of the check. Thus, it is advisable to endorse all checks "For Deposit Only" to avoid danger of loss.

## HOW TO BENEFIT FROM AUTOMATED BANKING

Most bank transactions today are handled by computer. If you examinc a check, for instance, you will see a series of oddly shaped numbers on the bottom of a check or deposit slip. These numbers identify your account and the bank as well. When checks are transferred from the bank that paid them, to the bank that carries the check writer's account, these numbers are used by the clearing house to identify the receiving bank. When the checks are received, these numbers are used to correct automatically the balance of the check writer. Since the numbers are magnetically coded, the computer can identify the bank involved, the account of the check writer, and even the date and amount of the check since that is recorded in code on the check by the receiving bank. At the same time, the money is transferred from the account of the paying bank.

A typical check and deposit slip with magnetic coding follow:

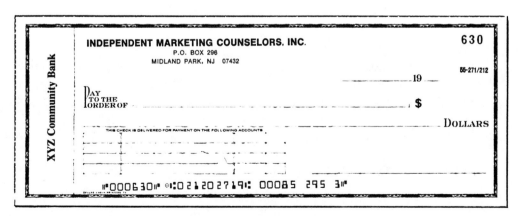

Magnetically Coded Check

**INDEPENDENT MARKETING COUNSELORS, INC.**
P.O. BOX 296
MIDLAND PARK, NJ 07432

XYZ Community Bank

55-271/212

**DEPOSIT TICKET**

DATE_____19____

Checks and other items are received for deposit subject to the provisions of the Uniform Commercial Code or any applicable collection agreement.

| | | |
|---|---|---|
| CURRENCY | | |
| COIN | | |
| TOTAL CHECKS | | |
| TOTAL ITEMS | TOTAL | |

⑆00112⑆ ⑈021202719⑈ 00085 295 3⑆

Magnetically Coded Deposit Slip

The use of coded checks and deposit slips requires that check writers and depositors use only those deposit slips and checks carrying their individual account codes. In case of necessity, the bank can print checks and slips on the spot.

Banks also require identification for clearinghouse purposes. Normally each check carries that number in the upper right-hand corner.

## Example   Specific bank number

City or State ——> 56-271/212 <—— Days required to clear check

Federal   District

Reserve   Branch

District

Banks often ask that the first set of numbers (56-271 in the example) be listed for each outside check shown on the deposit slip.

## Understanding Other Banking Methods

If your company is not concerned with making deposits rapidly, it may be convenient to handle deposits by mail. The bank will provide you with special slips and envelopes to use. To do this, you must endorse the checks for deposit, list them on the slip, and mail them to the bank. You should use registered mail for currency. You will, in turn, receive a receipt from the bank.

Although banks now offer longer business hours for their customers' convenience, it is possible to deposit money after hours in suitably equipped banks. Using a special bag (supplied by the bank) you may use the night depository, a special slot available after hours. The bank will receive your deposit the next day and either mail you a receipt or hold it for pick-up.

In recent years, many of the larger banks have installed automatic cash withdrawal equipment for customers' use after banking hours. To use the facility, you'll need a bank-issued credit card (which is inserted in the appropriate slot) plus your own secret code number, which is entered through a keyboard along with the amount of cash desired. You will then receive the cash with a charge notice indicating that your account has been charged with the withdrawal.

It is now possible to use your card and secret code at banks all across the country in principal cities, provided of course, that your bank belongs to the network.

## HOW TO PROFIT FROM A CHECKING ACCOUNT

So far we have confined our banking discussion to ways of making deposits. But banking is a two-way transaction and using the checkbook to make withdrawals is probably a more important step.

If you go to the bank to order a checkbook, you'll be faced with a wide variety of check types and forms. Many women and men seem to prefer the small book, just the size of a check for their personal accounts, because it fits readily into a purse or pocket. The information normally entered on the check stub is written on a series of lined pages in the front of the book. This is perhaps the only disadvantage of the small checkbook—it's difficult to include all the details for each check.

Businesses generally prefer the larger books with three checks to the page and the stubs alongside each check. These books are also provided with interleaved sheets for copying the checks as they are written. Business checks are generally a larger size than personal ones with spaces to enter invoice numbers or other transaction details. Personal checks usually provide the name, address, and phone number of the account holder. Business checks carry the company name and sometimes its trademark.

### How to Write Checks

Checks and stubs should be filled out completely at the time the checks are written. Be sure to include the check number, payee's name, invoice numbers, date, plus any special information such as part payment, payment on account, etc. An example is shown on page 124.

To insure proper credit to your company, follow the specific instructions on the face of the invoice regarding invoicing address, department, etc. If you are paying several invoices, list them on the check as well as the stub.

INDEPENDENT MARKETING COUNSELORS, INC.                    631
P.O. BOX 296
MIDLAND PARK, NJ  07432

XYZ Community Bank

Oct. 15 19 84          65-271/212

PAY TO THE ORDER OF  *Allen's Office Supplies*          $ 58.42

*Fifty eight and 42/100*                              DOLLARS

THIS CHECK IS DELIVERED FOR PAYMENT ON THE FOLLOWING ACCOUNTS

Inv. 201                    17.72
     212                    24.50
     221                    16.20          *Earl D Hitchcock*

⑈000631⑈ ⑇021202719⑇ 00085 295 3⑈

Some creditors offer discounts for prompt payment. If it's your company's policy to take advantage of these discounts, mail checks in time to earn them. For example, if an invoice says: "Terms: 1% 10 days, net 30," you can deduct 1% of the invoice amount if you mail the check within 10 days of receipt.

The actual preparation of the check must be done with care. After it is written, it becomes a negotiable instrument, so precautions should be taken to insure that the face value cannot be altered if it falls into the wrong hands. Although it's illegal to alter a check and the bank will not accept an altered one, you must use reasonable care to prevent the possibility of its being changed.

For instance, most businesses use a checkwriter to prepare their checks. This is the surest way to prevent alteration. However, if you have to type checks or write them by hand, be sure to leave no space in front of or behind the written amount so that digits cannot be added to either end of the amount. Use hyphens to fill out lines on a typewriter or a wavy line when using ink.

Consult the invoice or letterhead to get the exact name of the payee. If you make a mistake in preparing a check, do not cross out or erase the error to make a correction. Mark both check and stub "Void" and use a new one (see example on page 125).

Normally the bank will number your checks for you when they are printed. When reordering, you should specify where the new numbering should start. If your checks are not numbered, number them by hand from front to back before starting to use the checkbook.

When writing personal checks to withdraw cash or to pay small obligations, you may find it convenient to write the check to the order of cash. If you do so, bear in mind that such a check can be negotiated by whoever presents and endorses it. Use caution in preparing such checks. Either write them at the bank and cash them immediately or present them immediately.

| | | | | | | NUMBER |
|---|---|---|---|---|---|---|
| | | | | | | **167** |

INDEPENDENT MARKETING
COUNSELORS, INC.

10/20 19 84   55-728
212

PAY TO THE
ORDER OF _Ray Wright_____ $ 76 00

_Seventy six and 00/100_____ DOLLARS

VOID

**ABC BANK & TRUST CO.**

MEMO_____   Gail B Hitchcock

⑆⑈021207280⑈ ⑈880 481 6⑈ 0167

DELUXE CHECK PRINTERS DCIL

| | DEPOSITS | | RECORD OF CHECKS DRAWN | AMOUNT OF CHECKS |
|---|---|---|---|---|
| BALANCE FORWARD | | | NO. _167_ DATE _10/20_ 19 _84_ | |
| DATE | | | PAY TO _Ray Wright_ $ | |
| | | | Consultant's fee | 76 00 |
| | | | NO.____ DATE____ 19___ | |
| | | | PAY TO _____ $ | |

VOID

Canceled checks are convenient receipts for payment of bills, but a check made out to cash does not prove you made payment to a specific recipient unless he or she endorses it by name.

## HOW TO INTERPRET AND RECONCILE A BANK STATEMENT

Usually the bank will send you a monthly statement of account showing your opening balance at the beginning of the month; a list of withdrawals including checks, service charges, and any special charges (for checks drawn on insufficient funds, stop payment orders, new checkbook orders, etc.); a list of deposits and credits to your account; and your ending account balance.

As banking grows more automated, some banks are not keeping canceled checks, but are using microfilmed copies instead. In such case, the bank will send you a list of withdrawals with check numbers and amounts instead. If you need a canceled check to prove payment or for some other reasons, the bank will send you a photocopy of both sides of your canceled check.

Since the bank's ending balance will generally not agree with the corresponding balance in your checkbook, it's necessary to reconcile the difference. Although the subject was discussed briefly in Chapter 3, here we will provide you with a step-by-step procedure to insure that balances are reconciled, checks accounted for, and filed for future reference.

*Step A*—Check the bank statement first. See that the amount of each canceled check corresponds with the amount listed under withdrawals on the statement.

*Step B*—Be sure that the checks are in numerical order. Your bank should provide this service for you, particularly if you're dealing with large numbers of checks.

*Step C*—Check off entries on the check stubs against the returned checks. Make note of checks written and outstanding (not listed in the statement). List and total these outstanding checks.

*Step D*—Check your deposits against those listed in the statement. List and total any deposits not shown in the statement.

*Step E*—Correct the bank's ending balance by adding the unlisted deposits (Step D). Subtract the total of outstanding checks (Step C). The result is the bank's corrected balance.

*Step F*—Subtract all the bank service charges shown on the bank's statement from the balance shown in your checkbook on the closing date of the statement. The two balances should now be in agreement.

*Step G*—Correct the balance in your checkbook by subtracting these charges. To avoid changing all your check stubs, merely correct your current balance with a notation of the charges.

*Step H*—If the two balances do not agree, first check your reconciliation, then be sure all checks and deposits have been included. Next, check your computations in making out the check stubs. Be sure all your subtractions are correct and that the right balance has been carried from page to page. Finally, check the arithmetic in the bank statement (this is the least likely place to find a mistake). When you find the error, correct the entry itself and then correct your current balance. Always make note of the reconciliation date in your checkbook so you know where to start next month.

*Step I*—Bank statements and canceled checks should be filed by date. You'll need the last one for the next reconciliation, and the checks are useful as receipts for accounting and tax purposes.

*Step J*—If you find outstanding (uncashed) checks omitted from two successive statements, chances are the checks have strayed. Either the payees have lost them or never received them. After checking with the payees, the checks in question should be voided in the checkbook.

Next, a stop payment order should be directed to the bank. Such orders are issued when a check is lost or delivered merchandise is unsatisfactory or there is an error in the check.

Once the bank receives the order, it checks to establish that the check has not cleared and the order is then enforced. There is a bank charge for this service.

If you place the order by phone, the bank will require written confirmation.

Finally, you should write a new check to replace the lost item. (Samples of a canceled check and bank statement are shown below and on page 128.)

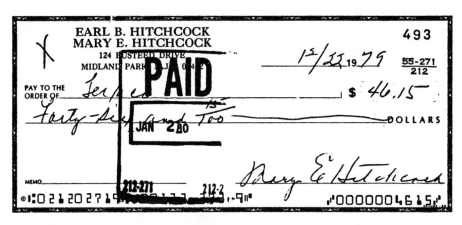

Canceled Check

## HOW TO USE OTHER BANKING SERVICES

You or your company may require other banking services, some of which are discussed here.

In the past few years, banks have been authorized to provide more and more investment-related services. They can now buy and sell stocks, bonds, mutual funds, U.S. Treasury bonds, certificates, and bills. They can act as custodians, provide investment advice, ship securities, collect coupons and dividends.

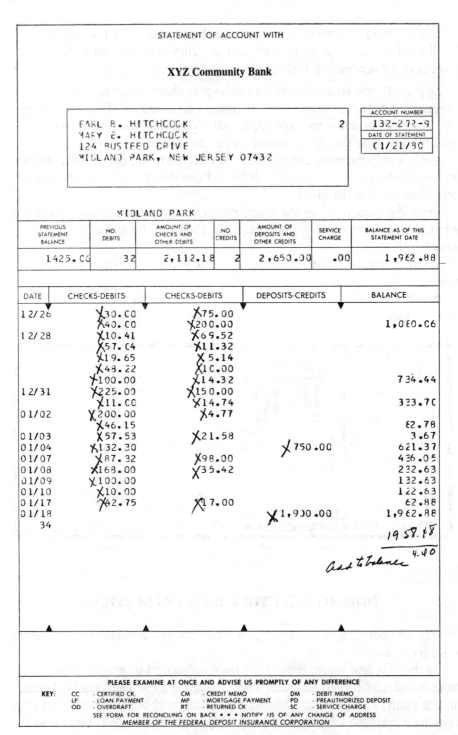

STATEMENT OF ACCOUNT WITH

## XYZ Community Bank

EARL B. HITCHCOCK                                              2
MARY E. HITCHCOCK
124 BUSTEED DRIVE
MIDLAND PARK, NEW JERSEY 07432

| ACCOUNT NUMBER |
|---|
| 132-272-9 |
| DATE OF STATEMENT |
| 01/21/80 |

MIDLAND PARK

| PREVIOUS STATEMENT BALANCE | NO. DEBITS | AMOUNT OF CHECKS AND OTHER DEBITS | NO CREDITS | AMOUNT OF DEPOSITS AND OTHER CREDITS | SERVICE CHARGE | BALANCE AS OF THIS STATEMENT DATE |
|---|---|---|---|---|---|---|
| 1425.06 | 32 | 2,112.18 | 2 | 2,650.00 | .00 | 1,962.88 |

| DATE | CHECKS-DEBITS | CHECKS-DEBITS | DEPOSITS-CREDITS | BALANCE |
|---|---|---|---|---|
| 12/26 | 30.00 | 75.00 | | |
|  | 40.00 | 200.00 | | 1,080.06 |
| 12/28 | 10.41 | 69.52 | | |
|  | 57.04 | 11.32 | | |
|  | 19.65 | 5.14 | | |
|  | 48.22 | 10.00 | | |
|  | 100.00 | 14.32 | | 734.44 |
| 12/31 | 225.00 | 150.00 | | |
|  | 11.00 | 14.74 | | 323.70 |
| 01/02 | 200.00 | 4.77 | | |
|  | 46.15 | | | 82.78 |
| 01/03 | 57.53 | 21.58 | | 3.67 |
| 01/04 | 132.30 | | 750.00 | 621.37 |
| 01/07 | 87.32 | 98.00 | | 436.05 |
| 01/08 | 168.00 | 35.42 | | 232.63 |
| 01/09 | 100.00 | | | 132.63 |
| 01/10 | 10.00 | | | 122.63 |
| 01/17 | 42.75 | 17.00 | | 62.88 |
| 01/18 | | | 1,900.00 | 1,962.88 |
| 34 | | | | |

1958.18
4.40
add to balance

**PLEASE EXAMINE AT ONCE AND ADVISE US PROMPTLY OF ANY DIFFERENCE**

| KEY: | CC - CERTIFIED CK. | CM - CREDIT MEMO | DM - DEBIT MEMO |
|---|---|---|---|
| | LP - LOAN PAYMENT | MP - MORTGAGE PAYMENT | PD - PREAUTHORIZED DEPOSIT |
| | OD - OVERDRAFT | RT - RETURNED CK | SC - SERVICE CHARGE |

SEE FORM FOR RECONCILING ON BACK • • • NOTIFY US OF ANY CHANGE OF ADDRESS
*MEMBER OF THE FEDERAL DEPOSIT INSURANCE CORPORATION*

Bank Statement

Banks may also provide payroll services, including direct deposit into employees' accounts, where desired. The company sends one check to the bank directing how it should be divided. Many banks also provide payroll check-cashing service to the employees of large customers.

Safe-deposit boxes are rented to customers for safeguarding such valuable documents as wills, insurance policies, notes, and securities. Jewelry, silverware, and other such items are also kept in safe-deposit boxes. (You will probably have to visit larger central banks to find safe-deposit boxes since most neighborhood branches do not make them available.) Bank regulations require that customers register at each visit. The user is escorted to the box where the bank's and customer's keys are used to open it. The user is then left to inspect the box in privacy.

## HOW TO PAY BILLS SYSTEMATICALLY

Unless you work in a very small office, you will not normally be asked to pay company bills. However, it's a skill that may prove valuable to your employer during emergencies or vacation periods.

It is more likely, however, that your employer may ask you to help with a personal checking account, particularly when he's traveling or extremely busy.

Here is a handy procedure to follow in either eventuality that will ensure the job is done right and earn your boss's appreciation.

*Step A:* Check each listing on all bills. Verify the arithmetic, note the date payment is required plus prompt payment discounts, if any.

*Step B:* Fill out check and stub simultaneously. Identify details of the payment on the stub for tax and other records.

*Step C:* Record check number, date and amount on the bill. Record invoice number on check face.

*Step D:* Remove payment stubs from bills. Attach to completed check and payment envelope.

*Step E:* Present for signature.

Requests for payment come in several forms. Bills are generally rendered for services such as utilities, messengers, package delivery, doctors, dentists, etc.

An invoice is presented when merchandise is delivered.

A statement is normally rendered monthly. It may sum up the services performed or merchandise delivered that month. Be sure not to pay a statement as well as the invoices it covers.

Check invoices to be sure

1. Merchandise has been received
2. It is as ordered
3. The price is as agreed

You may be asked, when paying monthly credit cards statements (for American Express, Mastercard, Visa, etc.) to verify the statement against the charge record for each transaction. Since credit card theft (and card number theft) is becoming increasingly common, it's important to insure that the statements only show actual transactions.

For certain types of payment, special check forms may be required, as in the purchase of a car, for instance. The most common of these is the certified check. Such a check requires a bank visit so that the teller can verify that the account contains funds to cover the check. The money is withdrawn at the time of certification, the check is then stamped and presented.

Cashier's or treasurer's checks are prepared by the bank upon presentation to the bank of cash equal to the check amount. The bank charges for both certified and cashier's checks.

Bank drafts and money orders are other instruments also used for payment.

## HOW TO HANDLE PETTY CASH

Often (particularly in small offices), you will be asked to be responsible for the petty cash box.

Rather than write checks for small amounts, most offices set aside a cash amount, generally $50 to $250 to pay small sums that come due without notice during the normal course of business. Such expenditures can include postage (but not for a postage meter), delivery charges, taxi fares, office supplies, etc.

The fund is established by writing a check to petty cash and placing the money in a locked receptacle. When money is withdrawn, a petty cash voucher is made up, containing the amount, the date, the purpose of the withdrawal and the signature of the person receiving the money.

When the fund is nearly depleted, a new check is drawn for the full amount of the fund less whatever remains. If, for example, the fund is for $100 and $7.50 is still on hand, the check would be written for $92.50.

At the same time, the petty cash custodian lists all the withdrawals with all the information from the vouchers. The total should, of course, correspond to the amount of the check. The list is turned over to the accounting department whenever a new petty cash check is written.

## ALTERNATIVE PAYMENT METHODS YOU CAN USE

In addition to checks and cash, there are other ways of paying for merchandise and services used in business.

A businessperson may, for instance, accept an interest-bearing note from a customer in payment. Since interest-bearing and discounted notes were discussed in Chapter 3, you can refer back to those pages to refresh your memory.

Cash on delivery (COD) terms are used sometimes with customers whose credit ratings are unsatisfactory. In such a case, the Post Office, United Parcel Service, or air or motor freight carrier collects from the consignee before making delivery.

Commercial drafts are used in a similar way. The bill of lading is sent with the draft to a bank near the consignee. When the merchandise is delivered, the buyer pays the draft, the bank turns over the bill of lading and the buyer can claim his goods.

When payments are made between countries, special forms of payment may be necessary. Most U.S. businesses demand letters of credit from their overseas customers. This document guarantees that U.S. funds are on deposit in the buyer's country and that the shipper can collect as soon as shipment is confirmed.

Banks can wire payments from one country to another for the account of their customers. This is the most expensive way of transferring cash.

You can also buy a bank draft payable in a foreign country. Your foreign customer can do likewise. It can be either a sight draft payable on presentation or payable against shipping documents.

# CHAPTER 7

# Taking the Mystery Out of Payroll and Business Taxes

In Chapter 3, the subject of payroll was discussed with emphasis on the arithmetic involved. In this chapter, the subject will be expanded and the actual procedures involved in maintaining wage and salary records as well as preparing the payroll will be dealt with in detail.

As a secretary, you may become involved in payroll procedures in several ways. First of all, in a small company it may become your responsibility. Or you may be asked to fill in for absent employees, who are on vacation or are absent for other reasons. If you are an executive secretary with administrative responsibilities, understanding the payroll procedure will enhance your qualifications and capabilities.

Business taxes play a dual role in the life of a secretary. First of all, he or she must understand social security, workmen's compensation, and unemployment tax concepts to handle the payroll effectively. Second, a familiarity with Federal and State income taxes from the payroll standpoint as well as from the employer's standpoint is necessary since the employer may well ask him or her to maintain records needed for tax preparation.

Remember in all this that a capable secretary is often a candidate for key executive positions in the company, particularly if a broad education and mastery of the important administrative and financial concepts involved in running a business are a reality.

When a secretary is able to demonstrate administrative skills, she is frequently asked to assume responsibilities in these areas. Since ability and discretion has been demonstrated, it is only natural for the boss to turn to her when help is needed.

Often these special administrative tasks are the stepping stones to broader responsibilities and permanent executive positions. So consider these chapters on administration as opportunities to grow in your job.

## THE PAYROLL

Needless to say, preparing the payroll and maintaining pay records are among the most important and potentially sensitive tasks in the company.

Employee morale can be quickly destroyed by shoddy payroll work. Employees depend heavily on their paychecks in many ways and when errors occur in preparation or checks are late, the reaction is quick and unfavorable.

The preparation of payroll records requires careful attention to detail and a thorough understanding of social security regulations, state and federal income tax requirements, unemployment and workmen's compensation rules, as well as the company's fringe benefit plans.

Whoever prepares the payroll is responsible for maintaining its confidentiality. Most employees want their wage and salary records kept secret. From the company's standpoint, great harm can be done by revealing such data to fellow employees. This is another way of hurting morale. Thus, in addition to careful computation of detailed records, security is vital to the payroll.

Ideally, it should be prepared in a private office but if that's not possible don't leave the records exposed when you leave your desk. Also, destroy the computations used in payroll preparation when you finish.

### Understanding and Handling Payroll Deductions

A variety of deductions are subtracted from the employee's check before it is received. Since the net effect is to reduce the amount of the check, employees are outraged by errors in deductions.

The biggest deduction is, of course, the withholding of federal income tax. You learned the method for computing withholding tax in Chapter 3, so this discussion will be confined to the forms needed and methods for depositing the taxes withheld.

Since the amount of tax withheld depends on the employee's marital and family status, he or she is required to complete a W-4 form when first hired and when the status changes.

The employee is entitled to a personal exemption for himself, one for the spouse (unless the spouse is employed and claims an exemption), one for each dependent child (unless claimed elsewhere by the spouse), plus additional exemptions if the employee (or spouse) is age 65 or older or is blind.

To comply fully with federal tax requirements, these records are needed:

1. W-2 forms (Wage & Tax Statement) for the employee at the end of the tax year or when he leaves the company's employment. The government receives a copy and the employer keeps a copy.

2. W-3 form is to summarize taxes withheld and accompany W-2 forms.

3. W-4—employee's exemptions (see earlier discussion).

4. 501 to accompany the employer's quarterly tax deposit.

5. 940—annual federal unemployment tax return.

6. 941—the employer's quarterly federal tax return.

In addition, some states require withholding for the payment of state income taxes.

It is of vital importance that social security taxes and federal income taxes withheld from employees be deposited quarterly in an authorized bank. The government regards this money as held in trust for the benefit of the employees and will hold the employer personally responsible if deposits are not made in a timely fashion.

Social Security payments are the next major paycheck deduction. Chapter 3 described the method for computing social security taxes but it should be added that these funds are to be deposited under the same conditions as income tax withheld. Note too, that there is a maximum amount of tax withheld every year beyond which no further payments are required.

Both employer and employee require Social Security numbers to identify their tax payments and insure that they are properly credited. If the employee has no Social Security number, he or she may receive one by filing Form SS-5 at the nearest regional office of the Social Security Administration.

To change a name, file Form OAAN-7003, and to receive a statement of earnings accumulated, file Form OAR-7004.

This form is particularly important since the vast size of the records makes for occasional errors. You, or any other employee should, from time to time, check to ensure that your records are being kept properly. If not, you may not receive the full amount due you upon retirement.

Social Security laws also require that companies with four or more paid employees contribute to the adminsitrative costs of state unemployment programs through payment of a federal tax. IRS Form 940 is used for this purpose.

The state unemployment tax is levied on employers to pay for benefits to unemployed workers. Some states also require a contribution from employees. If so, the tax is deducted from employee paychecks. Similar conditions govern the payment of taxes to support workmen's compensation to reimburse employees for time lost due to job-related injuries.

Check with your local chamber of commerce to learn the detailed requirements for state tax deductions in your area.

In addition to deductions for state and federal taxes, many companies require partial payment from their employees for the costs of fringe benefits such as group life, medical and dental insurance, or corporate pension plans. These payments normally take the form of payroll deductions.

Some employers also permit deductions for group savings plans, credit union payments, the purchase of U.S. Treasury savings bonds, and contributions to United Way organizations.

This wide range of deductions can make a serious dent in the size of paychecks and it is advisable that the person in charge of the payroll be prepared at all times to document each deduction clearly. Obviously, all voluntary deductions require an up-to-date signed release from the employee involved.

## AN EIGHT-STEP PLAN FOR PAYROLL PREPARATION

To assist you in keeping track of responsibilities involved in payroll preparation and the multitude of associated submissions, we have prepared a detailed month-by-month procedure for the entire calendar year.

*Step 1*—For new employees. Have each one fill out Form W-4 (employee's withholding exemption certificate).

*Step 2*—Remind current employees that changes in their personal status may require new Form W-4s (marriage, divorce, births, deaths, etc.). They may also wish to have more tax withheld by claiming additional dependents.

*Step 3*—When preparing paychecks, withhold the required amount of income and Social Security, plus all other deductions (use tax tables prepared by the IRS and state governments). Each employee should receive a record of his gross pay plus a list of deductions made with each paycheck.

*Step 4*—If withholding taxes plus Social Security amount to $200 or more in either of the first two months in a calendar quarter, that money must be deposited in an authorized bank by the fifteenth of the following month, using Form 501 to accompany the deposit.

If the amount if less than $200, it may be held until the quarterly return is filed (see Step 5).

*Step 5*—Within one month after the end of each calendar quarter (by Apr. 30, Jul. 31, Oct. 31, and Jan. 31), the Employer's Quarterly Federal Tax return must be filed including all the income and Social Security tax withheld plus the employer's contribution, but minus deposits previously made.

For convenience, any state unemployment tax is due at the same time.

*Step 6*—If an employee resigns or is terminated, he or she should receive Form W-2, indicating wages subject to federal income tax, amount of tax, and Social Security withheld.

*Step 7*—All employees must receive a completed Form W-2 by Jan. 31 of each calendar year indicating wage and tax information for the previous year. Two copies of the form are given to the employee; one copy is retained by the employer and one copy is sent to the IRS. If state or city income taxes are due (or withheld), these governmental bodies may also require a copy of the W-2 form.

*Step 8*—The Employer's Annual Federal Unemployment Tax Return (Form 940) and the Reconciliation of Income Tax Withheld from Wages (Form W-3) must also be filed by each Jan. 31.

## HOW TO UNDERSTAND AND HANDLE GOVERNMENT WAGE AND HOUR REQUIREMENTS

Under the provisions of the Fair Labor Standards Act, every employer must keep track of hours worked by employees paid on an hourly wage scale as well as non-managerial employees paid a weekly or monthly salary.

Such records are not required for managers, executives, and professional employees.

The records for non-exempt employees are subject to inspection by examiners from the Wage and Hour Division, U.S. Department of Labor. These inspectors will determine from the records that minimum wages are being paid and that employees who work more than forty hours per week are paid an overtime premium of 50 percent of their hourly rate (time and a half) for each overtime hour. These records must be kept open for inspection for a period of four years after they are completed.

Some companies require all non-exempt employees, both salaried and hourly workers, to use a time clock and cards to record times in and out of work. Others require all employees to sign in and out. Still others require time clocks for hourly workers and sign-in sheets for salaried employees.

It is important that the payroll supervisor insist that all employees sign or punch in and out just before their work starts and immediately after their working hours are completed.

Some employees habitually report early for work and others leave work late. Although these habits may be commendable from the employer's viewpoint, wage and hour examiners may well decide that the excess recorded is, in fact, overtime. If the practice has been permitted for some time, it may result in costly back payments and fines for the employer.

All companies, large and small, are obliged to keep complete payroll records for both current employees and past—at least for the four-year period demanded by the Fair Labor Standards Act.

Such records are also required to support Social Security and withholding tax returns as well as accounting records. Examples of several types of payroll records and individual employee records are shown later in this section. For small companies, standard forms are obtainable from business equipment suppliers.

Increasingly, even small offices are turning to computers to handle the payroll task. Once payroll information is recorded in the computer, the software package permits the total payroll to be called up on the screen as well as individual records, taxes due, quarterly and annual totals. The computer's disc storage permits records to be called up quickly and conveniently for the use of the accountant, the auditor, the Wage and Hour examiner, or the IRS.

The secretary who learns to use personal computers or who has access to a terminal in a larger company is acquiring skills that may lead to tasks and positions of greater and greater responsibility.

One such responsibility (particularly in a small office) is salary administration. Once you have demonstrated the capability for handling larger responsibilities, you may be asked to assist in establishing job descriptions and qualifications for performing specified jobs.

Such basic information is required to determine salary levels for various office positions and to ensure that positions requiring equal skills are equally compensated.

On this basis, fair recommendations for salary increases and promotions can be made. By the same token, evidence for termination or transfer to a position of lesser responsibility is available.

## HOW TO KEEP FAIL-SAFE INCOME TAX RECORDS

Here is where a capable secretary can be of great value to a boss. With proper guidance and the necessary background, she can provide, at a minimum, a carefully maintained file of supporting records to be available at tax-filing time.

With more experience, she can:

1. select material for the files from among personal and business bills and other financial records
2. maintain a calendar of filing times and tax payments due
3. keep track of changes in the tax laws that may affect a return.

It should be understood that this kind of work can be undertaken only if the employer suggests and encourages it. It's most definitely not a task that an executive would entrust to a newly hired employee.

But once you have earned the boss's confidence and you learn that such help might be useful, you should explain your qualifications and capabilities.

A typical business manager is generally confronted with a fairly complex tax return. For instance, a wide variety of business-related expenses, including travel, entertainment, meetings, gifts, charitable contributions, etc., may be incurred.

In addition, personal investments, deferred compensation, owned property, outside business ventures and family financial arrangements that materially affect a return may be involved.

Because of this complexity, most businesspeople today use full-time tax consultants to handle their returns. However, these experts step in at tax time and prepare the return based on records available.

Let's see specifically now, how you can assist your boss in preparing and filing a tax return.

### How to Maintain Records of Deductible Expenses

**1. Business Expenses**—Treatment will vary depending on whether or not the executive pays these expenses personally or is reimbursed by the company.

In the former case, all expenses are deductible on his own tax return, and detailed expense records are required to support the deductions. In the latter instance, the expenses are deductible on the company's tax return.

In 1985, the IRS has instituted new and more rigorous requirements for accounting records. In addition to bills, credit card statements, and receipts, each taxpayer is required to keep a "contemporaneous record" of travel, entertainment, business gifts, use of personal or company car, plus such personally-owned equipment as airplane, boat, or computer equipment.

To satisfy these requirements, accounting firms are suggesting the use of an expense log. Entries must be made at the time of use and include such information as:

- date of use
- name of user

- miles used (or time used, depending on equipment)
- purpose of use, for example: "sales call on customer"

If these records are not kept, deductions will not be allowed. Furthermore, a professional tax return preparer is required to advise clients of the new requirements and is not permitted to sign a tax return containing such deductions unless he's positive that the supporting records exist.

The new regulations offer you an excellent opportunity to be of special assistance to your boss. Since you are the person most familiar with his schedule, you can ensure that the expense log is kept up-to-date after each trip or appointment. In addition to ensuring that entries are made on time, you should file all bills, tickets, receipts, etc., relating to the expenses so that they are available at tax preparation time.

A suitable expense log designed for automobile use is shown in this section. If the number of entries is not large, one master log for all types of expenses may be used. However, if your boss is a frequent traveller, it may be advisable to keep separate logs for travel, car, entertainment, and use of boat, private plane, or computer equipment.

**2. Personal Deductions**—If you assist your boss in paying personal expenses, you can be of great assistance in preserving the necessary records to support deductions in these areas:

*A. Medical and dental expenses*—These may not be only for your boss, but for the family as well. They include doctor and hospital bills, equipment (eyeglasses, wheelchairs, braces, etc.), medical and dental insurance (reimbrusements must be subtracted).

Under certain conditions, doctor-ordered travel may also be deductible.

*B. Interest*—This is paid on installment purchases, personal loans, home and property mortgages.

*C. Taxes*—Some types of tax payment are deductible, including sales taxes, property taxes, and local income taxes.

*D. Contributions*—Those made to groups with charitable, religious, educational, or scientific objectives are deductible. These may include, for example, churches, hospitals, schools, foundations, United Way, Red Cross, etc.

If your boss incurs expenses on behalf of such an organization (travel, car, phone calls, postage, etc.) he's entitled to deduct such expenses provided that records are kept.

*E. Alimony and child care*—Parents may deduct child care costs if both are employed.

*F. Education*—Such expenses are deductible if required by the employer or are necessary in a present position. These include travel costs, tuition, books, etc. Educational expenses to acquire skills for a new job are *not* deductible.

*G. Bad debts*—Uncollectible debts, either personal or business-related, are deductible.

*H. Casualty and theft losses*—Unreimbursed damages to home, property or car, and due to fire, storm, flood or theft may be deducted.

## How to Know What Is Taxable and What Is Not

This is the other side of the coin. The average business executive often has numerous sources of income in addition to his salary. It's quite likely you may be asked to handle the records for some or all of this outside income and if you are able to keep them so that they're available at tax time, your efforts will be greatly appreciated.

These records will consist of such items as receipts, earnings statements, bank deposit slips (with notes to identify income sources), dividend statements, interest payments from savings or cash management accounts, rental income statements, etc.

To assist you here are the most common types of taxable income:

*A. Wages, salaries and other types of compensation for services performed* —This is the gross amount paid before deduction. Income from commissions, professional fees, tips, bonuses, awards, and money or merchandise prizes falls into this category.

*B. Dividends*—In most cases, cash dividends on stock owned are taxable. Stock dividends are normally not taxable (unless the stockholder had the option of taking cash instead).

Most companies send dividend statements to their stockholders of record before tax time. All such statements should be filed whether the income is taxable or not. The tax preparer should make the final judgment on this point.

*C. Interest*—With few exceptions, interest income is taxable. This includes bonds, mortgages, interest-bearing bank deposits, loans, savings, and money market accounts.

Although interest on certain types of Federal Government bonds, state, and municipal bonds is not taxable, these records should also be kept on file to assist the tax preparer.

*D. Profits from the sale of personal property*—These amounts are taxable either as current income or capital gain, depending on the length of time the property has been owned. Thus it's important to keep exact records of purchase and sale dates as well as prices paid and received. Personal property includes real estate, securities, jewelry, boats, cars, planes, etc.

*E. Returns from Annuities and Endowment Type Life Policies*—Depending on the type of policy owned, some part of the proceeds may be taxable, thus records should be kept.

*F. Rental income*—Although the income from rental property is taxable, the owner is permitted to deduct such costs as depreciation, mortgage payments, taxes, repairs, real estate agent's commissions, and insurance. Thus there is the necessity of keeping complete expense records.

*G. Royalties*—They are taxable, but the expenses associated with preparing patents, publishing books and music for instance, are deductible.

*H. Professional or business income*—The net income from either of these is taxable. Records of all normal operating expenses are required to substantiate deductions.

## HOW TO FILE INCOME TAXES

Your employer will no doubt use Form 1040 (long form) in preparing his income tax. It's a two-page form accompanied by a series of schedules including data to support deductions claimed and income earned. These include:

- Schedules A & B—Itemized Deductions and Interest and Dividend Income
- Schedule C—Profit or Loss from Business or Profession
- Schedule D—Capital Gains and Losses
- Schedule E—Supplemental Income
- Schedule SE—Computation of Social Security
- Self-Employment Tax
- Schedule W—Deduction for a Married Couple When Both Work

Each taxpayer receives one set of forms (two of certain pages). Additional copies or special forms, if required, may be obtained at banks, post offices, or your local IRS office.

Taxpayers who receive substantial amounts of income (over $500) from sources other than wages and salaries (or who do not have tax withheld from wages and salaries) are required to file Form 1040-ES, Declaration of Estimated Tax. Tax due must be paid either when filing the declaration or in four equal installments payable on Apr. 15, Jun. 15, Sept. 15, and Jan. 15. If income varies during this period, the declaration must be revised on these dates and additional tax paid, if due.

As a secretary, you can be of great assistance to your boss in reminding him to a) make the declaration, and b) pay the installments as they come due. Beyond that, you may be able to keep track of the outside income as it's received to ascertain how close it comes to the estimate.

If you are asked to prepare any of your boss's tax returns, remember that they contain confidential information. You will be responsible for the security of the tax return itself as well as the associated documents. If you have to leave your desk during the typing, all the papers involved should be placed in a secure location.

Use this checklist to determine the deductible status of expense items as they cross your desk:

|  | Deductible | |
|---|:---:|:---:|
|  | **Yes** | **No** |
| Alimony & Child Support | X | |
| Car, Business (unless reimbursed) | | |
| Gasoline Tax | | X |
| Operating Expenses | X | |
| Employer's Charge for Personal Use | | X |
| Car, Personal | | |
| Gasoline Tax | | X |
| Operating Expenses | | X |
| Interest on Car Payment Loan | X | |
| License Fees | | X |
| *Charitable Contributions to Qualified Organizations | X | |
| Dues to Clubs and Fraternal Groups | | X |
| Federal Excise Tax | | X |
| Federal Income Tax | | X |
| Fees Paid to Employment Agencies | X | |
| Gambling Losses (to offset winnings) | X | |
| Gifts | | |
| Personal | | X |
| *Business | X | |
| Taxes | | X |
| Home | | |
| Assessments (sewers, streets, etc.) | | X |
| Homeowner's insurance | | X |
| Loss (when sold) | | X |
| Mortgage Interest | X | |
| Rent | | X |
| Repairs | | X |
| Taxes | X | |
| Inheritance Taxes | | X |

| | | |
|---|---|---|
| Life Insurance Premiums | | X |
| Losses, Casualty (unless covered by insurance) | | |
|   Burglary | X | |
|   Earthquake | X | |
|   Fire | X | |
|   Flood | X | |
|   Lightning | X | |
|   Windstorm | X | |
| *Medical & Hospital Insurance Premiums | X | |
| *Medical Expenses | X | |
| *Prescription Drugs | X | |
|   Personal Loan Interest | X | |
| *Political Campaign Contributions | X | |
|   Property Taxes | X | |
|   Sales Taxes | X | |
|   Social Security Taxes | | X |
|   Traffic Fines | | X |
| *Travel Expenses, Business-Related | X | |
|   Travel Expenses, Commuter | | X |
|   Uniforms (required for work) | X | |
|   Union Dues | X | |
|   Wages Paid (household) | | X |

*Limited deductions, check tax instructions.

## NEW TAX INFORMATION

For 1985, the rules for reporting business expenses have been revised drastically. The IRS requires (starting with 1985 records) that taxpayers keep contemporaneous detailed records of business expenses including automobile, travel, entertainment, and the use of such personal property items as airplanes, boats, vacation homes, and even computer equipment. Of course, if the taxpayer makes no business use of such personal property, there is no record-keeping requirement.

The contemporaneous records must specify:

- the date of the use
- the name of the user
- number of miles driven (for a car) or the length of time used (for other property)
- purpose of the use

The taxpayer who drives a company-owned or leased car must, in the future, pay taxes on the personal use of that car. The amount of income is to be based on the monthly lease cost of the car and in proportion to the personal-use time.

These new rules are so strict and the amount of record keeping required so onerous that a great deal of protest has been made by the business community. In response, some easing of the regulations had been promised, but in the meantime the contemporaneous records should be kept.

It should also be noted that tax preparers (accountants, consultants, etc.) may not sign a tax return unless they are satisfied that the records (on which deductions are based) exist and are in order; and the taxpayer may be assessed a negligence penalty for claiming deductions without proper supporting records.

# CHAPTER 8

# Increasing Your Understanding of the Investment World

Investment transactions involve a great deal of paperwork and communication back and forth between investor, broker, bank, and adviser. With the proper background, you are in a position to relieve your boss of many of the tedious details involved in typical investment transactions. In addition, it may be helpful to you personally to understand the principles of investing as well as its risks and potential rewards. So for both reasons, this chapter is devoted to increasing your knowledge and understanding of the investment world.

From the tremendous choices offered to investors by those interested in raising capital, we have selected those of broadest interest. Far and away the most popular investment vehicle is common stocks, followed by bonds, mutual funds, stock options, and commodities. Real estate is such a fundamentally different way of investing that we have devoted a whole chapter to it.

## UNDERSTANDING AND WORKING WITH COMMON STOCK

When you own corporate stock, you actually own part of the corporation. That ownership gives you a right to vote on important issues at the stockholders' annual meeting where the corporation's board of directors reports to its owners on important developments of the year just completed.

Companies issue shares of common stock to raise capital, which is then used to operate the company and make it grow. These shares are bought and sold by investors at prices established by the market in which they are traded.

If the company makes a profit, they sometimes pay periodic cash dividends to their stockholders. If a company pays dividends regularly or if its sales grow rapidly, the price paid for its shares is likely to increase in the marketplace. The ultimate objective of an investor in common stocks is to buy stocks that are increasing in value and to sell them before their value declines.

Prices in the stock market are governed by many factors beyond the intrinsic value of the companies issuing the stocks. During periods of business prosperity, prices often increase rapidly (a "bull market") and during recessions stocks are likely to drop in price as a group (a "bear market").

Therein lies the fascination of the stock market. Investors who are able to anticipate changes in the market due to good or bad business news, international political developments, and other external influences, can make sizable profits. Others suffer serious losses.

Here is information you need to assist your boss effectively in executing any stock transactions efficiently.

Dividends are paid to stockholders of record on the date announced by the company. A stock is traded "ex-dividend" after the payment date so a buyer will not receive that dividend.

Occasionally, companies offer their stockholders "stock dividends." In effect, the company issues sufficient new shares to increase each holder's amount by 5 or 10 percent, for example. Thus, if you owned 100 shares before the dividend, you will have 105 or 110 shares after the dividend.

Companies will also announce a "stock split," generally after the price of the stock has risen substantially. If the split is 2-for-1, you will own 200 shares instead of the 100 you started with. The normal reason for a split is to reduce the price per share, thus making it more attractive to potential buyers.

Note that your stock does not immediately increase in value after either a stock dividend or a stock split. This is because in effect, the company has diluted the value of a share either by issuing new stock or splitting the share.

In normal market trading, stocks are bought and sold through a broker who collects a commission on both transactions. In today's markets, brokers are divided into two categories: the "full service" broker who collects a full commission and presumably offers investment advice and other services to earn it, versus the "discount broker" who collects a smaller commission but executes only the buy and sell transaction with no collateral services.

To make buying and selling easier, stocks are traded in several different markets:

*The New York Stock Exchange.* This is where the giants of American industry are traded. To be admitted to trading, companies must be of a certain size with a large enough stock issue to make a reasonable market.

*The American Stock Exchange.* This is for smaller companies that can't meet NYSE requirements.

*Regional Stock Exchanges* (Midwest, Pacific, etc.). This is for smaller companies of regional interest.

*Over the Counter Stocks.* These are for companies listed on no exchange but with sufficient trading interest so shares are bought and sold regularly. Prices are furnished by the National Association of Securities Dealers.

## Other Equity-Type Investments

In addition to common stock, there are other ways to participate in the ownership of U.S. industry.

Preferred stock is issued for the conservative investor who wishes to limit his risk. Normally this class of stock pays a high fixed-rate dividend, but the holder generally has no voting rights and the price of his stock will not fluctuate with the fortunes of the company. Thus, he does not benefit from growth or increased profits.

A special class called "convertible preferred" may, under certain conditions, be converted into common stock.

## UNDERSTANDING AND WORKING WITH RIGHTS AND WARRANTS

Closely related to common stocks, rights and warrants are issued by companies to raise capital quickly.

Rights permit a purchaser to buy company stock for a short period of time at a favorable price (in comparison to current market price). These rights may be exercised or sold to others during the allotted period of time.

Warrants are similar to rights except that they are issued to cover longer periods up to a year or more. Both of these vehicles are highly speculative when traded because they are so sensitive to changes in the basic stock price.

## HOW TO WORK WITH STOCK OPTIONS

These are ways of betting on a stock's projected rise or fall in value over a short period of time. A "put" is an option to sell a specified number of shares at a specified price during a given period. A "call" is a similar option to buy.

Options are traded primarily by speculators but are also traded by conservative investors to hedge against market changes and generate cash.

## THE SAFETY OF CORPORATE BONDS

Traditionally, bonds have been preferred by conservative investors to earn the interest they pay. Rather than buying an interest in the company, the bond buyer is lending the corporation who issues the bonds money at a predetermined interest rate for a fixed period of time.

Bonds are generally issued in $1,000 denominations. Market prices are quoted in terms of the bond's par value as 100. If, for instance, the bond is quoted at 95, the price is $950 or if the price is 103½, the price is $1,035.

The interest rate is expressed in terms of par value. If a later buyer pays more than $1,000 for the bond, he receives less interest, but if he pays less, the interest return is higher.

Since 1982, registered bonds are the only legal forms of bonds available. The issuing corporation sends periodic interest payments to the registered owner.

## GOVERNMENT SECURITIES: THE ULTIMATE IN SAFETY

From one point of view, U.S. Government obligations are undoubtedly the safest type of security you can buy. Very few people question the government's ability to pay its obligations since it controls the money supply from which the securities are paid. This does not mean that these securities will yield the maximum return on your investment. During periods of high inflation in 1980, for instance, government bonds offering 8 percent interest were a poor investment when the inflation rate was 9 percent.

Government securities may be bought from or sold to the twelve Federal Reserve Banks across the U.S. A broker or your bank can handle these transactions.

Since there are so many different types of securities available, a little clarification is in order.

Treasury bills are short-term obligations. Thirteen and twenty-six-week bills are auctioned off weekly and fifty-two-week bills are sold once a month. These bills are sold at a discount from par value, the difference being the interest accruing to the buyer. Minimum denomination sold is $10,000.

Treasury notes are sold with maturity dates ranging from one to ten years. Denominations run from $1,000 minimum for four to ten years and $5,000 minimum for other maturity dates. Yields are similar to those from treasury bills.

For longer term investors, treasury bonds are sold with normal maturities from ten to twenty-five years. Their denominations run from $1,000 to $1 million.

Some of these obligations may be redeemed early by the government upon four months' notice to the owner. Thus, a bond, labelled 5½% of 1989-95 may be called at any time during that period.

## WHY TAX-EXEMPT BONDS ARE IMPORTANT

Although Federal Government obligations are very safe investments with good yields in most times, the income is taxable. One class of government bonds, however, is attractive primarily because of its tax-exempt status. These are the obligations of state, county, and municipal governments. They have been given this status to allow local governments to attract investor capital at a somewhat lower rate of interest.

Since interest rates are lower, these bonds are primarily of interest to taxpayers in the higher brackets where the tax savings offset the loss in interest.

The table below shows the benefits to a high-bracket taxpayer.

| If you are in this tax bracket | Tax-exempt bonds paying these interest rates: | | |
|---|---|---|---|
| | 8% | 9% | 10% |
| | will actually yield these equivalents: | | |
| 33% | 11.43 | 12.86 | 14.29 |
| 42% | 13.33 | 15.00 | 16.67 |
| 49% | 15.39 | 17.31 | 19.23 |

Note that tax bracket refers to the highest tax rate in the IRS tax tables to which an individual taxpayer is subject and not the percentage of income actually paid in taxes.

Any investor who is considering the purchase of tax-exempt bonds should pay careful attention to the quality of the obligations. Some municipal governments have teetered on the edge of bankruptcy in recent years and the Washington State Power Authority has defaulted on certain issues.

Some bond issues offer municipal bond insurance to purchasers upon payment of a single premium at the time of purchase.

## MUTUAL FUNDS PROVIDE SAFETY AND CONVENIENCE

This is a convenient way to collectively refer to the many investment companies and trusts formed to cater to the interests of investors with specific objectives.

Such a company sells shares of its stocks to investors and, in turn, invests the capital in securities that meet the interests and needs of its shareholders. If the managers of the fund are successful, the value of each share of stock increases. If the fund is not successful, the share value decreases.

The advantages to the investor of a mutual fund are threefold:

1) He benefits from the market expertise of the fund's managers.
2) He dilutes his investment risk by spreading it over a variety of securities.
3) By proper selection of a fund, he is able to channel his investment into an area of the market (stocks of growing companies, for instance) that has the most profit potential. Or he can select a fund with specific investment objectives that suit his own needs (investments in stocks offering high current income, for instance).

By law, mutual funds (investment companies) are required to distribute at least 90 percent of their income annually to their shareholders. The remaining portion is applied to operating expenses and overhead. In this way, the individual shareholder pays most of the taxes on the fund's income.

Funds may not invest more than 5 percent of their assets in any single company or own more than 10 percent of its shares.

The attraction of funds lies in their diversity. Some people invest in high-risk growth stocks, others in public utility stocks that pay high dividends but little change in share value. There are funds for government securities, low-priced stocks, precious metals, municipal bonds (tax-exempt), even funds for investing in the money markets.

You will hear funds described as "load" versus "no load" funds. The load refers to the sales commission (8–10 percent) payable on purchases thus deducted from the investment.

Because of the number of funds on the market, it is generally possible to select a fund that meets the investor's needs without paying the front end commission, and there is no appreciable difference in performance between load and no load funds.

Far and away the largest number of funds specialize in common stocks. This doesn't mean that all the fund's cash under management is completely invested in stocks at all times. During declining markets or periods of uncertainty, the fund managers may decide to invest in the money markets or other short-term securities to preserve capital until conditions improve.

Even the common stock funds are diversified. Some funds specialize in aggressive growth stocks with proportionate risk, and others in growth stocks with fewer risks. Some try to combine income and growth (*Remember:* income results from dividends paid; growth as the price of the stock increases), still others concentrate on stocks that produce income regularly.

Here is a partial listing of funds that fall into each category. Although these funds are typical, the list is by no means complete:

**Growth Funds**
Guardian Mutual
Sequoia Fund
T. Rowe Price Growth

**Growth and Income**
Fidelity Equity—Income
Pine Street
Windsor Fund

**Income**
Dreyfus Tax Exempt
Northeast Investors Trust
Wellesley Income

**Aggressive Growth**
Fidelity Magellan
Lindner Fund
Partners Fund

Note that most funds are restricted by their charters to pursue these stated objectives and are limited as to the amount of money they can invest in securities that don't conform to those objectives.

## WORKING WITH THE SPECIALIZED FUNDS

As time goes on, mutual funds are developed to meet more and more specific needs. Here are some of those:

*Money Market Funds*–These became especially popular during a period of very high interest rates, offering investors an opportunity to cash in on these rates with maximum flexibility and by investing relatively small dollar amounts.

Even though rates have declined substantially since 1975, money market funds have proven to be extremely popular places to leave money for short periods of time. Funds can be easily withdrawn by writing a check and interest rates are higher than those that savings accounts and short-term certificates of deposit offer.

For security-minded investors, there are also money market funds that concentrate on U.S. Government securities and still others that specialize in tax-exempts.

*Index Funds*—They are designed to follow the results of the Standard & Poor's 500 Composite Stock Price Index. In other words, the Fund attempts to duplicate the performance of the stock market as a whole. Since most stock funds attempt to outperform the market averages—and many of them succeed—it's difficult to understand the attraction of such funds.

*Managed Municipal Bond Funds*—Since 1976, it's been possible to pass on tax-exempt interest to shareholders so this new class of fund has grown up to offer managed investment in tax-free local government issues. Under capable management, such funds can be expected to minimize the hazards of such issues.

*Specialty Funds*—These concentrate on stocks in specific industry segments such as chemicals, high technology, metals, aerospace, etc. They cater to the interests of investors who have reason to specialize in these fields.

*Foreign Funds*—These enable investors to benefit from diversified holdings of stocks in foreign countries. Such companies as the Japan Fund and the Canadian Fund specialize by country, others diversify in various countries.

*Gold Funds*—During the period of high inflation in the mid-70s, investors turned toward shares in gold-mining companies as an inflation hedge. As inflation has declined, so have gold prices and mining stock prices.

## YOUR ROLE IN THE INVESTMENT PROCESS

So far we've concentrated on acquiring a short education in securities available to the investor. With this background you'll be able to understand your boss when he talks about investment and also be able to invest your own money better if the opportunity offers.

Just how far you'll be able to assist him in handling his investment program depends, of course, on the kind of help he asks for. But if you demonstrate your familiarity with the concepts, he may very well give you additional responsibilities as time goes on.

As we've indicated earlier, the successful handling of greater responsibility can lead you to positions commensurate with your new abilities—either within your own company or elsewhere.

Areas where you can help might include help with annual reports. Often reading a company's annual report is the first step toward investing. Your boss might ask you to obtain annual reports of companies he's interested in. Generally, this involves writing to or phoning the company's headquarters. Most companies will respond quickly since they're interested in promoting their own stock. You might also want to ask for Form 10-K, an addition to the report containing information required by the Securities and Exchange Commission. If it's a new issue, you may also get a prospectus or a Wall Street analyst's report.

Since your employer is a busy person, you may be asked to digest this information for him, particularly if there's a lot of it! So maybe you should know something about annual reports.

First of all, don't judge the report by its graphics. Beautiful pictures and fancy artwork won't increase the price of the stock by a nickel. Remember that the report is designed to impress the stockholders, so if the numbers aren't too good, the thinking is that maybe the pictures will distract the reader.

Generally the report opens with a letter to the stockholders from the chief executive officer. Its purpose is to summarize the previous year's events and forecast the business trend for the coming year. Disregard the flowery speeches and concentrate on the numbers. If you're told sales are up 15 percent, costs are down and profits are up 30 percent, take heart. If sales are up 5 percent and profits are down, watch out!

After the letter, you'll probably find a section describing the company's products, summarizing the performance of each division or business unit and perhaps something about its markets. This is important. If the company's markets are growing (aerospace, electronics), it may grow with them; if they're stagnant or declining (steel mills, chemicals, railroads), it may have to find new markets to replace them.

The numbers, however, are the key to the report. Normally, the report must include a balance sheet, income statement, accumulated retained earnings statement, source and application of funds statement, and an analysis of changes in working capital. Often the accounting firm that signs off on the report will include footnotes to the statements.

If you look at a typical balance sheet, it will normally be laid out with assets listed on the left and liabilities on the right.

Since assets represent what the company owns and liabilities what it owes, the difference must be the value of the company. For publicly-owned companies, that's called "stockholders' equity." On the balance sheet, assets are shown on the left and liabilities plus stockholders' equity on the right. Since both sides are equal, the sheet is in balance.

Here are definitions for the most common items listed on the balance sheet:

*Current Assets* (Those that can be readily turned into cash)

Cash—Money held by the company for payroll, accounts payable, etc. Includes cash in bank, short-term securities, and petty cash.

Marketable Securities—Stocks, bonds, and notes owned by the company, shown at cost.

Accounts Receivable—Money owed by customers.

Inventories—Raw materials, parts, finished goods, and supplies in stock.

### Fixed Assets

Land, Plant and Equipment—Generally shown at purchase cost.

Accumulated Depreciation—The cumulative loss in value of plant and equipment due to use.

Intangibles—The value of patents, franchises, etc.

Prepaid Expenses—Items paid for that will be used during the coming year.

Deferred Charges—Expenses added to the balance sheet rather than the income statement.

### Current Liabilities

Accounts Payable—Owed to vendors and suppliers.

Accrued Expenses—Unpaid taxes, wages, insurance, etc.

Notes and Loans Payable—Money owed to banks or creditors and payable within one year.

Long-term Debt Payable within One Year—Portion of long-term debts due within coming year.

Accrued Income Taxes—Payable in coming year.

### Long-Term Liabilities (Bonds issued by the company, notes, and bank debts payable in more than one year)

### Stockholders' Equity

Preferred Stock—Value of outstanding shares equal to number of shares times par value.

Common Stock—Par value.

Capital in Excess of Par Value—Value of stock over and above par.

Retained Earnings—Profit remaining after paying all dividends.

*Note:* The balance sheet figures are those taken from books at the end of the fiscal year. Most annual reports show figures from the previous as well as current year.

Much valuable information can be derived from a careful examination of the balance sheet. If assets increase from year to year, that's a healthy sign.

The ability of the company to pay its bills can be measured by the ratio of current assets to current liabilities. If the ratio is less than 1 to 1, the company has a problem. A ratio of 2 to 1 is considered satisfactory for most companies.

Working capital is the difference between current assets and liabilities. A growing company needs increased working capital from year to year.

Unduly large amounts of preferred stock and long-term debt may burden a company. If the stockholders' equity (without preferred stock) does not exceed long-term debt, the company may be unstable.

## HOW TO UNDERSTAND AN INCOME STATEMENT

In Chapter 3 we discussed both the balance sheet and the profit and loss statement. Now we turn to the income statement which is basically no different than the P & L Statement. It shows in capsule form, how well the company performed in the year of the report. The prior year is also reported on for the sake of comparison and some companies include a five-year condensed income history for information.

Here is a breakdown of the terms encountered in most income statements:

Net sales—Cash received in payment for the company's products or services less an allowance for returned material.

Cost of goods sold—Contains raw material costs, plant wages and salaries, maintenance costs, utilities plus factory overhead.

Depreciation—The charge for the current year that is added to the cumulative figure on the balance sheet.

Selling, general, and administrative expense—Those company expenses not involving manufacturing.

Interest expense—Paid to bondholders and other creditors.

The above expenses are subtracted from net sales to give "income before taxes." After income taxes are subtracted, the result is "net income."

Most reports show an additional figure: "net income per common share," which is obtained by dividing the current number of outstanding shares into net income.

Note that on the balance sheet and income statements for larger companies, the last three zeros are omitted when writing numbers in the millions to save space and make reading easier.

The income statement can yield some more obvious bits of information, particularly about the current year of operation. For instance, you can determine either the pre-tax or net profit margin if you divide either income figure by net sales. A 10 percent pre-tax profit margin is generally considered good performance, depending, of course, on the industry and the economic climate.

The stockholder is also interested in how much the company has earned on the stockholders' investment. That figure is obtained by dividing net income to the common stockholders (subtract any dividend payable on preferred stock from net income) by last year's stockholders' equity (see balance sheet). The resulting percentage should be greater than you could earn from bonds or a savings account to make the investment worthwhile.

### Other Information Sources in the Annual Report

The statement of retained earnings shows how much this quantity has increased or decreased during the year. Normally the increase comes from profits (after paying dividends). Increases in earnings help the company to grow and pay dividends.

The source and application of the funds statement shows where the company's money comes from and where it goes. A healthy company should be able to increase its working capital from year to year without resorting to increasing long-term debt.

The analysis of changes in working capital show where the money came from. Since working capital represents the difference between current assets and current liabilities, these are the figures analyzed. If the increase comes from inventory growth on accounts receivable, the capital available might be less than needed.

Although there is more information available in the annual report for the skilled financial analyst, these portions just discussed can form a basis for judgment even by financial novices.

## WHERE TO GET INVESTMENT ADVICE

It may be helpful to you if you know something about where your boss can get sound advice on investments.

Several kinds of information are available. Some sources will supply basic facts about a company and leave you to draw your own conclusions. More ambitious analysts will interpret the facts and provide specific advice for individual issues and groups of issues based on market facts and their own experience.

The individual investor can often, by using the market facts available from newspapers and magazines plus the more detailed information from other sources, make sound judgments on his own. Few businesspeople, however, have the time to make such detailed studies. This is why they turn to analysts and advisory services.

Here are some of the most widely-used information sources:

*Newspapers and Magazines*—A good deal of basic background information comes from such daily newspapers as the *New York Times, Washington Post,* and *Chicago Tribune.* The bigger papers carry daily price quotations from the various stock exchanges, over-the-counter markets, and on bonds and mutual funds. Quarterly earnings reports for the larger companies as well as news of mergers and acquisitions and treasury issues are included.

For more detailed daily financial information, *The Wall Street Journal* is available.

Such weekly magazines as *Forbes* and *Business Week* supply news of company developments, growth, and financial problems for the investor.

*Standard & Poor's and Moody's*—These financial publishers furnish standard references on financial history, market trends, earnings reports, and annual report summaries for companies listed on the major exchanges and some over-the-counter stocks. Their information is so detailed that they are used primarily by investors who do their own research. Both companies provide ratings for both corporate and government bond offerings. Although subscriptions for their services are expensive, most libraries carry the information for reference purposes.

*Stockbrokers*—Their advisory service depends heavily on the quality of their own research. The larger firms publish studies of the market, industry groups, and individual companies. Since they live on commissions, they may stress trading rather than long-term investments.

*Banks*—Many of them are now able to act as brokers, but their strongest suit is their custodial service that will take possession of securities, keep accounting records, and execute transactions all at the investor's direction. Banks are not noted for their investment advice since it tends to be extremely conservative.

*Advisory services*—All types and varieties exist, from sensation-seeking individuals who are either prophets of doom or highly optimistic.

The more reliable services such as Value Line, United Business, United Mutual Fund Selector, and Dow Theory Forecasts all depend on good research and a reputation for reliability, which does not, however, make them omniscient.

## HOW TO HANDLE SECURITIES TRANSACTIONS

One of the ways that a secretary can be of most help to a boss is in facilitating the transactions involving securities: buying, selling, physical storage, conveyance, etc. To handle these tasks, it will be helpful to know a little about stock and bond markets and their workings.

Since most investors buy and sell securities in the open market, we'll limit our discussion to the various stock exchanges and the over-the-counter market.

On the exchanges, buyers and sellers (or their representatives) trade shares in an auction. The largest and most prestigious is the New York Stock

Exchange. Only members of the Exchange, which include brokerage firms, floor brokers, specialists, and registered traders are allowed to participate.

Brokerage firms buy and sell for their customers and sometimes for their own account.

Specialists make the market work for the stocks they are responsible for. They ensure that their stocks are always available at fair prices, sometimes by buying or selling them themselves.

Floor brokers assist brokerage firms when necessary to keep them from being swamped with orders when the market is busy.

Registered traders help keep the market liquid by buying and selling for their own account.

The American Stock Exchange works in a similar fashion except that it deals with stocks of smaller and newer companies.

In addition to these exchanges, there are smaller regional exchanges that handle stocks important to the particular geographic area.

A very large number of stocks (primarily smaller companies) are traded by brokers and dealers among themselves in the over-the-counter market.

## Understanding the Types of Investment Orders You Can Place

There are several ways investors can place their orders to buy and sell. Most often, a market order is placed with the broker. The broker then tries to buy at the lowest current price or sell at the highest price.

With a market order, the transaction can be completed immediately although the exact price is not guaranteed. You can be sure of not missing a market increase or decrease.

Limit orders are placed at a pre-determined price. The order is not executed by the specialist until the stock reaches that price. Sometimes, of course, that never happens but you are always sure of the price for the stock.

Stop loss orders require that the stock be bought or sold when it reaches a given price. They are used to prevent excessive losses.

Day orders are good for one day only.

Open orders are placed for a specified time period.

Occasionally, investors will place discretionary orders leaving the brokers to decide when to buy or sell. These orders must be placed in writing.

## How to Pick a Securities Broker

The basic choice is between a full service and a discount broker. If your boss is starting on an investment program, he may have to rely heavily on the broker at the outset just to learn the ropes. In that case, the full service broker can offer investment advice and financial guidance as well as storing stock certificates, handling dividend checks, and executing special transactions. The full service broker can also assist with tax shelters, Keogh and IRA plans, money market funds, and insurance programs.

If a full service broker is chosen, choose one who is a member firm in the New York Stock Exchange as well as the legally required account protection insurance.

Discount brokers, on the other hand, have cut out all extra services and run low overhead offices so they are able to offer lower commissions rates on stock transactions than the full service type. For knowledgeable, sophisticated investors who simply need representation in buying and selling securities, discount brokers perform a valuable service at very reasonable cost.

## How to Protect Securities

Safeguarding securities after they're bought is a concern of every investor. If you wish, the broker will send stock certificates to the owner to be held. This method ensures that the owner can always lay hands on his possessions when they're needed. If stocks are to be held for some time, this method is quite satisfactory.

However, the certificates must be stored in a safe place; this is generally a safe deposit box. If they are sold or used as loan collateral they must be removed and transferred to the broker or lender.

To avoid this inconvenience, many investors turn over their certificates to a bank or lawyer for custody. To transfer shares under custody, a stock power is signed and sent to the custodian.

A full service broker can hold your securities in your name. He can execute transactions upon receipt of a stock power.

Investors who trade frequently often use street accounts, where securities are held in the broker's name and can be transferred without endorsement.

It is wise to choose a reputable established broker in any case, but most particularly when he has custody of the investor's shares. In case of financial difficulty or insolvency, it may take time and paperwork to recover this property.

To protect investors, the Securities Investor Protection Corporation (a government agency) requires brokers to carry insurance that protects customers for losses up to $500,000.

If securities are lost or destroyed, the process for recovery is long, time-consuming, and expensive. As a secretary, you can help expedite this process by keeping careful record of certificate numbers and location of all your employer's securities.

Now that you have a reasonable understanding of the stock markets, how brokers operate, and how securities are handled, you can be of real value in handling the details of any investment program.

# CHAPTER 9

# How to Master Real Estate and Insurance Transactions

Since real estate is a subject of importance to the executive, it follows that the secretary should be reasonably familiar with the principles, terminology, and transactions involved.

Real estate is important to the businessperson in several ways. First of all, the land and buildings needed to operate the business may be bought, sold, or leased. If the business expands, more land and buildings may be needed. Branches, retail outlets, franchise stores, and other facilities require land and buildings.

Companies and individuals also invest in real estate for business purposes or simply for gain.

Again, for the secretary, the benefit of acquiring skill in real estate transactions, math, and terminology lies in better service to the employer and prospects for advancement.

## TEN IMPORTANT REAL ESTATE CONCEPTS

- Real property consists of land and whatever structures are built on the land, provided the structures are intended to be permanent. It encompasses minerals that lie under the surface and limited rights to the air above.

- Fixtures are items incorporated into the structure and intended to be permanent. They thus become part of the real property. However, fixtures installed by a tenant to carry on his business may be removed and are thus personal property.

- Contractual rights are those that convey certain capabilities to the parties to a contract. A lease, for instance, gives the tenant the right to control and possess real property. A mortgage gives rights to both parties. Both such contracts are personal property items.

- Title is held by the owner of real property; it confers full control and possession as well as the capability of challenging in court any infringement of rights.

- Easement is a right to use part of the land for right of way or other purposes. For example, the local government may have an easement to install sidewalks or the telephone company to install wires.

- Contract is an agreement to sell real property. A contract is reached when the buyer makes an offer that is accepted by the seller. Terms agreed to by both parties must be included in writing. The contract also includes a description of the property, the selling price, the instrument of conveyance (deed, land contract, etc.), evidence of title, survey, encumbrances (easements, building restrictions, mortgages, leases, etc.). A time for closing the transaction is also required.

- Deed is a written document conveying title to real property.

- Mortgage pledges real property as security for a debt. Generally the debt is incurred in payment for the property.

- Lien expresses the right of a creditor to sell the property of a debtor if he fails to pay the creditor as agreed.

- Lease is a contract in which the property owner (lessor) delivers control and possession in return for rent paid by the tenant (lessee).

## HOW TO UNDERSTAND AND WORK WITH INVESTMENT PROPERTY

The primary advantage to the investor of real estate is that the land supply is fixed while the demand grows. As the population grows, it requires more housing as well as commercial establishments to meet its needs and industry to provide jobs.

As the population grows wealthier, there are demands for resort property and vacation homes, not to mention new highways to reach these facilities.

Because of these demands, real estate becomes an excellent hedge against inflation because its value grows faster than inflation. Because of its intrinsic value, it has excellent borrowing power. Loans up to 75 percent of its value are often made.

In judging the value of a real estate investment, consideration must be given to the future income it can produce. The term "cash flow" is used to describe the continuing income from real estate. The ability to generate cash flow is based on what has been achieved in the past and how stable the flow will be in the future as well as prospects for growth.

The amount of money required for a real estate investment is often smaller than that for other ventures simply because so much of the purchase price can be borrowed. The loan is, of course, secured by the property itself. But if the value of the property or the income increases, the investor gets the full benefit.

This use of debt to finance property is called "leverage." How well it works depends on the difference between income and the cost of borrowing.

## SELECTING A REAL ESTATE INVESTMENT

A real estate investment trust is one way that small investors may buy for investment purposes. The trust operates much like a mutual fund for stocks except that shareholders' money is invested in real estate. By law, at least 95 percent of annual income must be distributed to its shareholders.

Until recently, buying a home was one of the most popular methods of real estate investment. However, in the recent past, escalation of prices for homes plus higher mortgage rates have driven many people out of the market.

Since the purchase of a home is one of the biggest investments most people will make, it is one that requires great care, particularly in view of prices and mortgage rates. The average family must make a substantial financial commitment that will last 20 or 30 years. Obviously, the property must retain its suitability for the family and its market value for at least that period of time.

Three factors are involved in selecting a home either for personal use or as an investment:

Site

Building

Location

Since the land is a major portion of the price, the building site is a key consideration. The size of the house with relation to the lot, lot size, location on the lot, privacy, and grading all influence site suitability.

The building must be large enough to fit the family's present and future size. Efficiency of layout, size of rooms, storage space, type of heating, and other features add or detract from the house's desirability.

The location is important for the present and future of a residential estate. Ideally, for most people, the home should be situated in an area of buildings similar in age, size, and appearance. It should be convenient to transportation, shopping, schools, parks, and playgrounds. In locating a new home, consideration must be given to the development of the area, its rate and type of growth. In older neighborhoods, the possible decline in property value as commercial development encroaches should be taken into account. Even though buying a home is a very personal decision, rising real estate values can make it a sound investment as well when the house is outgrown or the time for retirement approaches.

Commercial real estate entails similar considerations but on a broader scale. The user is interested in a site closely related to the market he or she serves. For example, a retail store must be convenient and accessible to the largest number of customers and a doctor wants to be close to his patients and a hospital. The investor has to bear these interests in mind when choosing a location. Regardless of the type of business involved there are a number of factors involved in choosing a sound business location.

## SIX CRITICAL POINTS FOR CHOOSING A SOUND BUSINESS LOCATION

- Community information has the widest influence from an environmental standpoint on the area surrounding it. This information should include form of government, zoning and other restrictions, quality of fire and police protection, educational system, hospitals, street and road conditions, ethnic composition, and recreational facilities. Also important is information on newspapers, TV, and radio stations.

- The economic base should include information on number of business firms and people employed, payroll, amount of bank deposits, assessed property valuation, taxation, and amount of new construction. Just as important is the trend of employment, bank deposits, new companies, etc.

- Population data on rate of growth or decline should also be considered. These include seasonal population shifts in resort areas, consumer shopping habits, and size of area they come from.

- Traffic data is important particularly for businesses dependent on drive-in customers (discount houses, furniture stores, restaurants, etc.).

- Site information should include availability of utilities on a favorable basis (electric, gas, water, phone, and sewerage), necessary parking space in proportion to the total, satisfactory financial terms, the number and quality of competitive enterprises.
- Factors that can influence a site adversely include smoke, dust, and noise, poor sidewalks and streets, and a deteriorating neighborhood.

## NINE POINTS TO CONSIDER WHEN EVALUATING INDUSTRIAL REAL ESTATE

Industrial real estate involves choices even more complex than those for commercial. An investor planning to purchase land for industrial development must base his decision on a series of basic considerations. These include:

sites available

labor market

industrial fuel—power and water supply

transportation facilities

availability of raw materials

market and distribution facilities

living conditions

present tax structure and availability of tax relief

climate

Beyond these, the condition of the site itself becomes critical based on other physical factors.

## EIGHT PHYSICAL FACTORS IN SITE SELECTION

topography and soil conditions

drainage

sanitary conditions

rail and truck service

local streets and interstate highways

telephone service

airline connections

water, gas and electric power

Finally, to make the selected area favorable for industrial development, it must be located in a community that has planned for industrial growth. Such growth usually attracts related personnel, services, and supplies for which provisions should be made in a master plan.

## EVERYTHING YOU NEED TO KNOW TO SELECT CO-OPS AND CONDOMINIUMS WISELY

Cooperatives and condominiums have become an important factor in the real estate market, particularly in urban areas. The trend has been accelerated by the boom in buying of private homes that has driven prices up sharply. They are generally thought of in terms of apartments or cluster housing.

The cooperative is generally a corporation with shareholders who occupy its buildings. They pay monthly fees covering each one's share of taxes, mortgage payments, and maintenance costs.

Shareholders are entitled to lease the property they occupy from the corporation. Since leases all expire simultaneously, shareholders as a group can decide on the future of the co-op at expiration time. Furthermore, the group may limit the resale of stock to a buyer they approve.

Co-ops should be cheaper than rental housing since there is no landlord profit, but the tenant has no real property rights although his equity in the corporation increases as the mortgage is paid off. Generally, the tenant may deduct his share of real estate taxes and mortgage interest from his income tax.

Condominiums, on the other hand, provide for individual ownership of the space occupied as well as a share of the land and facilities used in common with other occupants.

The condominium form of ownership that originated in Europe has spread rapidly in the U.S., particularly in urban areas. At present, they are offered in apartment buildings, garden apartments, detached single-family homes, town houses, office buildings, industrial plants and parks, even ski resorts, golf clubs, and marinas.

Each owner receives a deed to his or her property and pays taxes on the property owned including a share of common areas.

When the condominium group is formed, the prospective owners prepare an agreement covering maintenance costs, building management, and any restrictions on the right of resale.

The condo owner has several advantages over the renter. First of all, he or she gradually acquires an equity in the property. Also, a share of property taxes and interest on the mortgage are tax deductible. The owner avoids rent increases and the value of his property may increase in time. Generally, the costs of ownership are less than the costs of renting.

There are also advantages over co-ops. The co-op lease provides no ownership and the tenants' resale rights are more restricted.

The condo owner enjoys all the tax advantages of a homeowner. If a co-op tenant defaults on his rent payments, other tenants are required to meet the obligation. The condo owner negotiates his own mortgage and has no responsibility for other owners' debts.

In view of the growing housing shortage, the future for condominium real estate looks bright, particularly for living space but also for office, commercial, and industrial use.

## BUYING RESORT AND RECREATION PROPERTY

Resort real estate is yet another growth area. In spite of the recent energy crisis, Americans are turning to travel and second resort homes.

This trend has benefited the recreational vehicle industry, motels and hotels, and property in seaside and mountain areas.

Vacation condominiums are a growing element in resort real estate. Investors who rent their condos part-time can deduct insurance, repairs, maintenance, and depreciation for the rental period, and can look forward to a capital gain upon resale.

This overview of real estate investment provides a background for the secretary interested in assisting the boss with an investment program. In addition, it gives a perspective for her own investment objectives.

In addition, a group of math principles used in real estate may be helpful. For that reason, we've included some basic examples here.

## UNDERSTANDING THE MATH OF REAL ESTATE

### How to Figure Profit and Loss

Let's first talk about the profit or loss in a simple real estate transaction. Normally the expressed return is based on cost.

Since we're talking about percentages, the profit (or loss) can be expressed as:

Profit = cost × rate of profit, or
P = BR (rate of profit = percent of profit)

**Example:** If a house sells at a profit of 30 percent of cost and that cost is $60,000, how much is the profit in dollars?

*Answer:* P = BR = 60,000 × .30 = $18,000 profit

A loss is computed the same way: If a house sells at a loss of 20 percent of the cost, how much is the loss if the cost is $50,000?

*Answer:* Loss = BR = $50,000 × .20 = $10,000

If you know the cost and profit, you can easily figure the selling price by adding profit to cost. From the first example:

$60,000 + $18,000 = $78,000 selling price

Knowing cost and loss, you can figure the selling price by subtracting the loss from cost:

$50,000 − $10,000 = $40,000 selling price

We can use a handy shortcut to get the selling price if we know the cost and rate of profit (or loss). If profit is based on cost, then cost equals 100 percent. If profit is 30 percent (first example) then the selling price would be 100% + 30% of the cost or

$$\begin{aligned} \text{Selling price} &= \text{cost} \times (100\% + \text{profit}) \\ &= \text{cost} \times (1 + \text{rate of profit}) \\ &= \$60,000 \times (1 + .30) \\ &= \$60,000 \times 1.3 \\ &= \$78,000 \end{aligned}$$

## How to Compute the Rate of Profit

To find the rate or percent of profit (or loss), start with the equation

$$P = BR \text{ and solve for R}$$
$$R = \frac{P}{B}$$

Stated otherwise, the rate of profit is the ratio of profit to cost.

**Example:** If a house is bought for $60,000 (cost) and sold for $78,000, what is the rate of profit?

*Answer:* Profit = 78,000 − 60,000 = $18,000

$$R = \frac{18,000}{60,000} = \frac{18}{60} = \frac{3}{10} = .3 = 30\%$$

Finding cost. In this case, the equation is solved for B (base or cost)

$$B = \frac{P}{R}$$

**Example:** If a house sells at a profit of $6,000 and the rate of profit is 10 percent, what's the cost?

$$Answer:\ B = \frac{P}{R} = \frac{6,000}{.10} = \$60,000$$

The same procedure may be used if the property is sold at a loss.

If the selling price is known as well as the profit percentage, cost can be found by using P in the formula for selling price. But the rate must be changed correspondingly. If cost is 100 percent then the selling price is 100% + 10%. The formula then becomes:

$$Cost = \frac{Selling\ Price}{1 + Rate} \text{ or (using the example above)}$$

$$Cost = \frac{66,000}{1.1} = \$60,000$$

If there is a loss on the sale, the formula becomes:

$$Cost = \frac{Selling\ Price}{1 - Rate}$$

## How to Compute Commissions

Commissions on the sale of real estate are an important part of the transactions since they can materially affect the amount of return.

Normally, the commission is figured as a percentage of the gross sales price for property or percentage of gross rental on a lease.

The computation of commission is again, a simple percentage problem.

Commission = Gross Selling Price × Rate of Commission,
or C = SR

The formula can be used to find the sales price if the commission and rate are known. First, the basic formula C=SR must be solved for S:

$$S = \frac{C}{R}, \text{ then using the example above,}$$

$$S = \frac{8750}{.07} = \$125,000$$

Again by solving for R in the formula, we can find the commisson rate if we know the sales price and commission amount:

$$C = SR, \text{ and solving for R, } R = \frac{C}{S}$$

**Example:** If a house sells for $80,000 and the commission is $6,400, what's the rate?

$$Answer: R = \frac{6,400}{80,000} = 0.08 = 8\%$$

Commissions are sometimes paid on a graduated scale, particularly for long-term leases where the rental may change.

**Example:** A thirty-year lease is negotiated by a broker at an annual figure of $15,000 for the first fifteen years and $12,000 for the second fifteen-year period. A commission rate of 5 percent for the first two years, 3 percent for the next five and 1 percent for the remaining term of the lease is agreed on. Complete the total commission.

First 2 years:   $C = SR = 2 \times 15,000 \times .05 = \$1,500$
Next 5 years:    $C = 7 \times 15,000 \times .03 = \$3,150$
Next 8 years:    $C = 8 \times 15,000 \times .01 = \$1,200$
Last 15 years:   $C = 15 \times 12,000 \times .01 = \$1,800$
Total commission:   $= 1,500 + 3,150 + 1,200 + 1,800 = 7,650$

Commissions are sometimes split between the salesperson and the broker who employs him or between brokers who cooperate on a sale. If the commission split is 50/50, the computation is quite simple, but if the split is 40/60 for instance, it's generally easier to convert each commission to a portion of the gross.

**Example:** If a house is sold for $120,000 with a commission rate of 8 percent, which is split 40/60 between salesperson and broker, how much does each earn?
   *Answer:*

Salesperson's commission $= 40\%$ of $8\% = .4 \times .08 = .032$
Broker's commission:   $= 60\% \times 8\% = .6 \times .08 = .048$
Amount of commission   $= 120,000 \times .08 = \$9,600$
Salesperson's share   $= 120,000 \times .032 = \$3,840$
Broker's share   $= 120,000 \times .048 = \$5,760$

## HOW TO UNDERSTAND MORTGAGES

The detailed math involved in mortgage financing is necessarily complex. However, we'll discuss some of the simpler mortgage types and show how tables are used to simplify more complex calculations.

Normally, mortgage payments are made in two parts. One part pays the interest due at the date of payment on the unpaid balance of the loan. The other part pays a portion of the loan so that at the end of the mortgage term, the loan is completely paid. This process is called "amortization."

The first and simplest type of mortgage makes no provision for amortization. Instead it provides for regular payments of interest and repayment of the loan either in full at the end of the term or, if agreed to, in installments.

Payment calculations are relatively simple.

**Example:** A $15,000 simple mortgage at 9 percent interest is to be repaid in five years. Interest payments are due every six months on the unpaid balance. Repayment of the principal is to be made annually in five equal installments of $3,000. Calculate the first, third, and last interest payments.

*Answer:* For the first payment, the unpaid balance is $15,000, the interest due is on $15,000 at 9 percent for six months—

$$\text{Interest} = 15,000 \times \frac{.09}{2} = \$675$$

For the third payment, the unpaid balance is $12,000

$$\text{Interest} = 12,000 \times \frac{.09}{2} = \$540$$

For the last payment, the unpaid balance is $3,000

$$\text{Interest} = 3,000 \times \frac{.09}{2} = \$135$$

Such mortgages are used infrequently today except for short-term periods and smaller amounts of money.

Amortized mortgages, where equal monthly payments are made for the life of the mortgage, are far and away the most widely used in today's market. In the beginning, interest makes up the largest part of the payment with a small contribution to the principal. Toward the end of the mortgage term, the payment is mostly principal with a small amount of interest.

In recent years, partially amortized mortgages have become more popular, particularly on the west coast. In this case, only a part of the principal is paid off during the life of the mortgage, the rest coming due in a "balloon" payment at the end of the term.

Home buyers were attracted to these loans by lower payments and the concept that property values would increase sufficiently during the mortgage term that refinancing would be easy. Unfortunately, rising interest rates and declines in property values on the west coast caused many people to lose their homes.

The more common fully amortized loan is paid in equal installments spread over the life of the mortgage. A system known as "Constant Annual Percent" is used to determine the amount paid each year to satisfy the loan.

The work necessary to recompute the interest and principal payment each year would be tedious and complex. Instead, Constant Annual Percent tables have been prepared for various principal amounts, interest rates and mortgage terms. A portion of such a table is shown below:

| Interest Rate | 15 | 20 | 25 | 30 ◄── Term |
|---|---|---|---|---|
| 8% | 11.47 | 10.04 | 9.27 | 8.81 |
| 9 | 12.18 | 10.80 | 10.08 | 9.66 |
| 10 | 12.90 | 11.59 | 10.91 | 10.54 |
| 11 | 13.64 | 12.39 | 11.77 | 11.43 |

The figures in the table show the percentage of the principal that must be paid off each year to retire the loan.

**Example:** How much is the annual payment of interest and principal required to retire a $50,000 twenty-year mortgage at 10%?

*Answer:* From the table, the percentage for 20 years at 10 percent is 11.59.

Mortgage Amount × Constant Annual Percent = Annual Payment
50,000 × .1159 = $5,795

To establish the monthly mortgage payment, this figure is divided by twelve:

5,795 ÷ 12 = $482.92

## MASTERING THE MATH OF REAL ESTATE INSURANCE

Since the whole subject of insurance was covered at length in earlier chapters, we'll limit our discussion here to insurance as related to the subject of real estate.

Fire insurance is a fundamental topic in real estate. A property owner needs fire insurance protection against loss of home or business not only after he takes possession but also during the time between signing a contract and closing. The institution holding the mortgage also requires to have its interest in the property protected.

Single fire insurance policies have largely been replaced by package policies (such as Homeowners'), which cover a number of risks. However, the terminology involved is similar.

The cost of insurance for a specified period of time is called the "premium." Normally the period is one to three years. The premium is calculated by multiplying the insurance rate by the face value (amount of coverage) of the policy.

Establishing rates is a complicated procedure using the laws of probability and statistics. For the most part they are established by rating bureaus operating in each state or group of states.

To compute the premium, use the following formula:

$$\text{Premium} = \text{Rate} \times \text{Insurance Amount (face value)}$$

The rate is expressed as a cost per \$100 of coverage; for example: 75 cents per \$100. In the formula it is convenient to write it as a ratio:

$$\frac{.75}{100}$$

Here is an example of a premium computation: If a home needs to be insured for \$85,000 and the rate is 65 cents per \$100, what's the premium?
*Answer:*

$$P = RA \quad \text{or}$$

$$P = \frac{.65}{100} \times 85,000 = \$552.50$$

Three-year policies generally earn a discount of 10 percent to 20 percent. To compute this discount, multiply the annual premium by three and subtract 10 percent. Using the previous example (discount is 10%):

$$552.50 \times 3 = \$1657.50$$
$$1657.50 \times .1 = \$165.75$$
$$1657.50 - 165.75 = \$1491.75 \text{ net premium}$$

If the premium and the face value are known, the rate of insurance can be found by solving the equation $P = RA$ for R:

$$R = \frac{P}{A}$$

Here's an example: If a building is insured for $175,000 and the premium is $822.50, what is the rate?

$$R = \frac{822.50}{175,000} = 0.0047$$

This is the rate per dollar and must be multiplied by 100 to give the rate per $100:

$$0.0047 \times 100 = .47 \text{ per } \$100.$$

Again, if the premium and rate are unknown, the face value can be calculated by rearranging the formula.

$$A = \frac{P}{R}$$

**Example:** If a shopping center is insured at a premium of $4,950 and the rate is 90 cents per $100, what is the total amount of insurance?

$$A = \frac{P}{R} = \frac{4950}{\frac{.9}{100}} = \frac{495,000}{.9} = \$550,000$$

Since few property owners are willing to pay the full cost of insuring their property, the tendency is to underinsure somewhat, on the theory that some value will remain after the casualty.

Insurance companies, on the other hand, insist that if the property is underinsured, the insurance party must share in any loss. In Chapter Three, we discussed the subject of co-insurance and this is an extension of that subject.

Almost all fire insurance policies contain a co-insurance clause that states that the insured party must carry sufficient insurance to equal a fixed percentage (usually 80 percent) of the full value of the property. Otherwise he bears a certain amount of responsibility for the insurance. In other words, he becomes a co-insuror and in case of loss he will only be compensated in proportion to the amount of insurance carried in relation to the amount required (80 percent of full value).

To compute that amount, this formula is used:

$$\text{Amount paid} = \text{actual loss} \times \frac{\text{insurance carried}}{\text{insurance required}}$$

Here's an example: A property valued at $140,000 is covered by a policy with a face value of $90,000 with an 80 percent co-insurance clause. The property is damaged to the extent of $60,000. What kind of settlement can be expected from the insurance company?

*Answer:* Required insurance is 80 percent of $140,000 or $140,000 \times 0.8 = $112,000.

$$\text{Amount paid} = 60,000 \times \frac{90,000}{112,000} = \$48,214$$

Note that if insurance carried had amounted to $112,000, the claim would be paid in full.

When a company carries fire insurance on its property with several other insurance companies, it is said to use contributing insurance. In this way, the risk is spread among several companies. Each company is liable for that amount of the loss proportional to its coverage in relationship to the total amount of insurance and provided the 80 percent clause is met.

To compute any of the participating companies' loss share, the following formula is used:

$$\text{Share of Loss} = \text{Loss Amount} \times \frac{\text{Policy Amount}}{\text{Total Insurance Carried}}$$

The following example shows the formula at work.

A shopping center has policies with four different companies, each with an 80 percent co-insurance clause. The center is valued at $1,250,000 and the insurance is split as follows: Company A, $300,000; Company B, $275,000; Company C, $400,000; Company D, $150,000. A fire caused $460,000 in damage. Is the owner fully covered? If so, what is each company's share of the loss?

*Answer:* Insurance required to meet 80 percent clause:

$$\$1,250,000 \times .8 = \$1,000,000$$

Total coverage: $300,000 + 275,000 + 400,000 + 150,000 = \$1,125,000$

Coverage is complete.

$$\text{Co. A share} = 460,000 \times \frac{300,000}{1,125,000} = \$122,667$$

$$\text{Co. B share} = 460,000 \times \frac{275,000}{1,125,000} = \$112,444$$

$$\text{Co. C share} = 460,000 \times \frac{400,000}{1,125,000} = \$163,556$$

$$\text{Co. D share} = 460,000 \times \frac{150,000}{1,125,000} = \$61,333$$

The total amount of shares adds up to $460,000, so the owner is compensated in full.

If either the insurance company or the insured party cancels the insurance before the end of the term of coverage, the company must determine its earned premium.

When the company cancels, it can, by law, retain only that amount of premium that will cover the time the policy was in force. This is called "pro rata cancellation."

Here's how it works:

If a one-year policy with a premium of $280 went into effect on April 7 and was cancelled by the insurance company on November 10, what portion of the premium does the company retain?

*Answer:* First calculate the number of days the policy was in force:

$$\text{April 7 to November 10} = 218 \text{ or } \frac{218}{365} \text{ year}$$

$$\frac{218}{365} \times 280 = \$167.23 \text{ earned premium.}$$

When the insured party cancels, short-rate cancellation is used (this also applies when insurance is bought for a period of less than a year). Short-term rates are figured by the insurance company to include a small penalty.

## HOW TO MANAGE THE MATH OF REAL ESTATE TAXES

Although this subject was covered briefly in an earlier section, here we will also discuss how tax rates are calculated.

Real estate taxes are collected by various governmental units, most often by state, county, or municipal elements. The amount of the tax is established by the tax rate.

It is based on the total value of the taxable real estate in the area being taxed. That amount is called the "assessed valuation" and it in turn is based on a value established by appraisal of each piece of property. The assessed valuation is a percentage of appraised value.

When the community decides how much money it needs to operate in the forthcoming year, it estimates a tax rate using the following formula:

$$\text{Tax Rate} = \frac{\text{Required Amount}}{\text{Assessed Valuation}}$$

For example: If a town wants to raise $1,575,000 in taxes and the assessed valuation of its property is $48,275,620, what must be the tax rate?

$$\text{Tax rate} = \frac{1,575,000}{48,275,620}$$

$$= 0.0326251$$

To make this number easier to use, some of the digits are dropped and the last figure kept is raised to the next highest value.

For added convenience, the tax rate is often expressed in terms of hundreds of dollars of assessed valuation. If the rate just computed is multiplied by 100 it becomes:

$$\$3.26 \text{ per } \$100$$

At one time or another, the assessed value of a piece of property must be determined by a tax appraiser. Sometimes, the appraiser values the property at the current market price using a predetermined tax ratio to establish the assessed valuation. This ratio is a percentage of market value in the range of 40 percent to 70 percent.

Going back to the formula for tax rates, we can determine assessed valuation if we know the amount of taxes and the tax rate:

$$\text{Assessed Valuation} = \frac{\text{Tax}}{\text{Tax Rate}}$$

As an example: If a home is taxed at $2,210 per year and the tax rate is $3.40 per $100, what is the assessed valuation?

*Answer:*

$$\text{A.V.} = \frac{2210}{.034} = \$65,000$$

If we need to find the taxes payable and know the assessed valuation, we can rewrite the formula.

$$\text{Tax Payable} = \text{Assessed Value} \times \text{Tax Rate}$$

Here's an example: What are the taxes on a property with an assessed valuation of $52,000 and a tax rate of $2.75 per $100?

*Answer:*

$$\begin{aligned}
\text{Tax} &= \$52,000 \times .0275 \\
&= \$1,430
\end{aligned}$$

If we want to use the $2.75 per $100 directly we can divide 52,000 by 100 and write the equation:

$$\begin{aligned}
\text{Tax} &= 520 \times 2.75 \\
&= 1,430
\end{aligned}$$

# CHAPTER 10

# More Math Shortcuts to Save You Time and Effort

Here are a number of additional shortcuts that will make your use of arithmetic in your daily work easier. We've concentrated on such basic subjects as addition and subtraction, percentages and proportions.

Some of these basic operations can be tedious and time-consuming. Here's how to speed them up.

## ADDITION SHORTCUTS

### How to Speed Up Addition With Repeated Numbers in the Same Column

Certain types of numbers tend to repeat digits, particularly in the hundred and thousand-dollar columns. These include payroll, statistics, averages, and performance figures. For instance, the number of miles covered by a salesperson covering a regular route every week might vary by only a few miles each week. If you were asked to figure the average number of miles covered by the salesperson during a ten-week period, the problem might look like this:

| Week of | Miles Traveled |
|---------|----------------|
| 5/3     | 695            |
| 5/10    | 702            |
| 5/17    | 698            |
| 5/24    | 712            |
| 5/31    | 684            |
| 6/7     | 705            |
| 6/14    | 720            |
| 6/21    | 691            |
| 6/28    | 689            |
| 7/5     | 694            |

Obviously, to get the average, you will have to add up the column of miles traveled and divide by ten. Before you start, note that each week's totals are similar. Thus in the tens column, 9 appears four times and 8 twice. In the hundreds column, 6 appears six times and 7 shows up four times. As you add each column, multiply these figures by the number of times they appear, rather than adding them individually (6, 12, 18, 24, etc.). Your job becomes much easier:

| | | | |
|---|---|---|---|
| Total of Units Column | | | 40 |
| Total of Tens Column | $9 \times 4 = 36$ | | |
| | $8 \times 2 = 16$ | | |
| Other Digits | 0 | | |
| | 1 | | |
| | 0 | | |
| | 2 | | |
| | 55 | 55 | |
| Total of Hundreds Column | $6 \times 6 = 36$ | | |
| | $7 \times 4 = 28$ | | |
| | 64 | 64 | |
| | | 6,990 | |

If we divide 6,990 by 10, the average number of miles per week is 699.

If you are dealing with long columns it may be difficult to carry the multiplications in your head. If you use a piece of scratch paper, you will still save time over doing the addition digit by digit.

### How to Add Long Columns of Large Numbers Without Mistakes

When faced with the task of adding large numbers in long columns, it's pretty easy to lose your place or forget to carry the right number. You can keep your place easily and eliminate the carrying problem by using the method accountants use. Add each column, record the result. Then add the next column and record the result under the first but moved one place to the left.

Here's how it works: You're asked to total the quarterly sales figures of eight districts. They are:

| District | Quarterly Sales |
|:--------:|:---------------:|
| 1 | $462,785. |
| 2 | 604,112. |
| 3 | 712,006. |
| 4 | 561,475. |
| 5 | 621,892. |
| 6 | 491,642. |
| 7 | 512,817. |
| 8 | 772,015. |

You can start by adding columns from the left or right. If you wish, you can check your results by starting on the opposite side a second time. Here's what starting from the right side would look like:

$$
\begin{array}{r}
34 \\
31 \\
3\,4 \\
15 \\
32 \\
\underline{4\,4\phantom{0}} \\
4{,}738{,}744
\end{array}
$$

Note how fast the column addition goes and how easy it is to add up the columns.

Now try it from the other side:

$$
\begin{array}{r}
4\ 4 \\
32 \\
15 \\
3\ 4 \\
31 \\
\underline{34} \\
4{,}738{,}744
\end{array}
$$

You can make the addition of long columns easier by dividing the long column into a series of short columns, adding these separately and combining the subtotals to get a grand total.

Here's an example:

| | |
|---|---|
| 6,415 | |
| 7,220 | |
| 1,567 | |
| 4,025 | |
| 3,891 | 19,227 |
| 5,621 | |
| 8,001 | |
| 6,219 | |
| 4,434 | 23,732 |
| 6,294 | |
| 7,056 | |
| 5,593 | |
| | 23,377 |
| | 66,336 |

## Adding Across

Often you need to add up rows of data in a table across the columns to come up with a total. This may seem difficult because you're used to adding in columns, but with a little care you can add horizontal rows of figures and save time by not rewriting them in columns. Look at the following example.

Receipts from your company's four stores for the first five months of the year are as follows:

| Store | Jan. | Feb. | Mar. | Apr. | May | Total |
|-------|------|------|------|------|-----|-------|
| 1 | 2,512.63 | 791.50 | 1,507.69 | 1,221.25 | 974.50 | 7,007.57 |
| 2 | 3,051.15 | 1,117.41 | 1,820.00 | 1,472.56 | 1,005.60 | 8,466.72 |
| 3 | 4,002.65 | 1,268.71 | 2,407.60 | 3,257.80 | 1,792.41 | 12,729.17 |
| 4 | 2,971.15 | 1,056.12 | 1,291.45 | 2,430.50 | 1,257.86 | 9,007.08 |
|   | 12,537.58 | 4,233.74 | 7,026.74 | 8,382.11 | 5,030.37 | 37,210.54 |

You are asked to total receipts from each store for the five-month period. In addition, your boss wants to know total receipts for each month. Add the rows across by treating each row as if it were a column. Start with Store 1 and add the first digit in January's sales to the February number and so on. Say 3, 12, 17. Put the 7 in the total column and carry the 1. Continue through each digit in this fashion. After some practice you will be able to do it as easily as adding vertically.

Tabular data such as this can be checked easily by totalling the figures at the bottom of each column. They should, of course, add up to the total at the bottom of the right-hand column.

This method of horizontal addition can save you time and effort for a good deal of tabular data including payrolls, engineering data, statistical compilations, and various types of accounting records.

## Methods of Checking Your Results in Addition

There are several ways of checking your work in addition. The most common and well-known method is to add each column in reverse order. Since you would normally work from top to bottom, you can check your answer by adding in reverse order. Note that if you broke the column into shorter parts, you will have to check the short sections as well as your partial sums.

If you're facing long columns with many digits, you'll save time by using the accountant's method previously described. In that case, you can check your work by starting on the opposite side and adding the columns in reverse order.

Casting out 9s is a traditional way of checking all arithmetic problems. The first step in the check is to eliminate the 9s from the numbers you're dealing with. Here is an example:

To cast out the 9s from a number such as 5,791, first add up the digits $5+7+9+1=22$. By inspection you can tell that there are two 9s in 22 with a remainder of 4. If you prefer to do the arithmetic, divide 22 by 9:

$$\frac{2}{9)\,22} \text{ remainder 4}$$

Since we're casting out 9s, eliminate the 2 but recall the remainder 4, that's the check number.

In addition problems, answers can be checked by casting out the 9s for each number in the column, adding up the check numbers, eliminating 9s from that total and comparing it with the check number for the sum. Here's how it works:

|  |  | Casting out 9s leaves |
|---|---|---|
| 4,781 | 4 + 7 + 8 + 1 = 20 | 2 |
| 5,379 | 5 + 3 + 7 + 9 = 24 | 6 |
| 2,147 | 2 + 1 + 4 + 7 = 14 | 5 |
| 6,747 | 6 + 7 + 4 + 7 = 24 | 6 |
| 19,054 | Casting out 9s leaves | 19 |
| 19,054 | 1 + 9 + 0 + 5 + 4 = 19 | 1 |
|  |  | 1 |

Since the check numbers are equal, it's safe to assume that the answer is correct.

Please note there are some loopholes in this method. If you had arrived at an answer of 19,045 instead of 19,054, it would have checked out just as well as the right answer. Since it's unlikely you would have made two errors in adjacent columns, the odds are good that your answer is right. Just remember that a reversal of the numbers will not show up.

## SUBTRACTION SHORTCUTS

One of the easiest subtraction problems to solve involves the subtraction of 10 or its decimal multiples such as 100, 1,000, 10,000, etc. You can make subtraction easier by remembering that fact and also noting that if you add the same number to two different numbers, the difference between these two remains the same. Think about this example:

The difference between 8 and 6 is 2. If we add 3 to both of them, they become 11 and 9. But the difference is still 2.

Now see how you can use these facts to solve a problem in subtraction without writing any numbers down.

You've been offered a trade-in allowance of $800 on your old car when you buy a new one for $6,500. Here's how to do it in your head. First increase the $800 allowance to $1,000 so it's easy to subtract. Since you added $200 to do that you'll have to add $200 to the price of the car. It becomes

$6,700. Now it's easy to subtract $1,000 from $6,700 and get $5,700, which is what your new car will cost. Remember when you add $200 to both prices, the difference between the two stays the same.

You can even use this method without 10s or 100s. Simply adjust the number you're subtracting to one that's easier to work with and make the same adjustment to the number you're subtracting from. Here's an example:

You're buying a travel clock and you find one that's priced at $10.46 and another that's priced at $14.70. If you want to know the exact difference in price, add .04 to the $10.46 price making it $10.50. Then add .04 to the $14.70 price and you can subtract in your head: $14.74 - 10.50 = $4.24. (If you wish, and it makes the subtraction easier for you, subtract the adjusted lower figure (+ .04) from the original price and add the adjustment afterward: $14.70 - 10.50 = 4.20 + .04 = $4.24).

## Balancing Accounts

Occasionally, as a secretary you may get involved in accounting work and one of the things you may be asked to do is balance accounts. Literally, this means adding up what's owed (debits) and what's due (credits) and finding the difference between the two.

Here's a quicker way to get the same result: First of all, decide which of the two amounts is larger. Set up all the debits in one column and the credits in another. In most cases, the credits will be larger but you will generally be able to tell by inspection. If the difference is very small you may not be able to use this method.

After you decide which amount is larger, debit or credits, add up that column. Then, leaving room for the balance figure, draw a line under the column representing the smaller account. Put the sum of the larger amount at the bottom of both columns, since adding the balance to the smaller amount will make both columns equal. Here's how it will look.

|  | **Debits** |  | **Credits** |
|---|---|---|---|
|  | $ 2,524. |  | $ 8,047. |
|  | 671. |  | 946. |
|  | 5,043. | 15,032 | 4,161. |
|  | 1,485. | − 10,044 | 586. |
|  | 321. | 4,988 | 1,292. |
| Balance | 4,988 |  | $15,032. |
|  | $15,032 |  |  |

Since, in this case the credits are higher than the debits, the balance line is placed on the debit side. Now if we add up the debit side column by column, we can compute the balance by figuring what number must be added to each column to get the bottom line total. You can do this in your head:

For example, add the right-hand column in the usual way: $4+1+3+5+1=14$. Ask yourself what must be added to 14 to get a 2 on the bottom line. The answer is 8, of course, which gives 22. Carry the 2 to the next column and continue: $2+2+7+4+8+2=25$. What must be added to 25 to get a 3 on the bottom line? The answer is again 8: $8+25=33$. Carry the 3 to the next column and continue as before. The final result is $4,988, which is the balance.

The first time you use this method of figuring a balance, you may want to check your work by adding up both debits and credits to get the difference ($15,032 credits − $10,044 debits = $4,998 balance). With practice, you'll be able to use this technique quickly and accurately.

### Checking Your Answers in Subtraction

The time-honored way of checking your subtraction is to add back the result you obtained to the number subtracted. You should, of course, get the number from which you subtracted. It should look like this:

$$\begin{array}{r} \$6,753.76 \\ -\ 2,421.09 \\ \hline 4,332.67 \end{array}$$

If we add back
$$\begin{array}{r} 4,332.67 \\ +\ 2,421.09 \\ \hline 6,753.76 \end{array}$$

Since this is the top number, our answer is right.

It's hard to figure a situation where this method would not be sufficient, but just so you can show off to your friends, we'll demonstrate how to check subtraction by casting out 9s. It's similar to the method used to check addition, except that check numbers are subtracted. For example,

|  |  | Casting out 9s leaves |
|---|---|---|
| 6,753.76 | $6 + 7 + 5 + 3 + 7 + 6 = 34$ | 7 |
| −2,421.09 | $2 + 4 + 2 + 1 + 0 + 9 = 18$ | −0 |
| 4,332.67 | $4 + 3 + 3 + 2 + 6 + 7 = 25$ | 7 |

Since the subtraction of the check numbers works, the subtraction is assumed to be correct.

You may run into situations where the top check number is smaller than the bottom one. In that particular event, simply add 9 to the top number.

|        |                        | Casting out 9s leaves |          |
|--------|------------------------|-----------------------|----------|
| 8,461  | 8 + 4 + 6 + 1 = 19     | 1 add 9 to make       | 10       |
| −6,342 | 6 + 3 + 4 + 2 = 15     | 6                     | − 6      |
| 2,119  | 2 + 1 + 1 + 9 = 13     | 4                     | 4        |

## SHORTCUTS IN MULTIPLICATION

Some numbers are easier to multiply by than others. If you learn how to use them, you can save time and solve some problems in your head.

Since this is a long list, we suggest you learn a few at a time and practice them until you know them cold. If you try to learn them all at once, results may be confusing and you may not retain them all.

First of all, it will help to remember that in a multiplication problem, the number being multiplied is the *multiplicand* and the number doing the multiplying is the *multiplier.*

### How to Multiply by Numbers Ending in Zeros

In this case, you need to count the zeros in the multiplier first, then add the same number to the result after you finish. Then proceed with the rest of the multiplication, ignoring the zeros. For example:

$$584 \quad \text{Note the zero before you start}$$
$$\times 70 \quad \text{but multiply as if it weren't there}$$
$$4,088$$

*Answer:* 40,880 Then when you're finished, add the zero to
the result.

When you multiply by 10, 100, 1,000, etc., it's even easier. Since multiplying by 1 doesn't change the result, all you have to do is add the zeros.

$$375 \times 10 \quad = \quad 3,750$$
$$21 \times 100 \quad = \quad 2,100$$
$$15 \times 1000 = 15,000$$

## How to Multiply by 5

Since five is half of ten, we can make use of that fact to simplify multiplication. There are several ways:

First, you can multiply by 10 and divide the answer by 2. Like this:

$$64 \times 5 = \frac{64 \times 10}{2} = \frac{640}{2} = 320$$

You can also divide the multiplicand by two and multiply the result by 10.

$$\frac{64}{2} = 32 \times 10 = 320$$

Which of these methods you use will depend on the problem you're solving. If you can look at the multiplicand and divide it by 2 in your head, you can solve the problem quickly.

## How to Multiply by 7½

7½ is a good number to know because it's three-quarters of ten. So you can first multiply by 10 and then find ¾ of the answer or you can figure ¾ of the multiplicand and multiply the result by 10.

$$64 \times 7\frac{1}{2} = \frac{64 \times 10 \times 3}{4} = \frac{1{,}920}{4} = 480, \text{ or}$$

$$\frac{64 \times 3}{4} = 48 \times 10 = 480$$

Another way is to multiply by 10 and subtract one-quarter of the answer:

$$54 \times 7.5 \qquad 54 \times 10 = 540$$

$$\frac{540}{4} = 135$$

$$540 - 135 = 405$$

## Multiplying by 11

Here you can take advantage of the fact that 11 is 1 greater than 10. The simplest way is to multiply by 10 and add the multiplicand to the result. Here's how:

$$57 \times 11 = 57 \times 10 + 57 = 570 + 57 = 627$$

This is by far the simplest way to multiply by 11 but just so that you know all the ways, here's another: If you are multiplying a two-digit number whose digits add up to 9 or less, you can use a trick method. If the 11 members of a football team each run 21 laps, you can find the total number of laps run by putting down 2 1 with a space between them and inserting the sum of the digits, like this: 231.

You can even use this method (modified) to multiply three-digit numbers, provided the last two add up to 9 or less.

*Example:* 934 × 11. First multiply the last two digits as above: 3 4 or 374. Now multiply 900 by 11 and add the two figures:

$$11 \times 900 = 9,900$$
$$9,900 + 374 = 10,274$$

## How to Multiply by 15

If you think about 15 as a combination of 10 and 5, it's easy to see how a way can be found to simplify the multiplication operation. First we can multiply by 10 and then add half of that result to itself. Here's how:

$$264 \times 15$$

| | |
|---|---|
| First multiply by 10 | 2,640 |
| Then add half that number | 1,320 |
| | 3,960 |

## Using Combinations of Numbers

Many multiplication problems can be simplified by breaking the multiplier into a combination of numbers. Here are some examples:

*Multiply 56 × 12.* 12 can be broken into a combination of 10+2, making a mental solution possible.

$$56 \times 10 = 560$$
$$56 \times \phantom{0}2 = \underline{112}$$
$$672$$

*Multiply 84 by 14.* Since 14 is one less than 15, we can use the technique described above and subtract the multiplicand.

$$84 \times 15$$

|  | | |
|---|---|---|
| | $84 \times 10 =$ | 840 |
| plus half of 840 | | 420 |
| | | 1,260 |
| minus multiplicand | | −84 |
| | | 1,176 |

*Multiply 182 × 98.* Since 98 is two short of 100, we can multiply by 100 and subtract twice the multiplicand.

$$182 \times 100 = 18,200$$
$$\text{minus } 2 \times 182 = \underline{-364}$$
$$17,836$$

The trick to simplifying multiplication problems is to convert the multiplier into something you can handle quickly and easily.

There are often several ways to accomplish this. Think of the number 25, for instance. If the problem is to multiply 68 × 25, if you think of 25 as a quarter of 100, you could multiply by 100 and divide by 4, like this:

$$68 \times 100 = 6,800, \text{ and}$$
$$6,800 \text{ divided by } 4 = 1,700$$

Another method would be to think of 25 as a combination of 20 and 5, then:

$$68 \times 20 = 1,360, \text{ and}$$
$$68 \times 10 = 680 \text{ divided by } 2 = 340$$

$$1,360$$
$$\underline{\phantom{0}340}$$
$$1,700$$

Remember, the right way is what's easiest for you.

Another way to simplify some multiplication problems is to remember that if you multiply the multiplicand and divide the multiplier by the same number, then carry out the multiplication the answer will be unchanged. For instance:

$$6 \times 4 = 24$$

multiply 6 by 2 and divide 4 by 2 and you have:

$$12 \times 2 = 24$$

You can do it the other way around as well: 6 divided by 2 = 3 and 4 multiplied by 2 = 8:

$$3 \times 8 = 24$$

All this means is that if you multiply a number and then divide it by the same number, you don't change the original number. But using this method you can sometimes save time and work. Think about the problem of multiplying $24 \times 2\frac{1}{2}$. $2\frac{1}{2}$ is a little awkward to deal with, but remember $2 \times 2\frac{1}{2} = 5$. If we then divide 24 by 2 to get 12, we should get the right answer:

$$12 \times 5 = 60$$

You can use this method to eliminate fractions from multiplication problems, as for example:

$12\frac{1}{4} \times 8$. If we multiply $12\frac{1}{4}$ by 4 and divide the multiplier by 4, the problem is much simpler:

$$12\frac{1}{4} \times 4 = 49 \quad 8 \div 4 = 2 \quad 49 \times 2 = 98$$

## Tables of Multiples

Occasionally you will run into situations where you need to multiply the same number by a series of other numbers over and over. In such cases, it may be convenient to set up a table of multiples to facilitate a tedious job.

Let's assume for example, you have been asked to convert the cost of products in inventory to add overhead. The cost of each product in inventory must be multiplied by 3.25 to make the conversion.

There are two ways to set up the table. First, consider that you can obtain the multiples by adding the multiplicand to the previous figure in the table as you go from 1 to 10. Here's how:

| | Multiplier | Product |
|---|---|---|
| 1 | | 325  (1 × 325) |
| 2 | 325 + 325 | 650  (2 × 325) |
| 3 | 650 + 325 | 975  (3 × 325) |
| 4 | 975 + 325 | 1,300  (4 × 325) |
| 5 | 1,300 + 325 | 1,625  (5 × 325) |
| 6 | 1,625 + 325 | 1,950  (6 × 325) |
| 7 | 1,950 + 325 | 2,275  (7 × 325) |
| 8 | 2,275 + 325 | 2,600  (8 × 325) |
| 9 | 2,600 + 325 | 2,925  (9 × 325) |
| 10 | 2,925 + 325 | 3,250 (10 × 325) |

In constructing the table, it's more convenient to omit the decimal point and insert it after the multiplication is done.

To use the table, consider that you have a product in stock costed at $6,724. To arrive at the burden cost, multiply 3.25 by 6,724. Use the table of multiples as follows:

| | |
|---|---|
| 4 × 325 | 1300 |
| 2 × 325 | 650 |
| 7 × 325 | 2 275 |
| 6 × 325 | 1 9 50 |
| | 2 1,853.00 |

Since there were two decimal places in the factor of 3.25, there should be two decimal places in the answer.

You could also set up your table of multiples by simply multiplying out each of the ten positions. With more complex multipliers, this method might be easier.

## Using Factors in Multiplication

If you multiply two numbers together to get a third, mathematicians call the first two numbers factors of the third. For example, 4 and 3 are factors of 12, but so are 2 and 6. Some numbers have several factors (like 12), others have none, 3 or 7 for instance.

We can sometimes use factors to simplify multiplication problems. Multiplying 345 × 32 is a somewhat tedious problem, for instance. But since 8 and 4 are factors of 32, we can get the answer by multiplying 345 first by 8 and then by 4:

$$345 \times 8 = 2{,}760 \times 4 = 11{,}040$$

Larger numbers can have three or more factors and we can use the same process for solving sticky problems. For instance, 4, 3, and 6 are factors of 72. To multiply 864 by 72, simply proceed as follows:

$$864 \times 4 = 3{,}456$$
$$3{,}456 \times 3 = 10{,}368$$
$$10{,}368 \times 6 = 62{,}208$$

*Note:* In these examples, we have chosen those factors that make multiplication easier, but both multipliers also have other factors. For instance, in addition to 8 and 4, other factors of 32 are 2 and 16; and 72's other factors are 2, 8, 9, and 12.

It will be helpful, now that you have learned these various multiplication shortcuts, to practice using them. To help you do that we've set up a series of problems, each to be solved by a specific shortcut. In each case, we've indicated the shortcut to use and the answer to the problem, but it's up to you to apply the shortcut:

| Problem | Shortcut | Answer |
|---|---|---|
| 750 × 356 | Multiply 356 by 1,000 and take ¾ of result. | 267,000 |
| 55 × 2,112 | Multiply by 5 and 11; use special techniques for these numbers. | 116,160 |
| 35 × 872 | 35 = 25 + 10; multiply 872 first by 25, then by 10 and add the results. | 30,520 |
| 45 × 461 | Multiply first by 50, then by 5 and subtract the second product from the first. | 20,745 |

| Problem | Shortcut | Answer |
|---|---|---|
| 48 × 771 | Break 48 down into its factors and multiply by those you choose (their product must be 48). | 37,008 |
| 180 × 475 | Since 180 is 20 less than 200, first multiply by 200, then subtract one-tenth of the answer. | 85,500 |
| 125 × 783 | On these next problems, select your own shortcuts. See if you can find more than one. | 97,875 |
| 64 × 512 | | 32,768 |
| 44 × 842 | | 37,048 |
| 27 × 406 | | 10,962 |
| 95 × 108 | | 10,260 |
| 84 × 522 | | 43,848 |
| 65 × 388 | | 25,220 |
| 18 × 427 | | 7,686 |

### How to Check Your Answers in Multiplication

The accepted way to check multiplication answers is to divide the multiplier into the product. If your work is accurate, the answer will be the multiplicand.

**Example:** Multiply 34 × 665 and check your answer.

$$34 \times 665 = 22,610$$

```
                665
To check:  34)22610
               204
               221
               204
               170
               170
                 0
```

And, as you might guess, casting out 9s is another way to check your multiplication. To check the same answer by casting out 9s, proceed as follows:

First, cast 9s out of both the multiplicand and the multiplier. Multiply both check numbers together and the result (with 9s cast out) should equal the check number of the product:

|  | | Casting out 9s |
|---|---|---|
| 665 | 6 + 6 + 5 = 17 | 8 |
| × 34 | 3 + 4 = 7 | 7 |
| 2,660 | | |
| 1,995 | Multiplying the product of 8 and 7 | |
| 22,610 | and casting out 9s: 8 × 7 = 56, 5 | |

and casting out 9s: 8 × 7 = 56, 5 + 6 = 11 or 2 + 2 + 6 + 1 + 0 = 11, casting out 9s: $\frac{2}{2}$

## HOW TO FIND THE FACTORS OF LARGER NUMBERS

Before we go on to discuss shortcuts in division, let's extend our discussion of factoring by talking about larger numbers. It's fairly easy to find the factors of numbers like 12, 24, 28, 36, 48, etc., if we remember the multiplication tables. But larger numbers are not so easy; in fact, you should know that some of these larger numbers are simply not factorable.

Here are some ways to find those that are:

If a number is even, it is divisible by 2, thus 2 is always a factor of even numbers (a number is even if its final digit is 2, 4, 6, 8, or 0).

If the sum of the digits of a number is divisible by 3, then 3 is a factor of the number.

A number ending in 00 or a number whose final two digits are divisible by 4, has 4 as a factor.

5 is a factor of any number ending in 0 or 5.

If the sum of a number's digits is divisible by 3 and it is an even number, 6 is a factor.

If the three right-hand digits of a number are divisible by 8 or if those three digits are 000 then 8 is a factor.

If the sum of the digits of a number is divisible by 9, then 9 is a factor.

Here are some examples of these rules:

1.  5,892—An even number, so 2 is a factor. Also digits add up to 24, so 3 and 6 are factors.
2.   797—Not factorable.
3.   384—Even number, last two digits divisible by 4. 2 and 4 are factors.
4.   435—Last digit is 5, sum of digits divisible by 3. 3 and 5 are factors.
5. 27,000—5, 10, 9, and 3 are factors.
6.  4,480—10 is a factor. Note that 8 is also a factor since 3 digits are divisible by 8 and the zero does not affect factorability. 2 and 4 are also factors.
7.  4,962—2, 6, and 3 are factors.
8. 72,565—5 is a factor.


## DIVISION SHORTCUTS

First, let's see how the use of factors can make division problem-solving easier. Remember that division is simply the reverse process of multiplication. If we could make multiplication problems easier by breaking the multiplier down into factors and multiplying by those factors, we should be able to do the same thing in division.

Here's an example: Your company has just bought 24 desks for $4,440. Since your department will be charged for two of them, you want to know the cost of each desk.

By breaking 24 down into its factors of 4 and 6, you can solve the problem quickly.

$$
\begin{array}{r}
4\overline{)\,4440} \\
6\overline{)\,1110} \\
185
\end{array}
$$

Each desk costs $185 and your department will be charged $370.

Here's another example: Your office spent a total of $285,648 in the last four years. Your boss wants to know the average monthly expense. You could do it this way: Since there are 48 months in four years, divide $285,648 by 48:

$$
\begin{array}{r}
5{,}951 \\
48\overline{)285{,}648} \\
\underline{240} \\
456 \\
\underline{432} \\
244 \\
\underline{240} \\
48 \\
\underline{48} \\
0
\end{array}
$$

Or, you could have used the factors of 48, 6, and 8 as follows:

$$
\begin{array}{r}
6)\ \underline{285{,}648} \\
8)\ \ \underline{47{,}608} \\
5{,}951
\end{array}
$$

## Using the Double and Double Method

This way of solving division problems makes use of the principle that you can multiply the divisor and dividend by the same number without affecting the quotient (answer). For example:

$12\overline{)48}\!\phantom{}^{\,4}$ , multiplying 12 and 48 by 2 we get

$24\overline{)96}\!\phantom{}^{\,4}$

This method makes it easier to solve problems containing numbers with fractions (mixed numbers).

Consider this case: You have a piece of lumber 18′ long from which you want to make pieces 1½″ long. How many pieces can you make?

First, convert feet to inches, multiplying $18 \times 12 = 216$, next divide as follows:

$$216 \div 1\frac{1}{2}$$

then, multiply both numbers by 2

$$432 \div 3 = 144 \text{ pieces}$$

These problems illustrate the method further:

$$6,448 \div 1\frac{1}{3}\text{—multiply both numbers by 3}$$

to eliminate the fraction:

$$6,448 \times 3 = 19,344$$
$$1\frac{1}{3} \times 3 = 4$$
$$19,344 \div 4 = 4836$$

$$2,590 \div 5\frac{5}{6} \text{ —multiply by 6}$$
$$2,590 \times 6 \quad = 15,540$$
$$5\frac{5}{6} \times 6 \quad = 35$$
$$15,540 \div 35 \quad = 444$$

$$16,337 \div 7\frac{3}{4}\text{—multiply by 4}$$
$$16,337 \times 4 \quad = 65,348$$
$$7\frac{3}{4} \times 4 \quad = 31$$
$$65,348 \div 31 = 2,108$$

## How to Divide Numbers Ending with Zeros

You will recall that multiplying by 10, 100, or 1,000 was easy. We simply added the required number of zeros to the multiplicand, like this:

$$553 \times 10 \quad = \quad 5,530$$
$$553 \times 100 = 55,300, \text{ etc.}$$

In division, we can reverse the process by removing zeros:

$$5,530 \div 10 = 553$$
$$55,300 \div 100 = 553$$

To divide a number by 10, 100, or 1,000 if there are no zeros to remove, we can move the decimal place to the left as many places as there are zeros:

$$553 \div 10 = 55.3$$
$$553 \div 100 = 5.53$$

In dividing numbers that end in zeros, we can accomplish a similar result by dropping the zeros in the dividend and moving the decimal place to the left in the divisor. Example:

$$6,720 \div 12$$
$$becomes \quad 672 \div 1.2 = 560$$

## How to Divide with the Help of a Table of Multiples

Just as with multiplication, a table of multiples is helpful in certain types of division problems, especially where a series of numbers is to be divided by a common divisor. This example will show how it works.

One of the salespeople in your office sells regularly to 157 accounts. Over the last four months, he has sold $28,103, $33,598, $19,782, and $36,895 per month to these accounts. Your boss now wants to know what his average sales per customer were for each month.

Setting up a table of multiples for the divisor will speed up this task. In addition, you can easily check in the table to see how well the number you have estimated for the quotient fits. Here's the table:

| Multiplier | Product |
|:---:|:---:|
| 1 | 157 |
| 2 | 314 |
| 3 | 471 |
| 4 | 628 |
| 5 | 785 |
| 6 | 942 |
| 7 | 1,099 |
| 8 | 1,256 |
| 9 | 1,413 |
| 10 | 1,570 |

Here's how the division goes:

```
          179  Average sale/customer first month's sales
157)28,103
    157
    1240
    1099     7 × 157 from the table
    1413
    1413
       0
```

Performing the same division on each month's sales (and using the tables of multiples) gives:

$$1st\ month\ =\ 179$$
$$2nd\ month\ =\ 214$$
$$3rd\ month\ =\ 126$$
$$4th\ month\ =\ 235$$

## How to Check Your Work in Division

The most obvious way to check a division problem result is by multiplication. Multiplying the quotient (answer) by the divisor should give you the dividend if your work is correct. Looking back at the problem

```
        179
   ×    157   and using our Table of Multiples
      1413  157 × 9
      1099  157 × 7
   ×    157
     28,103  the answer checks
```

We can always fall back on casting out 9s, which works as well for division as it does for multiplication. Here is the procedure:

```
             235
157) 36,895
     314
     549
     471
     785
     785
       0
```

First cast 9s out of the quotient; then the divisor, and find the product of the two check numbers.

|  |  | Casting out 9s |
|---|---|:---:|
| Quotient: $2 + 3 + 5 = 10$ | | 1 |
| Divisor: $1 + 5 + 7 = 13$ | | 4 |
| Product: $4 \ \times \ 1 = 4$ | | 4 |

Now cast 9s out of the dividend; its check number should equal the above:

$$3 + 6 + 8 + 9 + 5 = 31 \quad 3 + 1 = 4$$

# APPENDIX

LUMP SUM REQUIRED TO EQUAL $100,000 AT THE END
OF A SPECIFIED PERIOD—VARYING RATES

|     | 5 Yrs. | 10 Yrs. | 15 Yrs. | 20 Yrs. | 25 Yrs. | 30 Yrs. | 35 Yrs. | 40 Yrs. |
|-----|--------|---------|---------|---------|---------|---------|---------|---------|
| 1%  | 95,147 | 90,529  | 86,135  | 81,954  | 77,977  | 74,192  | 70,591  | 67,165  |
| 2%  | 90,573 | 82,348  | 74,301  | 67,297  | 60,953  | 55,207  | 50,003  | 45,289  |
| 3%  | 86,261 | 74,409  | 64,186  | 55,526  | 47,761  | 41,199  | 35,538  | 30,656  |
| 4%  | 82,193 | 67,556  | 55,367  | 45,639  | 37,512  | 30,832  | 25,341  | 20,829  |
| 5%  | 78,353 | 61,391  | 48,102  | 37,689  | 29,530  | 23,138  | 18,129  | 14,205  |
| 6%  | 74,726 | 55,839  | 41,727  | 31,180  | 23,300  | 17,411  | 13,011  | 9,722   |
| 7%  | 71,299 | 50,835  | 36,245  | 25,842  | 18,425  | 13,137  | 9,367   | 6,678   |
| 8%  | 68,058 | 46,319  | 31,524  | 21,455  | 14,602  | 9,938   | 6,763   | 4,603   |
| 9%  | 64,993 | 42,241  | 27,454  | 17,842  | 11,597  | 7,537   | 4,899   | 3,184   |
| 10% | 62,092 | 38,554  | 23,940  | 14,864  | 9,230   | 5,731   | 3,558   | 2,209   |
| 11% | 59,345 | 35,218  | 20,900  | 12,403  | 7,361   | 4,368   | 2,592   | 1,538   |
| 12% | 56,743 | 32,197  | 18,270  | 10,367  | 5,882   | 3,340   | 1,894   | 1,075   |
| 13% | 54,276 | 29,460  | 15,989  | 8,678   | 4,710   | 2,557   | 1,388   | 753.12  |
| 14% | 51,937 | 26,974  | 14,010  | 7,276   | 3,780   | 1,963   | 1,019   | 529.43  |
| 15% | 49,718 | 24,718  | 12,289  | 6,110   | 3,040   | 1,510   | 750.89  | 373.32  |
| 16% | 47,611 | 22,683  | 10,792  | 5,139   | 2,447   | 1,163   | 354.59  | 364.49  |
| 17% | 45,611 | 20,804  | 9,489   | 4,379   | 1,974   | 900.38  | 410.67  | 187.31  |
| 18% | 43,711 | 19,107  | 8,352   | 3,651   | 1,596   | 697.49  | 304.88  | 133.27  |
| 19% | 41,905 | 17,560  | 7,359   | 3,084   | 1,292   | 541.49  | 226.91  | 95.10   |
| 20% | 40,188 | 16,151  | 6,491   | 2,610   | 1,048   | 421.27  | 169.30  | 68.04   |
| 21% | 38,554 | 14,864  | 5,731   | 2,209   | 851.85  | 328.43  | 126.62  | 48.82   |
| 22% | 37,000 | 13,690  | 5,065   | 1,874   | 693.43  | 256.57  | 94.93   | 35.12   |
| 23% | 35,520 | 12,617  | 4,482   | 1,592   | 565.42  | 200.84  | 71.34   | 25.34   |
| 24% | 34,112 | 11,635  | 3,969   | 1,354   | 461.80  | 157.52  | 53.72   | 18.33   |
| 25% | 32,768 | 10,737  | 3,512   | 1,153   | 377.78  | 123.79  | 40.56   | 13.30   |

## ONE DOLLAR PRINCIPAL COMPOUNDED ANNUALLY

| End of Year | 3% | 5% | 8% | 10% | 12% | 15% |
|---|---|---|---|---|---|---|
| 1 | $ 1.0300 | $ 1.0500 | $ 1.0800 | $ 1.1000 | $ 1.1200 | $ 1.1500 |
| 2 | 1.0609 | 1.1025 | 1.1664 | 1.2100 | 1.2544 | 1.3225 |
| 3 | 1.0927 | 1.1576 | 1.2597 | 1.3310 | 1.4049 | 1.5209 |
| 4 | 1.1255 | 1.2155 | 1.3605 | 1.4641 | 1.5735 | 1.7490 |
| 5 | 1.1593 | 1.2763 | 1.4693 | 1.6105 | 1.7623 | 2.0114 |
| 6 | 1.1941 | 1.3401 | 1.5869 | 1.7716 | 1.9738 | 2.3131 |
| 7 | 1.2299 | 1.4071 | 1.7138 | 1.9487 | 2.2107 | 2.6600 |
| 8 | 1.2668 | 1.4775 | 1.8509 | 2.1436 | 2.4760 | 3.0590 |
| 9 | 1.3048 | 1.5513 | 1.9990 | 2.3579 | 2.7731 | 3.5179 |
| 10 | 1.3439 | 1.6289 | 2.1589 | 2.5937 | 3.1058 | 4.0456 |
| 11 | 1.3842 | 1.7103 | 2.3316 | 2.8531 | 3.4785 | 4.6524 |
| 12 | 1.4258 | 1.7959 | 2.5182 | 3.1384 | 3.8960 | 5.3503 |
| 13 | 1.4685 | 1.8856 | 2.7196 | 3.4523 | 4.3635 | 6.1528 |
| 14 | 1.5126 | 1.9799 | 2.9372 | 3.7975 | 4.8871 | 7.0757 |
| 15 | 1.5580 | 2.0789 | 3.1722 | 4.1772 | 5.4736 | 8.1371 |
| 16 | 1.6047 | 2.1829 | 3.4259 | 4.5950 | 6.1304 | 9.3576 |
| 17 | 1.6528 | 2.2920 | 3.7000 | 5.0545 | 6.8660 | 10.7613 |
| 18 | 1.7024 | 2.4066 | 3.9960 | 5.5599 | 7.6900 | 12.3755 |
| 19 | 1.7535 | 2.5270 | 4.3157 | 6.1159 | 8.6128 | 14.2318 |
| 20 | 1.8061 | 2.6533 | 4.6610 | 6.7275 | 9.6463 | 16.3665 |
| 21 | 1.8603 | 2.7860 | 5.0338 | 7.4002 | 10.8038 | 18.8215 |
| 22 | 1.9161 | 2.9253 | 5.4365 | 8.1403 | 12.1003 | 21.6447 |
| 23 | 1.9736 | 3.0715 | 5.8715 | 8.9543 | 13.5523 | 24.8915 |
| 24 | 2.0328 | 3.2251 | 6.3412 | 9.8497 | 15.1786 | 28.6252 |
| 25 | 2.0938 | 3.3864 | 6.8485 | 10.8347 | 17.0001 | 32.9190 |
| 26 | 2.1566 | 3.5557 | 7.3964 | 11.9182 | 19.0401 | 37.8568 |
| 27 | 2.2213 | 3.7335 | 7.9881 | 13.1100 | 21.3249 | 43.5353 |
| 28 | 2.2879 | 3.9201 | 8.6271 | 14.4210 | 23.8839 | 50.0656 |
| 29 | 2.3566 | 4.1161 | 9.3173 | 15.8631 | 26.7499 | 57.5755 |
| 30 | 2.4273 | 4.3219 | 10.0627 | 17.4494 | 29.9599 | 66.2218 |
| 31 | 2.5001 | 4.5380 | 10.8677 | 19.1943 | 33.5551 | 76.1435 |
| 32 | 2.5751 | 4.7649 | 11.7371 | 21.1138 | 37.5817 | 87.5651 |
| 33 | 2.6523 | 5.0032 | 12.6760 | 23.2252 | 42.0915 | 100.6998 |
| 34 | 2.7319 | 5.2533 | 13.6901 | 25.5477 | 47.1425 | 115.8048 |
| 35 | 2.8139 | 5.5160 | 14.7853 | 28.1024 | 52.7996 | 133.1755 |
| 36 | 2.8983 | 5.7918 | 15.9682 | 30.9127 | 59.1356 | 153.1519 |
| 37 | 2.9852 | 6.0814 | 17.2456 | 34.0039 | 66.2318 | 176.1246 |
| 38 | 3.0748 | 6.3855 | 18.6253 | 37.4043 | 74.1797 | 202.5433 |
| 39 | 3.1670 | 6.7048 | 20.1153 | 41.1448 | 83.0812 | 232.9248 |
| 40 | 3.2620 | 7.0400 | 21.7245 | 45.2593 | 93.0510 | 267.8635 |
| 41 | 3.3599 | 7.3920 | 23.4625 | 49.7852 | 104.2171 | 308.0431 |
| 42 | 3.4607 | 7.7616 | 25.3395 | 54.7637 | 116.7231 | 354.2495 |
| 43 | 3.5645 | 8.1497 | 27.3666 | 60.2401 | 130.7299 | 407.3870 |
| 44 | 3.6715 | 8.5572 | 29.5560 | 66.2641 | 146.4175 | 468.4950 |
| 45 | 3.7816 | 8.9850 | 31.9204 | 72.8905 | 163.9876 | 538.7693 |
| 46 | 3.8950 | 9.4343 | 34.4741 | 80.1795 | 183.6661 | 619.5847 |
| 47 | 4.0119 | 9.9060 | 37.2320 | 88.1975 | 205.7061 | 712.5224 |
| 48 | 4.1323 | 10.4013 | 40.2106 | 97.0172 | 230.3908 | 819.4007 |
| 49 | 4.2562 | 10.9213 | 43.4274 | 106.7190 | 258.0377 | 942.3103 |
| 50 | 4.3839 | 11.4674 | 46.9016 | 117.3909 | 289.0022 | 1083.6574 |

## $10,000 LUMP SUM AT VARYING RATES COMPOUNDED ANNUALLY—
## END-OF-YEAR VALUES

|      | 5th Yr. | 10th Yr. | 15th Yr. | 20th Yr. | 25th Yr. |
|------|---------|----------|----------|----------|-----------|
| 1%   | 10,310  | 11,046   | 11,609   | 12,201   | 12,824    |
| 2%   | 11,040  | 12,189   | 13,458   | 14,859   | 16,406    |
| 3%   | 11,592  | 13,439   | 15,579   | 18,061   | 20,937    |
| 4%   | 12,166  | 14,802   | 18,009   | 21,911   | 26,658    |
| 5%   | 12,762  | 16,288   | 20,789   | 26,532   | 33,863    |
| 6%   | 13,382  | 17,908   | 23,965   | 32,071   | 42,918    |
| 7%   | 14,025  | 19,671   | 27,590   | 38,696   | 54,274    |
| 8%   | 14,693  | 21,589   | 31,721   | 46,609   | 68,484    |
| 9%   | 15,386  | 23,673   | 36,424   | 56,044   | 86,230    |
| 10%  | 16,105  | 25,937   | 41,772   | 67,274   | 108,347   |
| 11%  | 16,850  | 28,394   | 47,845   | 80,623   | 135,854   |
| 12%  | 17,623  | 31,058   | 54,735   | 96,462   | 170,000   |
| 13%  | 18,424  | 33,945   | 62,542   | 115,230  | 212,305   |
| 14%  | 19,254  | 37,072   | 71,379   | 137,434  | 264,619   |
| 15%  | 20,113  | 40,455   | 81,370   | 163,665  | 329,189   |
| 16%  | 21,003  | 44,114   | 92,655   | 194,607  | 408,742   |
| 17%  | 21,924  | 48,068   | 105,387  | 231,055  | 506,578   |
| 18%  | 22,877  | 52,338   | 119,737  | 273,930  | 626,686   |
| 19%  | 23,863  | 56,946   | 135,895  | 324,294  | 773,880   |
| 20%  | 24,883  | 61,917   | 154,070  | 383,375  | 953,962   |
| 21%  | 25,937  | 67,274   | 174,494  | 452,592  | 1,173,908 |

# POST OFFICE-AUTHORIZED TWO-LETTER STATE ABBREVIATIONS

| | | | | | |
|---|---|---|---|---|---|
| Alabama | AL | Hawaii | HI | Missouri | MO |
| Alaska | AK | Idaho | ID | Montana | MT |
| American Samoa | AS | Illinois | IL | Nebraska | NE |
| Arizona | AZ | Indiana | IN | Nevada | NV |
| Arkansas | AR | Iowa | IA | New Hampshire | NH |
| California | CA | Kansas | KS | New Jersey | NJ |
| Canal Zone | CZ | Kentucky | KY | New York | NY |
| Colorado | CO | Louisiana | LA | New Mexico | NM |
| Connecticut | CT | Maine | ME | North Carolina | NC |
| Delaware | DE | Maryland | MD | North Dakota | ND |
| Dist. of Col | DC | Massachusetts | MA | Northern Mariana Is. | CM |
| Florida | FL | Michigan | MI | Ohio | OH |
| Georgia | GA | Minnesota | MN | Oklahoma | OK |
| Guam | GU | Mississippi | MS | Oregon | OR |
| | | | | Pennsylvania | PA |

| | | | | | |
|---|---|---|---|---|---|
| Puerto Rico | PR | | | | |
| Rhode Island | RI | | | | |
| South Carolina | SC | | | | |
| South Dakota | SD | | | | |
| Tennessee | TN | | | | |
| Texas | TX | | | | |
| Trust Territories | TT | | | | |
| Utah | UT | | | | |
| Vermont | VT | | | | |
| Virginia | VA | | | | |
| Virgin Islands | VI | | | | |
| Washington | WA | | | | |
| West Virginia | WV | | | | |
| Wisconsin | WI | | | | |
| Wyoming | WY | | | | |

Also approved for use in addressing mail are the following abbreviations:

| | | | | | | | |
|---|---|---|---|---|---|---|---|
| Alley | Aly | Courts | Cts | Heights | Hts | Rural | R |
| Arcade | Arc | Crescent | Cres | Highway | Hwy | Square | Sq |
| Boulevard | Blvd | Drive | Dr | Lane | Ln | Street | St |
| Branch | Br | Expressway | Expy | Manor | Mnr | Terrace | Ter |
| Bypass | Byp | Extended | Ext | Place | Pl | Trail | Trl |
| Causeway | Cswy | Extension | Ext | Plaza | Plz | Turnpike | Tpke |
| Center | Ctr | Freeway | Fwy | Point | Pt | Viaduct | Via |
| Circle | Cir | Gardens | Gdns | Road | Rd | Vista | Vis |
| Court | Ct | Grove | Grv | | | | |

## COMMON FRACTIONS REDUCED TO DECIMALS

| 8ths | 16ths | 32ds | 64ths | | 8ths | 16ths | 32ds | 64ths | | 8ths | 16ths | 32ds | 64ths | |
|---|---|---|---|---|---|---|---|---|---|---|---|---|---|---|
|  |  |  | 1 | .015625 |  |  |  | 23 | .359375 |  |  |  | 45 | .703125 |
|  |  | 1 | 2 | .03125 |  |  | 12 | 24 | .375 |  |  | 23 | 46 | .71875 |
|  |  |  | 3 | .046875 |  |  |  | 25 | .390625 |  |  |  | 47 | .734375 |
|  | 1 | 2 | 4 | .0625 |  |  | 13 | 26 | .40625 | 6 | 12 | 24 | 48 | .75 |
|  |  |  | 5 | .078125 |  |  |  | 27 | .421875 |  |  |  | 49 | .765625 |
|  |  | 3 | 6 | .09375 |  | 7 | 14 | 28 | .4375 |  |  | 25 | 50 | .78125 |
|  |  |  | 7 | .109375 |  |  |  | 29 | .453125 |  |  |  | 51 | .796875 |
| 1 | 2 | 4 | 8 | .125 |  |  | 15 | 30 | .46875 |  | 13 | 26 | 52 | .8125 |
|  |  |  | 9 | .140625 |  |  |  | 31 | .484375 |  |  |  | 53 | .828125 |
|  |  | 5 | 10 | .15625 | 4 | 8 | 16 | 32 | .5 |  |  | 27 | 54 | .84375 |
|  |  |  | 11 | .171875 |  |  |  | 33 | .515625 |  |  |  | 55 | .859375 |
|  | 3 | 6 | 12 | .1875 |  |  | 17 | 34 | .53125 | 7 | 14 | 28 | 56 | .875 |
|  |  |  | 13 | .203125 |  |  |  | 35 | .546875 |  |  |  | 57 | .890625 |
|  |  | 7 | 14 | .21875 |  | 9 | 18 | 36 | .5625 |  |  | 29 | 58 | .90625 |
|  |  |  | 15 | .234375 |  |  |  | 37 | .578125 |  |  |  | 59 | .921875 |
| 2 | 4 | 8 | 16 | .25 |  |  | 19 | 38 | .59375 |  | 15 | 30 | 60 | .9375 |
|  |  |  | 17 | .265625 |  |  |  | 39 | .609375 |  |  |  | 61 | .953125 |
|  |  | 9 | 18 | .28125 | 5 | 10 | 20 | 40 | .625 |  |  | 31 | 62 | .96875 |
|  |  |  | 19 | .296875 |  |  |  | 41 | .640625 |  |  |  | 63 | .984375 |
|  | 5 | 10 | 20 | .3125 |  |  | 21 | 42 | .65625 | 8 | 16 | 32 | 64 | 1. |
|  |  |  | 21 | .328125 |  |  |  | 43 | .671875 |  |  |  |  |  |
|  |  | 11 | 22 | .34375 |  | 11 | 22 | 44 | .6875 |  |  |  |  |  |

3 (8ths, first block, at 64th 24 position) / 4 / 5

## DAYS BETWEEN TWO DATES

| DATE | JAN | FEB | MAR | APR | MAY | JUN | JUL | AUG | SEP | OCT | NOV | DEC | DATE | JAN | FEB | MAR | APR | MAY | JUN | JUL | AUG | SEP | OCT | NOV | DEC |
|---|---|---|---|---|---|---|---|---|---|---|---|---|---|---|---|---|---|---|---|---|---|---|---|---|---|
| 1 | 1 | 32 | 60 | 91 | 121 | 152 | 182 | 213 | 244 | 274 | 305 | 335 | 1 | 366 | 397 | 425 | 456 | 486 | 517 | 547 | 578 | 609 | 639 | 670 | 700 |
| 2 | 2 | 33 | 61 | 92 | 122 | 153 | 183 | 214 | 245 | 275 | 306 | 336 | 2 | 367 | 398 | 426 | 457 | 487 | 518 | 548 | 579 | 610 | 640 | 671 | 701 |
| 3 | 3 | 34 | 62 | 93 | 123 | 154 | 184 | 215 | 246 | 276 | 307 | 337 | 3 | 368 | 399 | 427 | 458 | 488 | 519 | 549 | 580 | 611 | 641 | 672 | 702 |
| 4 | 4 | 35 | 63 | 94 | 124 | 155 | 185 | 216 | 247 | 277 | 308 | 338 | 4 | 369 | 400 | 428 | 459 | 489 | 520 | 550 | 581 | 612 | 642 | 673 | 703 |
| 5 | 5 | 36 | 64 | 95 | 125 | 156 | 186 | 217 | 248 | 278 | 309 | 339 | 5 | 370 | 401 | 429 | 460 | 490 | 521 | 551 | 582 | 613 | 643 | 674 | 704 |
| 6 | 6 | 37 | 65 | 96 | 126 | 157 | 187 | 218 | 249 | 279 | 310 | 340 | 6 | 371 | 402 | 430 | 461 | 491 | 522 | 552 | 583 | 614 | 644 | 675 | 705 |
| 7 | 7 | 38 | 66 | 97 | 127 | 158 | 188 | 219 | 250 | 280 | 311 | 341 | 7 | 372 | 403 | 431 | 462 | 492 | 523 | 553 | 584 | 615 | 645 | 676 | 706 |
| 8 | 8 | 39 | 67 | 98 | 128 | 159 | 189 | 220 | 251 | 281 | 312 | 342 | 8 | 373 | 404 | 432 | 463 | 493 | 524 | 554 | 585 | 616 | 646 | 677 | 707 |
| 9 | 9 | 40 | 68 | 99 | 129 | 160 | 190 | 221 | 252 | 282 | 313 | 343 | 9 | 374 | 405 | 433 | 464 | 494 | 525 | 555 | 586 | 617 | 647 | 678 | 708 |
| 10 | 10 | 41 | 69 | 100 | 130 | 161 | 191 | 222 | 253 | 283 | 314 | 344 | 10 | 375 | 406 | 434 | 465 | 495 | 526 | 556 | 587 | 618 | 648 | 679 | 709 |
| 11 | 11 | 42 | 70 | 101 | 131 | 162 | 192 | 223 | 254 | 284 | 315 | 345 | 11 | 376 | 407 | 435 | 466 | 496 | 527 | 557 | 588 | 619 | 649 | 680 | 710 |
| 12 | 12 | 43 | 71 | 102 | 132 | 163 | 193 | 224 | 255 | 285 | 316 | 346 | 12 | 377 | 408 | 436 | 467 | 497 | 528 | 558 | 589 | 620 | 650 | 681 | 711 |
| 13 | 13 | 44 | 72 | 103 | 133 | 164 | 194 | 225 | 256 | 286 | 317 | 347 | 13 | 378 | 409 | 437 | 468 | 498 | 529 | 559 | 590 | 621 | 651 | 682 | 712 |
| 14 | 14 | 45 | 73 | 104 | 134 | 165 | 195 | 226 | 257 | 287 | 318 | 348 | 14 | 379 | 410 | 438 | 469 | 499 | 530 | 560 | 591 | 622 | 652 | 683 | 713 |
| 15 | 15 | 46 | 74 | 105 | 135 | 166 | 196 | 227 | 258 | 288 | 319 | 349 | 15 | 380 | 411 | 439 | 470 | 500 | 531 | 561 | 592 | 623 | 653 | 684 | 714 |
| 16 | 16 | 47 | 75 | 106 | 136 | 167 | 197 | 228 | 259 | 289 | 320 | 350 | 16 | 381 | 412 | 440 | 471 | 501 | 532 | 562 | 593 | 624 | 654 | 685 | 715 |
| 17 | 17 | 48 | 76 | 107 | 137 | 168 | 198 | 229 | 260 | 290 | 321 | 351 | 17 | 382 | 413 | 441 | 472 | 502 | 533 | 563 | 594 | 625 | 655 | 686 | 716 |
| 18 | 18 | 49 | 77 | 108 | 138 | 169 | 199 | 230 | 261 | 291 | 322 | 352 | 18 | 383 | 414 | 442 | 473 | 503 | 534 | 564 | 595 | 626 | 656 | 687 | 717 |
| 19 | 19 | 50 | 78 | 109 | 139 | 170 | 200 | 231 | 262 | 292 | 323 | 353 | 19 | 384 | 415 | 443 | 474 | 504 | 535 | 565 | 596 | 627 | 657 | 688 | 718 |
| 20 | 20 | 51 | 79 | 110 | 140 | 171 | 201 | 232 | 263 | 293 | 324 | 354 | 20 | 385 | 416 | 444 | 475 | 505 | 536 | 566 | 597 | 628 | 658 | 689 | 719 |
| 21 | 21 | 52 | 80 | 111 | 141 | 172 | 202 | 233 | 264 | 294 | 325 | 355 | 21 | 386 | 417 | 445 | 476 | 506 | 537 | 567 | 598 | 629 | 659 | 690 | 720 |
| 22 | 22 | 53 | 81 | 112 | 142 | 173 | 203 | 234 | 265 | 295 | 326 | 356 | 22 | 387 | 418 | 446 | 477 | 507 | 538 | 568 | 599 | 630 | 660 | 691 | 721 |
| 23 | 23 | 54 | 82 | 113 | 143 | 174 | 204 | 235 | 266 | 296 | 327 | 357 | 23 | 388 | 419 | 447 | 478 | 508 | 539 | 569 | 600 | 631 | 661 | 692 | 722 |
| 24 | 24 | 55 | 83 | 114 | 144 | 175 | 205 | 236 | 267 | 297 | 328 | 358 | 24 | 389 | 420 | 448 | 479 | 509 | 540 | 570 | 601 | 632 | 662 | 693 | 723 |
| 25 | 25 | 56 | 84 | 115 | 145 | 176 | 206 | 237 | 268 | 298 | 329 | 359 | 25 | 390 | 421 | 449 | 480 | 510 | 541 | 571 | 602 | 633 | 663 | 694 | 724 |
| 26 | 26 | 57 | 85 | 116 | 146 | 177 | 207 | 238 | 269 | 299 | 330 | 360 | 26 | 391 | 422 | 450 | 481 | 511 | 542 | 572 | 603 | 634 | 664 | 695 | 725 |
| 27 | 27 | 58 | 86 | 117 | 147 | 178 | 208 | 239 | 270 | 300 | 331 | 361 | 27 | 392 | 423 | 451 | 482 | 512 | 543 | 573 | 604 | 635 | 665 | 696 | 726 |
| 28 | 28 | 59 | 87 | 118 | 148 | 179 | 209 | 240 | 271 | 301 | 332 | 362 | 28 | 393 | 424 | 452 | 483 | 513 | 544 | 574 | 605 | 636 | 666 | 697 | 727 |
| 29 | 29 | – | 88 | 119 | 149 | 180 | 210 | 241 | 272 | 302 | 333 | 363 | 29 | 394 | – | 453 | 484 | 514 | 545 | 575 | 606 | 637 | 667 | 698 | 728 |
| 30 | 30 | – | 89 | 120 | 150 | 181 | 211 | 242 | 273 | 303 | 334 | 364 | 30 | 395 | – | 454 | 485 | 515 | 546 | 576 | 607 | 638 | 668 | 699 | 729 |
| 31 | 31 | – | 90 | – | 151 | – | 212 | 243 | – | 304 | – | 365 | 31 | 396 | – | 455 | – | 516 | – | 577 | 608 | – | 669 | – | 730 |

## UNIT CONVERSIONS

| To Convert | Into | Multiply By |
|---|---|---|
| Acre | hectare | 0.4047 |
| Acres | square feet | 43.560.0 |
| Acres | square miles | $1.562 \times 10^{-3}$ |
| Ampere-hours | coulombs | 3.600.0 |
| Angstrom unit | inch | $3.937 \times 10^{-9}$ |
| Angstrom unit | micron | $1 \times 10^{-4}$ |
| Astronomical unit | kilometers | $1.495 \times 10^{8}$ |
| Atmospheres | cms of mercury | 76.0 |
| Bolt (U.S. cloth) | meters | 36.576 |
| BTU | horsepower-hrs. | $3.931 \times 10^{-4}$ |
| BTU | kilowatt-hrs. | $2.928 \times 10^{-4}$ |
| BTU/hr. | watts | 0.2931 |
| Bushels | cubic inches | 2.150.4 |
| Calories, gram (mean) | BTU (mean) | $3.9685 \times 10^{-3}$ |
| Centares | square meters | 1.0 |
| Centimeters | kilometers | $1 \times 10^{-5}$ |
| Centimeters | meters | $1 \times 10^{-2}$ |
| Centimeters | millimeters | 10.0 |
| Centimeters | feet | $3.281 \times 10^{-2}$ |
| Centimeters | inches | 0.3937 |
| Chain | inches | 792.0 |
| Circumference | radians | 6.283 |
| Coulombs | Faradays | $1.036 \times 10^{-5}$ |
| Cubic centimeters | cubic inches | 0.06102 |
| Cubic centimeters | pints (U.S. liq.) | $2.113 \times 10^{-3}$ |
| Cubic feet | cubic meters | 0.02832 |
| Cubic feet/min. | pounds water/min. | 62.43 |
| Cubic feet/sec. | gallons/min. | 448.831 |
| Cubits | inches | 18.0 |
| Days | seconds | 86.400.0 |
| Degrees (angle) | radians | $1.745 \times 10^{-2}$ |
| Degrees/sec. | revolutions/min. | 0.1667 |
| Dynes | grams | $1.020 \times 10^{-3}$ |
| Dynes | joules meter (newtons) | $1 \times 10^{-5}$ |
| Ell | inches | 45.0 |
| Em. pica | inch | 0.167 |
| Ergs | BTU | $9.480 \times 10^{-11}$ |
| Ergs | foot-pounds | $7.3670 \times 10^{-8}$ |
| Ergs | kilowatt hours | $2.778 \times 10^{-14}$ |
| Faradays/sec. | amperes (absolute) | 96.500 |
| Fathoms | feet | 6.0 |

## UNIT CONVERSIONS (continued)

| To Convert | Into | Multiply By |
|---|---|---|
| Feet | centimeters | 30.48 |
| Feet | meters | 0.3048 |
| Feet | miles (nautical) | $1.645 \times 10^{-4}$ |
| Feet | miles (statute) | $1.894 \times 10^{-4}$ |
| Feet/min. | centimeters/sec. | 0.5080 |
| Feet/sec. | knots | 0.5921 |
| Feet/sec. | miles/hour | 0.6818 |
| Foot pounds | BTU | $1.286 \times 10^{-8}$ |
| Foot pounds | kilowatt hours | $3.766 \times 10^{-7}$ |
| Furlongs | miles (U.S.) | 0.125 |
| Furlongs | feet | 660.0 |
| Gallons | liters | 3.785 |
| Gallons of water | pounds of water | 8.3453 |
| Gallons/min. | cubic feet/hour | 8.0208 |
| Grams | ounces (avoirdupois) | $3.527 \times 10^{-2}$ |
| Grams | ounces (troy) | $3.215 \times 10^{-2}$ |
| Grams | pounds | $2.205 \times 10^{-3}$ |
| Hand | centimeters | 10.16 |
| Hectares | acres | 2.471 |
| Hectares | square feet | $1.076 \times 10^{-5}$ |
| Horsepower | BTU/min. | 42.44 |
| Horsepower | kilowatts | 0.7457 |
| Horsepower | watts | 745.7 |
| Hours | days | $4.167 \times 10^{-2}$ |
| Hours | weeks | $5.952 \times 10^{-3}$ |
| Inches | centimeters | 2.540 |
| Inches | miles | $1.578 \times 10^{-5}$ |
| International ampere | ampere (absolute) | 0.9998 |
| International volt | volts (absolute) | 1.003 |
| Joules | BTU | $9.480 \times 10^{-4}$ |
| Joules | ergs | $1 \times 10^{-7}$ |
| Kilograms | pound | 2.205 |
| Kilometers | feet | 3,281.0 |
| Kilometers | meters | 1,000.0 |
| Kilometers | miles | 0.6214 |
| Kilometers/hr. | knots | 0.5396 |
| Kilowatts | horsepower | 1.341 |
| Kilowatt-hours | BTU | 3,413.0 |
| Knots | feet/hour | 6,080.0 |
| Knots | nautical miles/hr. | 1.0 |
| Knots | statute miles/hr. | 1.151 |

## UNIT CONVERSIONS (continued)

| To Convert | Into | Multiply By |
|---|---|---|
| League | miles (approximately) | 3.0 |
| Light year | miles | $5.9 \times 10^{-12}$ |
| Links (surveyor's) | inches | 7.92 |
| Liters | cubic centimeters | 1,000.0 |
| Liters | cubic inches | 61.02 |
| Liters | gallons (U.S. liq.) | 0.264 |
| Liters | milliliters | 1,000.0 |
| Liters | pints (U.S. liq.) | 2,113 |
| Meters | centimeters | 100.0 |
| Meters | feet | 3.281 |
| Meters | kilometers | $1 \times 10^{-3}$ |
| Meters | miles (nautical) | $5.396 \times 10^{-4}$ |
| Meters | miles (statute) | $6.214 \times 10^{-4}$ |
| Meters | millimeters | 1,000.0 |
| Microns | meters | $1 \times 10^{-6}$ |
| Miles (nautical) | feet | 6,080.27 |
| Miles (statute) | feet | 5,280.0 |
| Miles (nautical) | kilometers | 1.853 |
| Miles (statute) | kilometers | 1.609 |
| Miles/hour | feet/min. | 88.0 |
| Milligrams/liter | parts/million | 1.0 |
| Milliliters | liters | $1 \times 10^{-3}$ |
| Newtons | dynes | $1 \times 10^{-5}$ |
| Ohms (international) | ohms (absolute) | 1.0005 |
| Ounces | grams | 28.349527 |
| Ounces | pounds | $6.25 \times 10^{-2}$ |
| Ounces (troy) | ounces (avoirdupois) | 1.09714 |
| Parsec | miles | $19 \times 10^{-12}$ |
| Parsec | kilometers | $3.084 \times 10^{-13}$ |
| Pints (liq.) | cubic centimeters | 473.2 |
| Pints (liq.) | cubic inches | 28.87 |
| Pints (liq.) | gallons | 0.125 |
| Pints (liq.) | quarts (liq.) | 0.5 |
| Pounds | kilograms | 0.4536 |
| Pounds | ounces | 16.0 |
| Pounds | ounces (troy) | 14.5833 |
| Pounds | pounds (troy) | 1.21528 |
| Pounds/sq. inch | grams/sq. cm. | 70.31 |
| Quarts (dry) | cubic inches | 67.20 |
| Quarts (liq.) | cubic inches | 57.75 |
| Quarts (liq.) | gallons | 0.25 |

## UNIT CONVERSIONS (continued)

| To Convert | Into | Multiply By |
|---|---|---|
| Quarts (liq.) | liters | 0.9463 |
| Quires | sheets | 25.0 |
| Radians | degrees | 57.30 |
| Radians | minutes | 3.438.0 |
| Reams | sheets | 500.0 |
| Revolutions | degrees | 360.0 |
| Revolutions/min. | degrees/sec. | 6.0 |
| Rods | meters | 5.029 |
| Rods | feet | 16.5 |
| Rods (surveyor's measure) | yards | 5.5 |
| Seconds | minutes | $1.667 \times 10^{-2}$ |
| Slug | pounds | 32.17 |
| Tons (long) | kilograms | 1.016.0 |
| Tons (short) | kilograms | 907.1848 |
| Tons (long) | pounds | 2,240.0 |
| Tons (short) | pounds | 2,000.0 |
| Tons (long) | tons (short) | 1.120 |
| Tons (short) | tons (long) | 0.89287 |
| Volt (absolute) | statvolts | $3.336 \times 10^{-3}$ |
| Watts | BTU/hour | 3.4129 |
| Watts | horsepower | $1.341 \times 10^{-3}$ |
| Watts (international) | watts (absolute) | 1.002 |
| Yards | meters | 0.9144 |
| Yards | miles (nautical) | $4.934 \times 10^{-4}$ |
| Yards | miles (statute) | $5.682 \times 10^{-4}$ |

## TABLES OF U.S. CUSTOMARY WEIGHTS AND MEASURES

### LINEAR MEASURE

| | |
|---|---|
| 12 inches (in.) | = 1 foot (ft.) |
| 3 feet | = 1 yard (yd.) |
| 5½ yards | = 1 rod (rd.), pole, or perch (16½ ft.) |
| 40 rods | = 1 furlong (fur.) = 220 yards = 660 feet |
| 8 furlongs | = 1 statute mile (mi.) = 1,760 yards = 5,280 feet |
| 3 land miles | = 1 league |
| 5,280 feet | = 1 statute or land mile |
| 6,076.11549 feet | = 1 international nautical mile |

### AREA MEASURE

Squares and cubes of units are sometimes abbreviated by using "superior" figures. For example, $ft^2$ means square foot, and $ft^3$ means cubic foot.

| | |
|---|---|
| 144 square inches | = 1 square foot |
| 9 square feet | = 1 square yard = 1,296 square inches |
| 30¼ square yards | = 1 square rod = 272¼ square feet |
| 160 square rods | = 1 acre = 4,840 square yards = 43,560 square feet |
| 640 acres | = 1 square mile |
| 1 mile square | = 1 section (of land) |
| 6 miles square | = 1 township = 36 sections = 36 square miles |

### CUBIC MEASURE

| | |
|---|---|
| 1,728 cubic inches | = 1 cubic foot |
| 27 cubic feet | = 1 cubic yard |

### LIQUID MEASURE

When necessary to distinguish the liquid pint or quart from the dry pint or quart, the word "liquid" or the abbreviation "liq." should be used in combination with the name or abbreviation of the liquid unit.

| | |
|---|---|
| 4 gills (gi.) | = 1 pint (pt.) = 28.875 cubic inches |
| 2 pints | = 1 quart (qt.) = 57.75 cubic inches |
| 4 quarts | = 1 gallon (gal.) = 231 cubic inches = 8 pints = 32 gills |

### APOTHECARIES FLUID MEASURE

| | |
|---|---|
| 60 minims (min.) | = 1 fluid dram (fl. dr.) = 0.2256 cubic inch |
| 8 fluid drams | = 1 fluid ounce (fl. oz.) = 1.8047 cubic inches |
| 16 fluid ounces | = 1 pint = 28.875 cubic inches = 128 fluid drams |
| 2 pints | = 1 quart = 57.75 cubic inches = 32 fluid ounces = 256 fluid drams |
| 4 quarts | = 1 gallon = 231 cubic inches = 128 fluid ounces = 1.024 fluid drams |

## TABLES OF U.S. CUSTOMARY WEIGHTS AND MEASURES (continued)

### DRY MEASURE

When necessary to distinguish the dry pint or quart from the liquid pint or quart, the word "dry" should be used in combination with the name or abbreviation of the dry unit.

| | |
|---|---|
| 2 pints | = 1 quart = 67.2006 cubic inches |
| 8 quarts | = 1 peck (pk.) = 537.605 cubic inches = 16 pints |
| 4 pecks | = 1 bushel (bu.) = 2.150.42 cubic inches = 32 quarts |

### AVOIRDUPOIS WEIGHT

When necessary to distinguish the avoirdupois dram from the apothecaries dram, or to distinguish the avoirdupois dram or ounce from the fluid dram or ounce, or to distinguish the avoirdupois ounce or pound from the troy or apothecaries ounce or pound, the word "avoirdupois" or the abbreviation "avdp." should be used in combination with the name or abbreviation of the avoirdupois unit.

(The "grain" is the same in avoirdupois, troy and apothecaries weights.)

| | |
|---|---|
| $27^{11}/_{32}$ grains | = 1 dram (dr.) |
| 16 drams | = 1 ounce (oz.) = $437\frac{1}{2}$ grains |
| 16 ounces | = 1 pound (lb.) = 256 drams = 7,000 grains |
| 100 pounds | = 1 hundredweight (cwt.)* |
| 20 hundredweights | = 1 ton (tn.) = 2,000 pounds* |

### APOTHECARIES' WEIGHT

| | |
|---|---|
| 20 grains | = 1 scruple (s. ap.) |
| 3 scruples | = 1 dram apothecaries (dr. ap.) = 60 grains |
| 8 drams apothecaries | = 1 ounce apothecaries (oz. ap.) = 24 scruples = 480 grains |
| 12 ounces apothecaries | = 1 pound apothecaries (lb. ap.) = 96 drams apothecaries = 288 scruples = 5,760 grains |

### TROY WEIGHT

| | |
|---|---|
| 24 grains | = 1 pennyweight (dwt) |
| 20 pennyweights | = 1 ounce (troy) (oz. t.) = 480 grains |
| 12 ounces troy | = 1 pound troy (lb. t.) = 240 pennyweights = 5,760 grains |

### GUNTER'S OR SURVEYOR'S CHAIN MEASURE

| | |
|---|---|
| 7.92 inches | = 1 link (li.) |
| 100 links | = 1 chain (ch.) = 4 rods = 66 ft. |
| 80 chains | = 1 statute mile = 320 rods = 5,280 ft. |

---

*When the terms "hundredweight" and "ton" are used unmodified, they are commonly understood to mean the 100-pound hundredweight and the 2,000 pound ton, respectively; these units may be designated "net" or "short" when necessary to distinguish them from the corresponding units in gross or long measure.

## TEMPERATURE CONVERSIONS

The table offers temperature conversions that range from the freezing point of water (32°F., 0°C.) to its boiling point (212°F., 100°C.). For conversions below or beyond that range, apply these formulas to convert Fahrenheit degrees into Centigrade, subtract 32, multiply by 5, and divide by 9; to convert Centigrade into Fahrenheit, multiply by 9, divide by 5 and add 32. A Fahrenheit degree is smaller than a Centigrade degree, one Fahrenheit degree being 5/9 of a Centigrade degree.

| °F | °C | °F | °C | °F | °C | °F | °C | °F | °C |
|---|---|---|---|---|---|---|---|---|---|
| 32 | 0 | 71 | 21.6 | 102 | 38.9 | 139 | 59.4 | 178 | 81 |
| 33.8 | 1 | 72 | 22.2 | 103 | 39.4 | 140 | 60 | 179 | 81.6 |
| 35.6 | 2 | 73 | 22.8 | 104 | 40 | 141 | 60.6 | 180 | 82.2 |
| 36.5 | 2.5 | 73.4 | 23 | 105 | 40.6 | 142 | 61.1 | 181 | 82.8 |
| 37.4 | 3 | 74 | 23.3 | 105.8 | 41 | 143 | 61.7 | 182 | 83.3 |
| 38 | 3.3 | 75 | 23.9 | 106 | 41.1 | 144 | 62.2 | 183 | 83.9 |
| 39 | 3.9 | 75.2 | 24 | 107 | 41.7 | 145 | 62.8 | 183.2 | 84 |
| 39.2 | 4 | 76 | 24.4 | 107.6 | 42 | 146 | 63.3 | 184 | 84.4 |
| 40 | 4.4 | 77 | 25 | 108 | 42.2 | 147 | 63.9 | 185 | 85 |
| 41 | 5 | 78 | 25.6 | 109 | 42.8 | 148 | 64.4 | 186 | 85.6 |
| 42 | 5.6 | 79 | 26.1 | 110 | 43.3 | 149 | 65 | 186.8 | 86 |
| 43 | 6.1 | 80 | 26.7 | 111 | 43.9 | 150 | 65.6 | 187 | 86.1 |
| 44 | 6.7 | 80.6 | 27 | 112 | 44.4 | 151 | 66.1 | 188 | 86.7 |
| 45 | 7.2 | 81 | 27.2 | 113 | 45 | 152 | 66.7 | 188.6 | 87 |
| 46 | 7.8 | 82 | 27.8 | 114 | 45.6 | 152.6 | 67 | 189 | 87.2 |
| 46.4 | 8 | 82.4 | 28 | 115 | 46.1 | 153 | 67.2 | 190 | 87.8 |
| 47 | 8.3 | 83 | 28.3 | 116 | 46.7 | 154 | 67.8 | 190.4 | 88 |
| 48 | 8.9 | 84 | 28.9 | 117 | 47.2 | 155 | 68.3 | 181 | 88.3 |
| 48.2 | 9 | 85 | 29.4 | 118 | 47.8 | 156 | 68.9 | 192 | 88.9 |
| 50 | 10 | 86 | 30 | 118.4 | 48 | 156.2 | 69 | 193 | 89.4 |
| 51 | 10.5 | 87 | 30.6 | 119 | 48.3 | 157 | 69.4 | 194 | 90 |
| 52 | 11 | 88 | 31.1 | 120 | 48.8 | 158 | 69.9 | 195 | 90.6 |
| 53 | 11.7 | 89 | 31.6 | 121 | 49.4 | 159 | 70.5 | 196 | 90.8 |
| 54 | 12.2 | 89.6 | 32 | 122 | 50 | 160 | 71.1 | 197 | 91.7 |
| 55 | 12.8 | 90 | 32.2 | 123 | 50.6 | 161 | 71.7 | 198 | 92.2 |
| 56 | 13.3 | 91 | 32.8 | 124 | 51.1 | 161.6 | 72 | 199 | 92.8 |
| 57 | 13.9 | 91.4 | 33 | 125 | 51.7 | 162 | 72.2 | 199.4 | 93 |
| 57.2 | 14 | 92 | 33.3 | 125.6 | 52 | 163 | 72.8 | 200 | 93.3 |
| 58 | 14.4 | 93 | 33.9 | 126 | 52.2 | 164 | 73.3 | 201 | 93.9 |
| 59 | 15 | 94 | 34.4 | 127 | 52.8 | 165 | 73.9 | 202 | 94.4 |
| 60 | 15.6 | 95 | 35 | 128 | 53.3 | 166 | 74.4 | 203 | 95 |
| 61 | 16.1 | 96 | 35.6 | 129 | 53.9 | 167 | 75 | 204 | 95.6 |
| 62 | 16.7 | 96.8 | 36 | 130 | 54.4 | 168 | 75.6 | 204.8 | 96 |
| 63 | 17.2 | 97 | 36.1 | 131 | 55 | 168.8 | 76 | 205 | 96.1 |
| 64 | 17.8 | 97.3 | 36.3 | 132 | 55.6 | 169 | 76.1 | 206 | 96.7 |
| 65 | 18.3 | 98 | 36.7 | 133 | 56.1 | 170 | 76.7 | 207 | 97.2 |
| 66 | 18.9 | 98.6 | 37 | 134 | 56.7 | 171 | 77.2 | 208 | 97.8 |
| 66.2 | 19 | 99 | 37.2 | 134.6 | 57 | 172 | 77.8 | 208.4 | 98 |
| 67 | 19.4 | 99.5 | 37.5 | 135 | 57.2 | 173 | 78.3 | 209 | 98.3 |
| 68 | 20 | 100 | 37.8 | 136 | 57.8 | 174 | 78.9 | 210 | 98.9 |
| 69 | 20.6 | 100.4 | 38 | 136.4 | 58 | 175 | 798.4 | 210.2 | 99 |
| 69.8 | 21 | 101 | 38.3 | 137 | 58.3 | 176 | 80 | 211 | 99.4 |
| 70 | 21.1 | 101.8 | 38.8 | 138 | 58.9 | 177 | 80.6 | 212 | 100 |

## TABLES OF METRIC WEIGHTS AND MEASURES

Linear Measure

| | |
|---|---|
| 10 millimeters (mm) | = 1 centimeter (cm) |
| 10 centimeters | = 1 decimeter (dm) = 100 millimeters |
| 10 decimeters | = 1 meter (m) = 1,000 millimeters |
| 10 meters | = 1 dekameter (dam) |
| 10 dekameters | = 1 hectometer (hm) = 100 meters |
| 10 hectometers | = 1 kilometer (km) = 1,000 meters |

Area Measure

| | |
|---|---|
| 100 square millimeters | = 1 square centimeter |
| 10,000 square centimeters | = 1 square meter = 1,000,000 square millimeters |
| 100 square meters | = 1 are (a) |
| 100 ares | = 1 hectare (ha) = 10,000 square meters |
| 100 hectares | = 1 square kilometer = 1,000,000 square meters |

Volume Measure

| | |
|---|---|
| 10 milliliters (ml) | = 1 centiliter (cl) |
| 10 centiliters | = 1 deciliter (dl) = 100 milliliters |
| 10 deciliters | = 1 liter (l) = 1,000 milliliters |
| 10 liters | = 1 dekaliter (dal) |
| 10 dekaliters | = 1 hectoliter (hl) = 100 liters |
| 10 hectoliters | = 1 kiloliter (kl) = 1,000 liters |

Weight

| | |
|---|---|
| 10 milligrams (mg) | = 1 centigram (cg) |
| 10 centigrams | = 1 decigram (dg) = 100 milligrams |
| 10 decigrams | = 1 gram (g) = 1,000 milligrams |
| 10 grams | = 1 dekagram (dag) |
| 10 dekagrams | = 1 hectogram (hg) = 100 grams |
| 10 hectograms | = 1 kilogram (kg) = 1,000 grams |
| 1,000 kilograms | = 1 metric ton (t) |

Cubic Measure

| | |
|---|---|
| 1,000 cubic millimeters | = 1 cubic centimeter |
| 1,000 cubic centimeters | = 1 cubic decimeter = 1,000,000 cubic centimeters |
| 1,000 cubic decimeters | = 1 cubic meter = 1 stere |
| | = 1,000,000 cubic centimeters |
| | = 1,000,000,000 cubic millimeters |

## TABLES OF EQUIVALENTS

The name of a unit enclosed in brackets [1 chain] indicates (1) that the unit is not in current use in the United States, or (2) that the unit is believed to be based on "custom and usage" rather than on formal definition. Equivalents involving decimals are, in most instances, rounded off to the third decimal place except where exact equivalents are so designated.

1 angstrom[1]
$$\begin{cases} 0.1 \text{ millimicron (exactly)} \\ 0.000\ 1 \text{ micron (exactly)} \\ 0.000\ 000\ 1 \text{ millimeter (exactly)} \\ 0.000\ 000\ 004 \text{ inch} \end{cases}$$

1 cable's length
$$\begin{cases} 120 \text{ fathoms} \\ 720 \text{ feet} \\ 219.456 \text{ meters (exactly)} \end{cases}$$

1 centimeter        0.3937 inch

1 chain (Gunter's or surveyor's)
$$\begin{cases} 66 \text{ feet} \\ 20.1168 \text{ meters (exactly)} \end{cases}$$

[1 chain] (engineer's)
$$\begin{cases} 100 \text{ feet} \\ 30.48 \text{ meters exactly)} \end{cases}$$

1 decimeter        3,937 inches
1 dekameter        32,808 feet

1 fathom
$$\begin{cases} 6 \text{ feet} \\ 1.8288 \text{ meters (exactly)} \end{cases}$$

1 furlong
$$\begin{cases} 220 \text{ yards} \\ \text{⅛ statute mile} \\ 201.168 \text{ meters (exactly)} \end{cases}$$

[1 hand]        4 inches
1 inch        2.54 centimeters (exactly)
1 kilometer        0.621 mile

1 league (land)
$$\begin{cases} 3 \text{ statute miles} \\ 4.828 \text{ kilometers} \end{cases}$$

1 link (Gunter's or surveyor's)
$$\begin{cases} 7.92 \text{ inches (exactly)} \\ 0.201\ 168 \text{ meter (exactly)} \end{cases}$$

[1 link (engineer's)]
$$\begin{cases} 1 \text{ foot} \\ 0.3048 \text{ meter (exactly)} \end{cases}$$

1 meter        39.37 inches

## TABLES OF EQUIVALENTS (continued)

1 mile (statute or land) $\begin{cases} 5{,}280 \text{ feet} \\ 1.609 \text{ kilometers} \end{cases}$

1 mile (nautical, international) $\begin{cases} 1.852 \text{ kilometers (exactly)} \\ 1.151 \text{ statute miles} \\ 0.999 \text{ U.S. nautical miles} \end{cases}$

1 millimeter          0.039.37 inch

1 millimicron (mm [the English letter
            m in combination with $\begin{cases} 0.001 \text{ micron (exactly)} \\ 0.000\ 000\ 039\ 37 \text{ inch} \end{cases}$
            the Greek letter mu])

1 point (typography) $\begin{cases} 0.013\ 837 \text{ inch (exactly)} \\ 1/72 \text{ inch (approximately)} \\ 0.351 \text{ millimeter} \end{cases}$

1 rod, pole, or perch $\begin{cases} 16\frac{1}{2} \text{ feet} \\ 5\frac{1}{2} \text{ yards} \\ 5.0292 \text{ meters (exactly)} \end{cases}$

1 yard          0.9144 meter (exactly)

## AREAS OR SURFACES

1 acre $\begin{cases} 43{,}560 \text{ square feet} \\ \phantom{4}4{,}840 \text{ square yards} \\ \phantom{4}0.405 \text{ hectare} \end{cases}$

1 are $\begin{cases} 119.599 \text{ square yards} \\ 0.025 \text{ acre} \end{cases}$

1 hectare          2.471 acres
[1 square (building)]          100 square feet
1 square centimeter          0.155 square inch
1 square decimeter          15,500 square inches
1 square foot          929.030 square centimeters
1 square inch          6.4516 square centimeters (exactly)

1 square kilometer $\begin{cases} 0.386 \text{ square mile} \\ 247.105 \text{ acres} \end{cases}$

1 square meter $\begin{cases} 1.196 \text{ square yards} \\ 10.764 \text{ square feet} \end{cases}$

1 square mile          258.999 hectares, or 2.59 square kilometers

## CAPACITIES OR VOLUMES AND WEIGHTS OR MASSES

<u>Capacities or volumes</u>

| | |
|---|---|
| 1 barrel, liquid | 31 to 42 gallons[2] |

1 barrel, standard for fruits
  vegetables, and other dry
  commodities except cranberries

$$\begin{cases} 7.056 \text{ cubic inches} \\ 105 \text{ dry quarts} \\ 3.281 \text{ bushels} \end{cases}$$

1 barrel, standard, cranberry

$$\begin{cases} 5.286 \text{ cubic inches} \\ 86\ 45/64 \text{ dry quarts} \\ 2.709 \text{ bushels, struck measure} \end{cases}$$

1 bushel (U.S.) struck measure

$$\begin{cases} 2,150.42 \text{ cubic inches} \\ 35.239 \text{ liters} \end{cases}$$

| | |
|---|---|
| 1 cord (firewood) | 128 cubic feet |
| 1 cubic centimeter | 0.061 cubic inch |
| 1 cubic decimeter | 61.024 cubic inches |

1 cubic foot

$$\begin{cases} 7.481 \text{ gallons} \\ 28.317 \text{ cubic decimeters} \end{cases}$$

1 cubic inch

$$\begin{cases} 0.554 \text{ fluid ounce} \\ 4.43 \text{ fluid drams} \\ 16.387 \text{ cubic centimeters} \end{cases}$$

| | |
|---|---|
| 1 cubic meter | 1.308 cubic yards |
| 1 cubic yard | 0.765 cubic meter |

1 cup, measuring

$$\begin{cases} 8 \text{ fluid ounces} \\ \frac{1}{2} \text{ liquid pint} \end{cases}$$

1 dram, fluid
  or liquid (U.S.)

$$\begin{cases} 0.226 \text{ cubic inch} \\ 3.697 \text{ milliliters} \\ 1.041 \text{ British fluid drachms} \end{cases}$$

1 dekaliter

$$\begin{cases} 2.642 \text{ gallons} \\ 1.135 \text{ pecks} \end{cases}$$

1 gallon (U.S.)

$$\begin{cases} 231 \text{ cubic inches} \\ 3.785 \text{ liters} \\ 0.833 \text{ British gallon} \\ 128 \text{ U.S. fluid ounces} \end{cases}$$

[1 gallon (British Imperial)]

$$\begin{cases} 277.42 \text{ cubic inches} \\ 1.201 \text{ U.S. gallons} \\ 4.546 \text{ liters} \\ 160 \text{ British fluid ounces} \end{cases}$$

## CAPACITIES OR VOLUMES AND WEIGHTS OR MASSES (continued)

1 gill $\begin{cases} 7.219 \text{ cubic inches} \\ 4 \text{ fluid ounces} \\ 0.118 \text{ liter} \end{cases}$

1 hectoliter $\begin{cases} 26.418 \text{ gallons} \\ 2.838 \text{ bushels} \end{cases}$

1 liter $\begin{cases} 1.057 \text{ liquid quarts} \\ 0.908 \text{ dry quart} \\ 61.025 \text{ cubic inches} \end{cases}$

1 milliliter $\begin{cases} 0.271 \text{ fluid dram} \\ 16.231 \text{ minims} \\ 0.061 \text{ cubic inch} \end{cases}$

1 ounce, fluid or liquid (U.S.) $\begin{cases} 1.805 \text{ cubic inches} \\ 29.573 \text{ milliliters} \\ 1.041 \text{ British fluid ounces} \end{cases}$

[1 ounce, fluid (British)] $\begin{cases} 0.961 \text{ U.S. fluid ounce} \\ 1.734 \text{ cubic inches} \\ 28.412 \text{ milliliters} \end{cases}$

1 peck      8.810 liters

1 pint, dry $\begin{cases} 33.600 \text{ cubic inches} \\ 0.551 \text{ liter} \end{cases}$

1 pint, liquid $\begin{cases} 28.875 \text{ cubic inches (exactly)} \\ 0.473 \text{ liter} \end{cases}$

1 quart, dry (U.S.) $\begin{cases} 67.201 \text{ cubic inches} \\ 1.101 \text{ liters} \\ 0.969 \text{ British quart} \end{cases}$

1 quart, liquid (U.S.) $\begin{cases} 57.75 \text{ cubic inches (exactly)} \\ 0.946 \text{ liter} \\ 0.833 \text{ British quart} \end{cases}$

[1 quart (British)] $\begin{cases} 69.354 \text{ cubic inches} \\ 1.032 \text{ U.S. dry quarts} \\ 1.201 \text{ U.S. liquid quarts} \end{cases}$

1 tablespoon $\begin{cases} 3 \text{ teaspoons} \\ 4 \text{ fluid drams} \\ \frac{1}{2} \text{ fluid ounce} \end{cases}$

1 teaspoon $\begin{cases} \frac{1}{3} \text{ tablespoon} \\ 1\frac{1}{3} \text{ fluid drams} \end{cases}$

## CAPACITIES OR VOLUMES AND WEIGHTS OR MASSES (continued)

Weights or Masses

1 assay ton[3]        29.167 grams

1 carat $\begin{cases} 200 \text{ milligrams} \\ 3.086 \text{ grains} \end{cases}$

1 dram, apothecaries $\begin{cases} 60 \text{ grains} \\ 3.888 \text{ grams} \end{cases}$

1 dram, avoirdupois $\begin{cases} 27^{11}/_{32} \ (= 27.344) \text{ grains} \\ 1.772 \text{ grams} \end{cases}$

1 grain      64.798 91 milligrams (exactly)

1 gram $\begin{cases} 15.432 \text{ grains} \\ 0.035 \text{ ounce, avoirdupois} \end{cases}$

1 hundredweight, gross or long[4] $\begin{cases} 112 \text{ pounds} \\ 50.802 \text{ kilograms} \end{cases}$

1 hundredweight, net or short $\begin{cases} 100 \text{ pounds} \\ 45.359 \text{ kilograms} \end{cases}$

1 kilogram      2.205 pounds
1 microgram (mg [the Greek letter mu
   in combination with the letter g])      0.000 001 gram (exactly)
1 milligram      0.015 grain

1 ounce, avoirdupois $\begin{cases} 437.5 \text{ grains (exactly)} \\ 0.911 \text{ troy or apothecaries ounce} \\ 28.350 \text{ grams} \end{cases}$

1 pennyweight      1.555 grams

1 pound, avoirdupois $\begin{cases} 7{,}000 \text{ grains} \\ 1{,}215 \text{ troy or apothecaries pounds} \\ 453{,}592.37 \text{ grams (exactly)} \end{cases}$

1 pound, troy, or apothecaries $\begin{cases} 5.760 \text{ grains} \\ 0.823 \text{ avoirdupois pound} \\ 373.242 \text{ grams} \end{cases}$

## CAPACITIES OR VOLUMES AND WEIGHTS OR MASSES (continued)

1 ton, gross, or long[4]
$$\begin{cases} 2{,}240 \text{ pounds} \\ 1.12 \text{ net tons (exactly)} \\ 1.016 \text{ metric tons} \end{cases}$$

1 ton, metric
$$\begin{cases} 2{,}204.623 \text{ pounds} \\ 0.984 \text{ gross ton} \\ 1.102 \text{ net tons} \end{cases}$$

1 ton, net, or short
$$\begin{cases} 2{,}000 \text{ pounds} \\ 0.893 \text{ gross ton} \\ 0.907 \text{ metric ton} \end{cases}$$

[1]The angstrom is basically defined as $10^{-10}$ meter.

[2]There are a variety of "barrels," established by law or usage. For example, federal taxes on fermented liquors are based on a barrel of 31 gallons: many state laws fix the "barrel for liquids" at 31½ gallons; one state fixes a 36-gallon barrel for cistern measurement; federal law recognizes a 40-gallon barrel for "proof spirits"; by custom, 42 gallons comprise a barrel of crude oil or petroleum products for statistical purposes, and this equivalent is recognized "for liquids" by four states.

[3]The assay ton bears the same relation to the milligram that a ton of 2,000 pounds avoirdupois bears to the ounce troy; hence the weight in milligrams of precious metal obtained from one assay ton of ore gives directly the number of troy ounces to the net ton.

[4]The gross or long ton and hundredweight are used commercially in the United States to only a limited extent, usually in restricted industrial fields. These units are the same as the British "ton" and "hundredweight."

## ROMAN NUMERALS AND BINARY NUMBERS

Roman Numerals

These are letter symbols used to represent numbers. The seven basic letters and their number equivalents are: I = 1, V = 5, X = 10, L = 50, C = 100, D = 500, M = 1,000. All other numbers (there is no zero) are formed using combinations of these letters (reading from left to right, highest to lowest) which, when added together, produce the desired total: MCLX = 1,160; LXXI = 71, XVIII = 18, etc.

In most cases, a subtraction principle is used to show numbers containing 4's and 9's. Thus, instead of using four consecutive similar letters (IIII, XXXX or CCCC), only one letter is shown, followed by a larger value letter from which the smaller is to be subtracted. Examples of these cases are: IV = 4, IX = 9, XL = 40, XC = 90, CD = 400, CM = 900, 494 is written CDXCIV, 1979 becomes MCMLXXIX.

Binary Numbers

The number system utilizes only two symbols, 1 and 0. The location of these symbols in the binary number indicates the presence (1) or absence (0) of a certain number of units which when added together, produce a total numerical value. The number of units to be added is determined by the length of the binary number and the location(s) of the 1 symbol. The extreme right-hand place stands for one unit: each successive place to the left represents double (2 times) the quantity of the place to its right.

| Number of Units | | 32 | 16 | 8 | 4 | 2 | 1 | Add | Total Value |
|---|---|---|---|---|---|---|---|---|---|
| BINARY | 1 = | | | | | | 1 | 1 | 1 |
| NUMBERS | 10 = | | | | | 1 | 0 | 2+0 | 2 |
| | 101 = | | | | 1 | 0 | 1 | 4+0+1 | 5 |

# WORLD CITIES: STANDARD TIME DIFFERENCES

When it is 12 noon in New York (Eastern Standard Time), the standard time in other cities is as follows:

| City | Time | City | Time |
|---|---|---|---|
| Alexandria | 7:00 p.m. | Kinshasa | 6:00 p.m. |
| Amsterdam | 6:00 p.m. | Lima | 12 Noon |
| Anchorage | 7:00 a.m. | Lisbon | 6:00 p.m. |
| Athens | 7:00 p.m. | London (Greenwich) | 5:00 p.m. |
| Bangkok | 12 Midnight | Los Angeles | 9:00 a.m. |
| Barcelona | 6:00 p.m. | Madrid | 6:00 p.m. |
| Basra | 8:00 p.m. | Manila | 1:00 a.m.* |
| Beirut | 7:00 p.m. | Melbourne | 3:00 a.m.* |
| Berlin | 6:00 p.m. | Miami | 12 Noon |
| Bogota | 12 Noon | Monrovia | 5:00 p.m. |
| Bombay | 10:30 p.m. | Montevideo | 2:00 p.m. |
| Boston | 12 Noon | Moscow | 8:00 p.m. |
| Brussels | 6:00 p.m. | New Orleans | 11:00 a.m. |
| Bucharest | 7:00 p.m. | Nome | 8:00 a.m. |
| Budapest | 6:00 p.m. | Noumea | 4:00 a.m.* |
| Buenos Aires | 2:00 p.m. | Oslo | 6:00 p.m. |
| Cairo | 7:00 p.m. | Papeete | 7:00 a.m.* |
| Calcutta | 10:30 p.m. | Paris | 6:00 p.m. |
| Cape Town | 7:00 p.m. | Peking | 1:00 a.m.* |
| Caracas | 1:00 p.m. | Phoenix | 10:00 a.m. |
| Chicago | 11:00 a.m. | Portland | 9:00 a.m. |
| Copenhagen | 6:00 p.m. | Rangoon | 11:30 p.m. |
| Dakar | 5:00 p.m. | Recife | 2:00 p.m. |
| Damascus | 7:00 p.m. | Reykjavik | 5:00 p.m. |
| Delhi | 10:30 p.m. | Rio de Janeiro | 2:00 p.m. |
| Denver | 10:00 a.m. | Rome | 6:00 p.m. |
| Dublin | 5:00 p.m. | Salt Lake City | 10:00 a.m. |
| Fairbanks | 8:00 a.m. | San Francisco | 9:00 a.m. |
| Frankfurt | 6:00 p.m. | San Juan | 1:00 p.m. |
| Frobisher Bay | 1:00 p.m. | Santiago | 1:00 p.m. |
| Geneva | 6:00 p.m. | Seattle | 9:00 a.m. |
| Glasgow | 5:00 p.m. | Seoul | 2:00 a.m.* |
| Halifax | 1:00 p.m. | Shanghai | 1:00 a.m.* |
| Hamilton (Bermuda) | 1:00 p.m. | Singapore | 12:30 a.m.* |
| Havana | 12 Noon | Stockholm | 6:00 p.m. |
| Helsinki | 7:00 p.m. | Suva | 5:00 a.m.* |
| Ho Chi Minh City (Saigon) | 1:00 a.m. | Sydney | 3:00 a.m.* |
| Hong Kong | 1:00 a.m.* | Tehran | 8:30 p.m. |
| Honolulu | 7:00 a.m.* | Tel Aviv | 7:00 p.m. |
| Houston | 11:00 a.m. | Tokyo | 2:00 a.m.* |
| Istanbul | 7:00 p.m. | Tucson | 10:00 a.m. |
| Jakarta | 12 Midnight | Valparaiso | 1:00 p.m. |
| Jerusalem | 7:00 p.m. | Vancouver | 9:00 a.m. |
| Johannesburg | 7:00 p.m. | Vienna | 6:00 p.m. |
| Juneau | 8:00 a.m. | Vladivostok | 3:00 a.m.* |
| Karachi | 10:00 p.m. | Warsaw | 6:00 p.m. |
| Ketchikan | 9:00 a.m. | Washington, D.C. | 12 Noon |
| | | Yokohama | 2:00 a.m.* |
| * = following day | | Zurich | 6:00 p.m. |

## D & B INFORMATION

| Estimated Financial Strength | | | HIGH | GOOD | FAIR | LIMITED |
|---|---|---|:---:|:---:|:---:|:---:|
| 5A | $50,000,000 and over | | 1 | 2 | 3 | 4 |
| 4A | 10,000,000 to | $49,999,999 | 1 | 2 | 3 | 4 |
| 3A | 1,000,000 to | 9,999,999 | 1 | 2 | 3 | 4 |
| 2A | 750,000 to | 999,999 | 1 | 2 | 3 | 4 |
| 1A | 500,000 to | 749,999 | 1 | 2 | 3 | 4 |
| BA | 300,000 to | 499,999 | 1 | 2 | 3 | 4 |
| BB | 200,000 to | 299,999 | 1 | 2 | 3 | 4 |
| CB | 125,000 to | 199,999 | 1 | 2 | 3 | 4 |
| CC | 75,000 to | 124,999 | 1 | 2 | 3 | 4 |
| DC | 50,000 to | 74,999 | 1 | 2 | 3 | 4 |
| DD | 35,000 to | 49,999 | 1 | 2 | 3 | 4 |
| EE | 20,000 to | 34,999 | 1 | 2 | 3 | 4 |
| FF | 10,000 to | 19,999 | 1 | 2 | 3 | 4 |
| GG | 5,000 to | 9,999 | 1 | 2 | 3 | 4 |
| HH | Up to | 4,999 | 1 | 2 | 3 | 4 |

The composite credit appraisal columns are headed HIGH, GOOD, FAIR, LIMITED.

### EXPLANATION

When the designation "1R" or "2R" appears, followed by a 2, 3, or 4, it is an indication that the Estimated Financial Strength, while not definitely classified, is presumed to be in the range of the ($) figures in the corresponding bracket, and while the Composite Credit Appraisal cannot be judged precisely, it is believed to fall in the general category indicated. "INV." shown in place of a rating indicates that Dun & Bradstreet is currently conducting an investigation to gather information for a new report. It has no other significance. "FB" (Foreign Branch), indicates that the headquarters of this company is located in a foreign country (including Canada). The written report contains the location of the headquarters.

### GENERAL CLASSIFICATION

| Estimated Financial Strength | Composite Credit Appraisal | | |
|---|:---:|:---:|:---:|
| | GOOD | FAIR | LIMITED |
| 1R $125,000 and over | 2 | 3 | 4 |
| 2R $50,000 to $124,999 | 2 | 3 | 4 |

ABSENCE OF A RATING—THE BLANK SYMBOL. A blank symbol (—) should not be interpreted as indicating that credit should be denied. It simply means that the information available to Dun & Bradstreet does not permit us to classify the company within our rating key and that further inquiry should be made before reaching a credit decision.

ABSENCE OF A LISTING. The absence of a listing in the Dun & Bradstreet Business Information File or in the Reference Book is not to be construed as meaning a concern is nonexistent, has discontinued business, nor does it have any other meaning. The letters "NQ" on any written report mean "not listed in the Reference Book." The letters "FBN" on any written report also mean that the business is not listed in the Reference Book and that the headquarters is located in a foreign country.

EMPLOYEE RANGE DESIGNATIONS IN REPORTS ON NAMES NOT LISTED IN THE REFERENCE BOOK—Certain businesses do not lend themselves to a Dun & Bradstreet rating and are not listed in the Reference Book. Information on these names, however, continues to be stored and updated in the D&B Business Information File. Reports are available on these businesses, but instead of a rating they carry an Employee Range Designation (ER) which is indicative of size in terms of number of employees. No other significance should be attached to this designation.

### Key to Employee Range Designations

| | |
|---|---|
| ER 1 | Over 1000 Employees |
| ER 2 | 500 – 999 Employees |
| ER 3 | 100 – 499 Employees |
| ER 4 | 50 – 99 Employees |
| ER 5 | 20 – 49 Employees |
| ER 6 | 10 – 19 Employees |
| ER 7 | 1 – 9 Employees |

## GROSS PROFIT AND INTEREST COMPUTING

| To Make a Gross Profit of: | Add to the Cost Price |
|---|---|
| 50% | 100% |
| 40% | 66⅔% |
| 35% | 53⅘% |
| 30% | 42⁶⁄₇% |
| 25% | 33⅓% |
| 20% | 25% |
| 15% | 17⅔% |
| 12½% | 14²⁄₇% |
| 10% | 11⅑% |
| 8% | 8⅔% |
| 5% | 5¼% |

### Rules for Computing Interest
### 360-Day Basis

The following will be found to be excellent rules for finding the interest on any principal for any number of days. When the principal contains cents, point off four places from the right of the result to express the interest in dollars and cents. When the principal contains dollars only, point off two places.

4%...Multiply the principal by the number of days in the contract term and divide by 90.

5%...Multiply by number of days and divide by 72.

6%...Multiply by number of days and divide by 60.

8%...Multiply by number of days and divide by 45.

9%...Multiply by number of days and divide by 40.

10%...Multiply by number of days and divide by 36.

11%...Multiply by number of days and divide by 32.73.

12%...Multiply by number of days and divide by 30.

18%...Multiply by number of days and divide by 20.

## GLOSSARY OF STOCK MARKET AND FINANCIAL TERMS

*Acid test*—A ratio of current assets (omitting inventory) to current liabilities. Also called the liquidity ratio. This ratio is considered a better measure of a company's health than the current ratio since inventory cannot always be disposed of in time to pay current indebtedness.

*Adjustable rate bonds* (also called preferred stock)—A security which pays a varying rate of interest which depends on some selected market rate (such as the prime rate).

*Advance-decline index*—The net cumulative result of increases and decreases on a stock exchange over a selected time period.

*Advisory service*—A group offering investment advice in return for a charge.

*American Depositary Receipts* (ADRs)—Receipts for foreign stock shares issued by the U.S. depositary bank. They indicate that a certain number of shares are on deposit with an overseas branch of the bank.

*American Stock Exchange*—The second largest exchange in the U.S., located in New York.

*Amortization*—An annual reduction of a portion in the cost of an intangible asset (a patent, for example).

*Annual report*—A corporation's annual accounting to its shareholders.

*Annuity*—A payment by contract to the holder at specified intervals for a given period of time, normally sold by life insurance companies.

*Arbitrage*—Buying a security in one market at one price and selling it elsewhere at the same time for a higher price.

*Assets*—Property of value, tangible or intangible. Authorized to sell according to its certificate of incorporation.

*Average, Weighted and Unweighted*—The average price of a group of stocks giving equal importance to all (unweighted); the weighted version emphasizes higher-priced stocks.

*Balanced Fund*—A mutual fund with a variety of securities including stocks, bonds, and other investments. The ratio of securities in the portfolio is varied according to market trends.

*Balance Sheet*—Shows a company's assets, liabilities, and equity as of any specified date.

*Basis Point*—A way of gauging changes in interest rates. A point is .01%.

*Bear*—A term applied to a trader who believes the market will decline.

*Bearer Bond*—Is not registered in the name of the owner.

*Bid Price*—Amount a buyer is willing to pay for stock at the time the price is quoted.

*Big Board*—The New York Stock Exchange.

*Blue Chip Stocks*—The stocks of those companies with good growth prospects and that have a good earnings and dividend record with sound management.

*Blue List*—Published daily specifically for municipal bond dealers, listing municipal bonds for sale by dealers nationwide.

*Blue Sky Laws*—Passed by states to protect investors against fraudulent transactions.

*Bond*—Securities issued by corporations as a promise to the holder of a fixed amount of interest for a predetermined time period as well as repaying the loan in full at maturity.

*Book Value*—The value of a company established by subtracting liabilities and liquidation value of preferred stock from assets.

*Broker*—One who buys and sells securities for clients on a commission basis.

*Bull*—a trader who believes the market will rise (opposite of bear).

*Business Cycle*—Describes the succession of economic events leading to growth, recession, and recovery.

*Callable*—A bond subject to redemption by the issuer prior to maturity.

*Call Option*—A contract by an investor to buy a fixed number of stock shares (or a commodity amount) within a certain time period and at a specific price.

*Capital Gain*—Profit realized when a capital asset is sold. (A capital loss is realized when the sale loses money.)

*Capital Goods*—Equipment used to manufacture other products.

*Capitalization*—All the securities issued by a corporation including stocks, bonds, notes, plus any retained earnings.

*Cash Flow*—The term applied to a company's earnings when augmented by such charges as depreciation and amortization which are not actually paid out.

*Certificate of Deposit*—Attests that money has been deposited in a bank for a fixed time period at a given interest rate.

*Chicago Board of Trade* (CBT)—A long-established U.S. Commodity Exchange dating back to 1859; it facilitates cash and futures trading.

*Clearing House*—A facility designed to provide an outlet for all trades. It can buy or sell as necessary.

*Commercial Paper*—Notes issued by major corporations on a short-term unsecured basis.

*Commission*—A fee payable to a broker or other intermediary to buy or sell securities.

*Commission Broker*—A broker with a stock exchange seat who conducts business on the exchange floor on behalf of his firm's customers.

*Commodity Contract*—An agreement between the clearing house and the buyer or seller.

*Commodity Futures Market*—Where contracts for future delivery of commodities are bought and sold.

*Common Stock*—A form of security representing ownership in a corporation.

*Confirmation*—Used to confirm in writing details of a completed transaction.

*Conglomerate*—A corporation which has acquired businesses serving a number of different markets.

*Convertible Security*—A bond or preferred stock which may be exchanged for some other security, generally common stock.

*Coupon Bond*—A bond containing interest coupons which indicate interest due on specified dates. They are presented for payment as they become due.

*Covered Option*—On securities owned by the issuer.

*Current Ratio*—Current assets to current liabilities. A measure of a company's financial condition.

*Custodian Account*—Any account maintained for the benefit of a second party.

*Cyclical Stocks*—Those stocks that move up and down in rhythm with the business cycle, such as construction materials and consumer goods.

*Day Order*—A buy or sell order valid one day only.

*Dealer*—One who buys and sells for his own account rather than on commission.

*Debenture*—An unsecured loan backed only by the company's own credit.

*Debt-to-Equity Ratio*—A comparison between long-term liabilities and stockholder's equity.

*Defensive Stocks*—Those which are less affected by variations in economic climate.

*Depreciation*—A charge against the corporation's earnings to account for the loss in value of an asset as it gets older. It does not represent an out-of-pocket expense.

*Discount*—The price for a security when below redemption value.

*Discount Broker*—One who charges less than a full-service broker and provides less service.

*Discount Rate*—The rate at which member banks may borrow from the Federal Reserve Board.

*Diversification*—A policy followed by a corporation to avoid concentration in one market or on cyclical products. Also an investment practice of buying securities in a variety of industries and varying the type of security bought.

*Dividend*—A distribution of cash to shareholders.

*Dollar Cost Averaging*—An investment policy of buying fixed dollar amounts of a specific security at regular intervals.

*Dow Jones Averages*—The average price for a group of stocks representative of the market as a whole. The Industrial Average consists of 30 blue chip industrial stocks, while the Transportation Average consists of 20 stocks in that field, and the Utility Average consists of 15 utility stocks.

*Dual Funds*—Sell two types of stock—capital and income. Holders of capital shares receive any capital appreciation, while the income shareholders receive only income earned by the securities owned.

*Dual Listing*—Said of stocks listed on the New York Exchange as well as another exchange.

*Efficient Market*—According to this theory, stock prices always take available market information into account.

*Exchange Privilege*—An offer by the owners of multiple funds to exchange shares from one fund for another at no cost.

*Ex-Dividend*—Said of a stock when it is sold after the dividend has been paid.

*Federal Reserve Board*—The official name of the seven governors of the Federal Reserve System.

*FIFO*—A way of valuing inventory which assumes that goods in inventory purchased first will be sold first.

*Fiscal Policy*—The method by which governments make use of financial resources.

*Fiscal Year*—For various reasons, businesses often work on a year different than the calendar year, and it is called by this name.

*Flower Bonds*—Treasury bonds which can be used to pay Federal estate taxes.

*Form 10-K*—Required by the SEC within 90 days after the end of a corporation's fiscal year. The report contains detailed financial information.

*General Obligation Bond*—A municipal bond fully backed by the issuing government.

*Good-til-Cancelled Order*—One which remains valid until completed or cancelled.

*Gross National Product*—The country's total output of goods and services.

*Growth Stock*—A term applied to the stock of a company with sales and earnings increasing faster than average.

*Hedge*—A technique for minimizing investment risk by taking an offsetting position.

*Hedge Funds*—Mutual funds that reserve a portion of their funds for investments that counter the market trend.

*High Technology Companies*—Those who sell products and services developed from advanced scientific research.

*Holding Company*—A company that owns a controlling interest in one or more other companies.

*Income Bond*—One which undertakes to repay principal only. Interest is paid as earned.

*Income Stocks*—Those that pay high dividends resulting in more income for shareholders.

*Indenture*—The agreement under which such securities as bonds are issued. Pertinent information such as interest rate, security, call provision (if any), and maturity date are included.

*Index Funds*—Those which attempt to match the performance of the stock market indexes (Standard & Poor's or Dow-Jones).

*Individual Retirement Account*—A government-sponsored method of tax-free savings until after retirement.

*Insider*—One who holds a position of responsibility in a corporation (directors, officers, and shareholders who own at least 10% of the company's stock). Under SEC regulations, insiders must report their stock holdings and any changes therein.

*Institutional Investors*—Life insurance companies, pension and profit sharing funds, or banks. Their stock holdings exert a major market influence.

*Investment Banker*—One who raises capital for the benefit of corporate borrowers.

*Investment Company*—Term used by the SEC to designate a mutual fund.

*Investment Tax Credit*—A method (designed by Congress) of permitting businesses to reduce income taxes by crediting a portion of new equipment costs against income tax.

*Junk Bonds*—Poorer quality bonds which generally yield a high interest rate, but with higher risk.

*Keogh Plan*—Established by law to permit self-employed businesspeople to set up retirement accounts.

*Lagging & Leading Indicators*—A series of indexes of economic activity which either lag behind or lead changes in business conditions.

*Leverage*—The result of using borrowed money to increase the return on an investment.

*LIFO*—Describes inventory valuation where the items bought most recently are sold first.

*Limit order*—Used to denote an order where the price at which the order is filled is specified by the client.

*Liquidation*—Converting real estate, commodity, or securities investments into cash.

*Liquidity*—A condition under which a corporation's assets are readily transferred into cash.

*Listed Stock*—One which is traded on a stock exchange.

*Load*—A sales charge paid by the buyer of certain mutual funds.

*Management Fee*—Paid by mutual funds to compensate fund managers. Generally deducted from gross income prior to distribution.

*Margin*—The amount of cash and securities in a brokerage account. May be used as security for later stock purchases.

*Margin Call*—A demand by the broker for a cash payment to bring the customer's account up to the minimum requirement by the exchange. The call is made necessary by a drop in stock value reducing the customer's account total.

*Market Order*—One which is placed at the best price available on the floor.

*Maturity*—The date when the face amount of a bond becomes due.

*Monetary Policy*—Established by a country's central bank to provide needed credit to meet monetary objectives.

*Money Market*—Where short-term credit needs are generally satisfied, generally by means of commercial paper, Treasury bills, bankers' acceptances, etc.

*Money-Market Funds*—Deal in the money market.

*Money Supply*—Amount of money available at any given time. Generally defined as currency in circulation plus money in checking accounts.

*Mortgage Bonds*—Those secured by a property lien.

*Municipal Bond*—One issued by a political entity other than the federal government and for which interest payments are exempt from federal income tax.

*Mutual Funds*—Designed for investors who want to place their funds into a professionally managed account.

*Net Asset Value*—The value of a single mutual fund share computed by subtracting liabilities from total market value and divided by the number of outstanding shares.

*New York Stock Exchange* (NYSE)—This country's largest and most prestigious stock exchange.

*NYSE Index*—Numerical average price of every stock listed on the NYSE.

*Open-End Investment Company*—A mutual fund which prices its shares at net asset value. Shares are sold as the market demands and may be bought back by the fund any time at net asset value.

*Option*—A contract giving the right to buy or sell a given security at a predetermined price within a fixed period of time.

*Over-the-Counter Market*—Where securities that are not listed on any exchange are traded.

*Par Value*—The face value of a security. For bonds, par is generally the amount paid at maturity. However, for common stock, par value has no special significance.

*Pink Sheet*—A daily publication listing approximate prices for over-the-counter stocks as well as the addresses and phone numbers of the dealers who handle them.

*Pit*—The commodity exchange floor where trades are made.

*Portfolio*—The group of securities owned by an investor.

*Preferred Stock*—One which has priority over common when dividends are paid.

*Premium*—The difference between the price paid for a bond and its redemption value if the difference is a plus.

*Price-Earnings Ratio*—The ratio of a stock's current price to annual earnings per share.

*Private Placement*—Occurs when securities are sold directly to key investors.

*Profit Margin*—The ratio of income to net sales. Usually designated pre-tax when income taxes are not deducted, otherwise after-tax.

*Prospectus*—A sales bulletin offering securities. It contains important information, both positive and negative, regarding the company.

*Put Option*—A contractual right to sell a fixed number of shares at a predetermined price within a specified period of time.

*Real Estate Investment Trust*—A group of real estate properties and mortgages under professional management.

*Record Date*—The time at which a stockholder must be registered with a company in order to receive dividends or vote his shares.

*Registered Bond*—One which is recorded by issuing the bond in the owner's name.

*Regulation Q*—A banking rule which limits the amount of interest that banks can pay on deposits.

*Resistance Level*—A stock price level high enough to encourage investors to sell. This has the effect of limiting increases.

*Retained Earnings*—The amount of profit kept by the company after dividends have been paid.

*Return on Equity*—Net income divided by current shareholders' equity.

*Round Lot*—A normal minimum trading amount: 100 shares of stock or $100,000 in bonds.

*Savings Bonds*—Issued by the U.S. Treasury for individual savers.

*Serial Bonds*—An issue with maturity dates in serial order and appropriate interest rates.

*Short Selling*—The practice of selling stock at current prices in anticipation of a lower future price. Since the seller does not own the stock, he borrows an amount sufficient to satisfy the buyer, hoping to pay for it at a future lower price.

*Single Premium Annuity*—An annuity paid for by a single payment.

*Sinking Fund*—An amount of money reserved by a company to repay bonds or preferred stock.

*Specialist*—A stock exchange member who conducts transactions to maintain an even market for those stocks he is responsible for.

*Speculation*—Making risky investments with the hope of large returns.

*Spin-Off*—The divestiture of one or more units of a corporation.

*Stock Dividend*—A stock dividend paid by issuing additional shares to stockholders of record.

*Stockholders' Equity*—A balance sheet figure showing the value of a company's assets minus the value of any preferred stock and liabilities (same as book value).

*Stock Split*—The exchange by a company of new shares for old, increasing the number of shares held by each stockholder. The increase reduces the stock's price, thus (in theory) making it more attractive to prospective buyers.

*Stop Order*—Used to buy a stock at a price above the current market or to sell at a price below the current market.

*Street Name*—Stock held by a broker in his name rather than the owner's.

*Striking Price*—Used with options. For a call, it refers to the price at which the stock may be sold. For a put, it indicates the selling price of the stock.

*Syndicate*—A group that underwrites and then sells a security.

*Tax-Free Rollover*—A method of transferring pension funds from one investment program to another without tax penalty.

*Tax Loophole*—A way of avoiding taxes by taking advantage of discrepancies in the tax law structure.

*Tax Shelter*—Describes a method of reducing income taxes.

*Technical Analysis*—Methods of forecasting stock price movement through examining internal factors in stock market data.

*Tender Offer*—Made by a company to acquire its own stock or by an outsider to acquire control.

*Transfer Agent*—A bank that acts as an independent source to keep records of stock transfers.

*Treasury Bills*—Government bonds with short maturity dates sold in weekly auctions.

*Treasury Bonds*—Those with five-year or longer maturity dates.

*Treasury Notes*—U.S. Bonds with one- to ten-year maturity dates.

*Treasury Stock*—Stock repurchased by the issuing company.

*Trust*—A legal agreement entrusting property to a third party (generally a bank or attorney) to be managed for the benefit of another.

*Trustee*—The property manager in a trust.

*Value Line Index*—Compiled from a list of 1,700 stocks and based on unweighted averages.

*Variable Annuity*—One where part of the principle is invested in stocks.

*Volume*—Total shares traded in one market for a specified time period.

*Warrant*—A certificate entitling the purchaser to buy stock at a given price within a predetermined time.

*Wash Sale*—One where similar quantities of the same stocks are bought and sold within 30 days. No tax benefit may be claimed on such sales.

*When Issued*—A stock issued but not yet consummated. Such stocks are traded, but transactions become final only after the issue.

*Withdrawal Plan*—Permits mutual fund investors to receive regular periodic payments of fixed amounts.

*Working Capital*—Defined as current assets minus current liabilities.

*Yield*—Amount paid to a holder of a stock or a bond in the form of dividend or interest and expressed as a percentage of or price paid (or face value of a bond).

*Zero Coupon Bonds*—Bonds with no stated interest rate. Instead, they are sold at a discount which comprises the investor's return.

# Math-O-Matic Guide